Boys Will Be Boys, and Other Myths

Boys Will Be Boys, and Other Myths

Unravelling Biblical Masculinities

Will Moore

scm press

Published in 2022 by SCM Press
Editorial office
3rd Floor, Invicta House,
108–114 Golden Lane,
London EC1Y 0TG, UK

www.scmpress.co.uk

SCM Press is an imprint of Hymns Ancient & Modern Ltd
(a registered charity)

Hymns Ancient & Modern® is a registered trademark of
Hymns Ancient & Modern Ltd
13A Hellesdon Park Road, Norwich,
Norfolk NR6 5DR, UK

British Library Cataloguing in Publication data
A catalogue record for this book is available
from the British Library

978-0-334-06300-1

Typeset by Regent Typesetting

Contents

Preface and Acknowledgements

I cannot even begin to describe how surreal it feels to have written a book and to have it openly available to be read by others. It is an achievement that I only ever imagined as an unlikely fantasy. I am grateful to God that I have had this opportunity to share my insights and reflections on masculinity and the Bible. I pray that my words will make at least a small ripple in the pool of the world, even if it only speaks to just one person who is struggling with what it means to be a Christian man today.

The main reason for writing this book was the fascination and captivation I had during my four years at university studying theology. I had been a Christian all my life and yet I barely knew anything about the Bible (rather typical of a Church of England upbringing, I must add). Yet, in those four years of research and study, my eyes were opened. I found a passion for a subject that was still relatively new to me. A lecturer's whizzing tour of the texts and overarching narrative of the Bible in no less than 50 minutes had me entranced. A couple of years later I had my undergraduate degree dissertation published as a chapter in an academic volume and my master's degree dissertation published as an academic journal article, with a few other publications and media and speaking appearances scattered along the way. I have been so lucky to have had these opportunities and they have always given me a hunger for more research, study and sharing of knowledge and experience. This yearning has led me to this book.

And so, first and foremost, I would like to thank all those people who have been a part of my academic journey so far, particularly at Cardiff University (alongside St Padarn's Institute and South Wales Baptist College) during my time studying for a BA and an MTh. Without those tutors, colleagues and friends who have intellectually challenged, aided and inspired me (and continue to do so), I would not have been so motivated in my writing and thinking as to be able to write a book. I hope such stimulation will carry on as I continue my research and study while at Westcott House in Cambridge, and within the Cambridge Theological Federation, for my ordination training and formation.

I realized, however, that much of what I was immersing myself in was unknown to the rest of the Christian community. Why should such information be locked away, only for the eyes of those within the academic sphere? More bluntly, why should such knowledge only be available for those who pay thousands of pounds to access it? When I particularly began to study masculinities in the Bible, I was mesmerized by the work that was being done. However, on the ground level, Christians in churches were only just coming to terms with feminist readings of the Bible, and even that kind of theology still oozes with controversy in some settings.

In the churches I had been to, no one had really heard of queer theology (or had associated it solely with arguments of LGBTQ+ affirmation), let alone masculinity studies. I wanted to share the knowledge I had learnt, studied and researched with my fellow-Christians and students. I acknowledge that in the academic world these subjects are much more advanced and intellectually challenging, but if feminist theology had shared its teaching with Christians in an accessible way, why not masculinity studies? And that is what I want this work to begin to rectify. If academic theology performed by those of faith is not for the benefit of other Christians and the wider Church, who is it for? If it is not practical and consequential to our Christian living, what is it for? In many ways, the book I have written is the book I was looking for as I began my research into gender and masculinity studies in the area of theology.

However, I worried that such research would be of no interest to many Christians. Most people have had enough of talking about men after centuries of it, within church history in particular. When I was in the final stages of the first draft of this book, unsure whether I would ever put it forward for publication, I participated in a Zoom book launch (thanks to Covid-19!) with the Centre for the Study of the Bible and Violence. I posed a question about the responsibility of men in situations of domestic abuse in which the Bible was used as justification. I suggested that remedying the root cause of such violence might require a re-education of 'Christian manhood'. After hearing some responses from the author and other academics and ministers, I received a private message from someone else in the Zoom meeting that I did not know. In their message, they applauded my question, suggesting that someone needed to write a book on this topic from a man's perspective and that they would be eager to read it. In that moment, with an early draft of this manuscript tucked away in a virtual folder, I knew that this book might actually have an impact. Christians needed to know about the violence that men have been (and are) doing to themselves and others. I sensed that such a book might fill a void, even satisfy a hunger for a healthy and progressive re-understanding of Christian masculinity in the light of what the Bible has to say about it.

During the writing, this book has had much review and revision. I have immense gratitude for all those who have undertaken a thorough reading of the typescript and given generous feedback of these pages and the thoughts that lie within them. I am particularly thankful to David Shervington and the SCM Press team for believing in my words, as well as my dear friends Olly Hearn and Lottie Trombin for all of your wisdom and guidance in the reading of and conversations about this book. Drawn together, I have been offered an expansive pool of experience, academic learning, interest, insight and faithfulness that has been invaluable. Any errors that remain within these pages are, of course, solely my own.

The constant support and love of my family and friends has

been integral to being able to write this book. My partner, Georgie Rose, has had incredible patience, love and grace to support me in this endeavour, while going through her own exciting journey of training to be a teacher. Her caring, listening ear, immeasurably loving heart, and fantastic sense of humour have been such a gift in my life that I can only hope to have returned half as much in hers. I look forward to seeing where God takes us together in the years to come. Thank you to my parents Gill and Barry Morgan for the stability, security and encouragement you have provided, particularly in recent years. I also wish to honour my Nana, Joan Cook. She has always been interested and engaged in my research and study, even if she does not always quite agree with its subject matter! She has a love for God that I will only ever be able to aspire to. Little did she know when she said 'I think you could write a book' that I was doing just that! I additionally want to thank my sister, dad and wider families for being a part of the journey of life that has made me who I am today.

The supportive friendship of many others has also been so valuable to me. I dare not begin naming them, for the list might never end and I will be sure to forget someone! However, I still wish to acknowledge the many conversations and much encouragement that I have had from friends in recent years, and I am sure many of them will know my appreciation for them, even if their names are not spelled out here.

I would also like to thank all those Christian communities of which I have been a part. Discussing ideas with others, as well as listening to thoughts and beliefs that are not your own, can be one of the most valuable ways to grow theologically and in faith. Particularly, I must thank all those from Lawford Church, Essex, who nurtured me as I grew up in the Christian Church, the several Christian communities and churches I was a part of in Cardiff, including the Anglican and Methodist University Chaplaincy, The Gathering, and St John the Baptist, as I flourished in my faith and theological study, and the communities of the North Hinckford Benefice in rural Essex where I have served as an Authorised Local Preacher (and a local pub bartender at The Half Moon!) in recent years. I also thank those in Cambridge, and particularly those at Westcott House and my placements, as they continue to nurture me as I undertake further postgraduate research and train for priesthood in the Church of England – I am so grateful for conversations, new friendships, love and support.

Lastly, and certainly not the least important, I must thank God. Every opportunity and joy in my life has come from God and my gratitude can never suffice to satisfy the blessings that have been given to me. In the last decade I have been through circumstances of real struggle, as well as times of joy and delight, during all of which I have found myself falling deeper into the arms of God, day by day, year by year, through this unexpected journey which we call life. Our God is full of surprises... and this book is certainly one of them!

And so, praise be to God the Creator of our very being, Christ the Redeemer who sets us free to live in love and compassion with each other each day, and the Holy Spirit who works through us in the most incredible and unforeseen ways.

I pray that this book speaks to you, the reader, profoundly about the Bible, revealing its beautiful complexity and wonders. I pray that this book might make you reassess the masculinity of yourself (if you are a man) and those around you (whether you are a man or not) with fresh eyes. I pray that this book will make you reconsider what might be toxic and unhealthy about what we think men should be and those characteristics that should be celebrated and encouraged. I pray that this book will draw people closer to Scripture and the Living Christ who continually transforms us all. If any of these things are achieved, I have all of those acknowledged above to thank.

I

Boys Will Be Boys: Introduction

Refocusing on masculinity

Phrases like 'boys will be boys' have reverberated around the walls of school halls, family homes, locker rooms and courts of law for far too many years in British society and their justification is wearing a little thin. In a country where seven times more men than women are arrested for crimes,[1] unhealthy traits found in modern masculinities have caused men to inflict violence on those close to them as well as in their surrounding communities. Yet, simultaneously, an inward-bound violence is being perpetrated on manhood and men themselves, with three times as many men than women committing suicide.[2] Toxic masculinity in modern Western society is a poison which, while infecting those who encounter it, is also crippling the very hosts that keep it in circulation. Men truly have become their 'own worst enemies'.[3] Our conversation in this book centres around these themes of violence and masculinity to be found in both modern society and the Bible, for it is this two-way stream of violence that is most prominent in the toxicity of how many masculinities have performed across history and cultures.

Although this violence may often be a choice,[4] we must also recognize the underlying and complex socialization of men that pushes them to feel that such behaviour towards themselves and others is appropriate. Many men will be enacting traits of toxic masculinity without any conscious awareness of it – why do men feel that they can act in such a way? Focusing on the causes rather than the consequences does not diminish the accountability of destructive masculinity but instead seeks to attain the deep-rooted answers for why it has become so normalized. Toxic masculinity has become so imbued within our societal make-up that men themselves need stirring, to awaken in them a realization of what is taking place in their own lives. If we do not strive to dig deeper into *why* men act in such a way, we will never deal with the pressing issues that they cause.

We have a dangerous gulf in society where so-called 'tough' and 'traditional' men are reproduced as the norm, while vulnerable shells of men are left behind when that standard is not achieved or maintained. Even worse, we have a cultural anxiety when it comes to discussing these problems sufficiently. Modern men do not want to talk about their own feelings or personal circumstances, let alone their own perception of what it means to be a man. We may be slowly repealing the shame around discussing masculinity, but we still have a long way to go. This book is an aid in that process, particularly from a Christian perspective. These issues are not just a concern for society as a whole but are urgently in need of tackling by the Church too. What part has the Church played in the history of masculinity that has led to the statistics above? At a quick glance, the Church of England has only begun to change the maleness of priestly and episcopal ministry in the last several decades, and the Roman Catholic Church has not even dared to budge on such issues. On the other side of the spectrum, in many conservative evangelical churches the headship of men is a fundamental aspect of their Christian teaching concerning family structures, church hierarchies and the responsibilities of Christian preaching and instruction. The androcentrism coming from all wings of the Church cannot be avoided and has undoubtedly had an impact on the way society has produced its men, whether we think it is theologically justified or not.

Church history and biblical interpretation have been steeped in masculinity for centuries. It will take centuries more to undo, or outbalance, this heavily masculine leaning. We have become almost oblivious of the extent to which men have dominated our history as well as our thinking. Until the last century, the vast majority of theologizing about God (at least that which has been considered creditable) was performed by well-off, straight, middle-class, cisgender white men in positions of power. As Stephen D. Moore says, 'masculinity was, at once, everywhere and nowhere in the discipline, so ubiquitous as to be ordinarily invisible'.[5] It was only with the emergence of liberation theologies that this changed, acknowledging our own identity markers such as gender, sex, race, ability and class, breaking away from what has been seen as mainstream biblical interpretation, which presumed neutrality when interpreting a text.

There is now, rightly, an acknowledgement that all scriptural reading is biased. No one can ever read the Bible objectively, for we always bring our own uniqueness of experience and circumstance to its interpretation, whether we are aware of it or not. Every encounter with Jesus that we have is rooted in our own life events and contexts. Appreciating our own individuality in understanding Scripture unveils a whole new way of approaching God. What might God look like to a black woman? Perhaps Jesus could look like her own black son, brother or father, rather than the arbitrary white man we see in much of art history. How might a child who lives in poverty understand the message of Jesus? Maybe they simply long for the day when the poor are exalted and the inequalities of the world are reversed. Will a transgender person understand the Genesis story of Adam and Eve differently to someone who has always identified with their biological sex from birth? Some have suggested that God made woman and man as markers within a spectrum of gender, with a plethora of possibility in between. But finally, and pertinently for this book, how does a man approach God, the Bible and theology? What aspects of masculinity make a man's theologizing unique to him? What experiences do men bring to their reading of biblical texts that offer distinctive points for discussion? What consequences have masculinist interpretations had in the past, including the abuse and subjugation of others, and what might be the potential for the future?

In a world where feminism has taken such giant leaps in the last century, further talk of masculinity might seem rather counterintuitive. Feminism has exposed the damning disparity of rights, pay and cultural attitudes shown towards women and men. Thankfully, these issues have been noticed and the world is starting to shift slowly towards making reparations. This has been the broader aim of identity-based politics and theology. If a certain type of person has dominated history, now is the time for more marginalized voices to be heard – including for example those of women, people of colour, those with disabilities, those who are LGBTQ+ (Lesbian, Gay, Bisexual, Transgender, and Queer or Questioning), or those who are working class. Not only should those voices be listened to, but changes to the way in which society operates should be made accordingly, in order to make space for these marginalized people and their input to be protected and encouraged. Theology *must* be practical, political and a force for change. In some ways, all theologies are these things – some theologians just misuse theology to uphold an existing hegemony that is corrupted with injustice and distrust.

Why then should we place men back in the centre of theological discussion if we are in an era when we are finally learning from the wisdom of those voices that have been historically overlooked? Well, part of the focus on identity has meant that masculinity has also required further assessment. This means acknowledging the privileges that men have had for centuries and coming at the issue of 'being a man' with an entirely new toolkit of questions and objectives. Precisely *because* our history has been almost invisibly veiled in maleness, what masculinity studies intend to do is probe the very essence of being a man rather than taking it for granted. It means asking questions of our unconscious assumptions of masculinity and the many myths that have arisen from them. Why are men conditioned differently to women? Why do we teach young boys to like sports and cars rather than crafts and baby dolls? Why are men less ready to express their emotions? Why do three times as many men commit suicide compared to women? Why are men more likely to be involved in crime and violence? It is these sorts of questions that studying masculinity deals with. The answers require a deconstruction of what we see manhood to be and an openness to reassessing (and reconstructing) our societal definitions.

Foundationally, this begins with the recognition of the process of socialization. Men are taught to be a certain way, right from their early upbringing and continually until the end of their lives. Masculinity is conditioned – it is recurrently formed, altered, broken down, and rebuilt. The 2019 Gillette advert entitled 'We Believe: The Best Men Can Be' caused a storm on national media because it was seen as a brutal attack on modern masculinity. It highlighted those behaviours of men, such as sexual predation, the patronizing of women and violence, that have been shrugged off by society for decades. These characteristics that have been considered 'manly' have been detrimental not only to the lives of women, but to men themselves. However, in hope for the future, the advert showed that if we are to change the way men act, it must begin with bringing up young boys in a healthier way, because they are the 'men of tomorrow'. In this book, we will work not with the fanciful premise that 'boys will be boys', but with 'boys will be who we raise them to be'.[6]

Defining masculinity

The sociologist Raewyn Connell has been one of the most prolific thinkers in the area of masculinity studies. Her book *Masculinities* was one of the first in-depth explorations into what culture understands about being a man, the lived experience of men themselves, and how men relate to one another in wider society.[7] There are specific points of Connell's argument that I want to raise briefly here to help underpin our ongoing discussion throughout this book.

First, there is never a singular masculinity or one type of man in a culture. Multiple masculinities are constantly at play.

As Natalie Collins states in terms of socializing children, 'there are as many ways to be a boy as there are boys in the world', and the same holds for the many options that men have for how they can perform their masculinities.[8] As such, to talk of 'masculinity' or 'masculinity studies' is rather misleading, for it implies there is just one monolithic and universal type of masculinity. I must emphasize that the use of the singular is usually for conceptual reasons rather than the denial of a plurality of masculinities.

This prompts a second finding of Connell, that these masculinities become categorized as ideal and unideal. This means that society tends to deem a certain masculinity as perfect and the aspirational aim, leaving other types of men insufficient. The technical term for a society's perfect masculinity is hegemonic masculinity. The term hegemonic comes from the Greek verb 'to lead' and so hegemony can be defined as a prevalent control or influence over others. This means that one type of masculinity becomes normative or, in other words, the default type of manhood to aspire to. However, this type of masculinity does not necessarily become the most common or frequently achieved. Succinctly, hegemonic masculinity is normative but not always the norm. In twenty-first-century Britain, the claim could be made that an example of normative hegemonic masculinity is a man with a highly-paid job with a good level of authority, a fair amount of material wealth, some of which he has spent on expensive cars, and a nice muscular body, who receives romantic and sexual attention from women – maybe, think James Bond?

Every man becomes measured against this ideal, in whatever form that ultimate model takes, meaning that most other masculinities fall below this standard. Whether that is someone who prioritizes fast food over exercise, or does not value sex as much as wider society does, there will always be ways in which the normative hegemonic model of manhood is not met by many who are enacting other masculinities. Connell describes these other masculinities as subordinate, marginalized and complicit – each with their own discrete definitions. They all act in relation to one another, leading to a central aspect of Connell's understanding of gender: that there is always a hierarchy of some sort.

Connell's idea of a singular hegemonic masculinity has been contested, however, and it might be more worthwhile to be receptive to the idea of many hegemonic masculinities competing for the top spot. Furthermore, the concept of hybrid masculinity has also emerged.[9] This is where a man may appear resistant to the ideal, but actually still benefits from the privileges that hegemonic masculinity provides (for example, patriarchal systems). Some might like to understand hybrid masculinity as like a wolf in sheep's clothing. As it may be becoming clear, once these many masculinities are at work, the hierarchy of gender becomes very complex. Masculinity studies is certainly not a simple endeavour!

Judith Butler has also been a key figure in gender studies. Notably, Butler devised the idea of gender performativity.[10] This means that gender should not be understood as an identity as such. Instead, gender concerns the way in which someone acts and interacts with others. This is constantly shifting: some performative acts are repeated so much that they become normalized and even glorified, whereas others seem so unique that they are viewed as odd or undesirable. As Gerard Loughlin states, 'masculinity is not one thing but many, and ... these masculinities should be understood as experiments or improvisatory performances'.[11] As humans we construct masculinity and femininity ourselves. We have associated certain characteristics with being male or female, which creates what we see as masculine or feminine traits, historically valuing one over the other. This will be explored more fully in the second chapter of this book, where the creation of sex and gender is discussed in relation to Adam and Eve. But, most importantly, we have to understand that if gender is constructed in this way, then it is changeable.

If to be masculine or feminine is something we design ourselves as a society, without even realizing it, and masculinity is dependent on what society idealizes, it is therefore also dependent on the time period, country, or culture one finds oneself in. Essentially, a man in one place or in one moment of history could be considered the epitome of masculinity but could be thought of as feminine in another. It is all circum-stantial. To realize this means opening our eyes beyond our closed box of the Western world in the twenty-first century. For example, men across cultures and centuries, including both Egyptians and Elizabethans, wore make-up as a symbol of their status and wealth; yet, by the twentieth century, it was seen as an exclusively feminine fashion choice. As we know, the fluidity continues even now as more men have started wearing make-up again in the pop culture of recent decades. Therefore, we must realize that masculinity is much more flexible than our own personal experiences and perceptions. Masculinities are continually transforming throughout history.

Other concepts regarding masculinity have come into wide-spread colloquial use in recent years. One of these is toxic masculinity, which is understood to be masculinities that exhibit toxic behaviours. These unhealthy traits may be violence, abuse, dominance, misogyny or homophobia. This toxicity may also involve the suppression of men's emotions, impacting issues of mental health and relationships. To be frank, these toxic behaviours have become so normalized that they are exhib-ited often, if not constantly, by most modern men. Toxicity has become heavily intertwined with masculinity, continually perpetuated by society. As will become clear as we journey through this book, I will argue that all men have been social-ized to exhibit some toxic behaviours in some way, whether we are wilfully aware of it or not. As such, much of modern (and particularly hegemonic) masculinity has become unhealthy in its very existence for those men who enact it, as well as for those around them who must interact with it. It is these toxic traits associated with masculinity that will be explored and critiqued in this book.

Though a little more disputed than at other times, the phrase 'a crisis of masculinity' is also often heard, usually referring to the shift of what it means to be a man, resulting in a lack of secure and dominant masculine identity. The implication is that men have lost their way in how to be a man. If masculinities are diversifying themselves, at the same time as the progression of women's rights, then some men assume there is some sort of present danger to their very identities. The word 'crisis' assumes that masculinity may potentially be threatened or even lost because of feelings of insecurity and lack of purpose. Because of this myth, Connell prefers the term 'crisis tendencies', by which she means that masculinity cannot be simply destroyed or lost in an act of crisis but that there are tendencies that disrupt and perhaps reimagine a masculinity. As we have already outlined, masculinity is not found or misplaced, but is rather continually re-moulding itself.

Within the media, the term has paradoxically caused a crisis itself, particularly because of its implication that any change in masculinity is a hazardous event. Whether the shifting of what we deem to be masculine is a threat is for the reader to decide; I think that the toxicity exhibited by many men, demonstrated in the statistics already outlined, rationalizes and advocates a re-evaluation in how we understand and produce men. Jack Urwin argues that modern masculinity is simply confused, but that this confusion gives the chance for a new masculinity (or, as I would prefer, masculinities) to emerge.[12] In other words, these crisis tendencies that unsettle our understanding of what it means to be a man are not a danger to masculinity but an essential opportunity for new hope. It means we can begin to imagine healthier perceptions of masculinity that pose no damage to men themselves nor to others around them.

This neatly leads on to the well-versed term of 'fragile masculinity'. This is the notion that men are so obsessed with maintaining their manhood that they overemphasize their masculinity and become hypermasculine in order to protect it. They do not want to 'look gay', seem 'girly' or 'act like a pussy'. This stems from the ideas outlined above that masculinity is in crisis and a change in our attitudes towards men must be a danger. The more masculinity is wrapped in red tape with *FRAGILE* printed across it, the more breakable it will then appear. In reality, however, masculinity (at least on a conceptual level) is a little more like playdough: malleable and ever-changing, and its appearance is in the hands of the sculptor. We, as society and individuals, are wholly responsible for what we sculpt.

In sum, masculinity is unequivocally unstable. To be clear, we cannot define masculinity. It is dependent on its context, culture, and it changes over time. Masculinity, and gender more broadly, are social constructs. We ourselves define what being feminine and masculine means as a society and as individuals. As Ovidiu Creangă outlines, observing masculinity means monitoring one's entire life, including societal institutions, relationships, roles, behaviours, emotions and the body, to name but a few.[13] In this way, it becomes rather complex to assess masculinity – we are acknowledging that we create gender norms and expectations ourselves, and yet are somewhat obliged to play into them in order to discuss them further. In the same way, it is not entirely helpful to talk about the 'manly' and 'unmanly' – which we will do – because it re-enforces those idealizations of right and wrong ways to be a man, but we have to see gender through the eyes of the ancient and modern worlds in order to understand, critique and reform it.

As these things are temporally set, both individually and more widely socially, we cannot transfer understandings of masculinity from one culture to another without serious consideration. This is important to remember as we approach men and masculinity in the Bible and discuss their implications for Christians and the Church today. There can, however, be likenesses of masculinities, even when they are millennia apart. For example, across history men have often been associated with power, authority, strength, violence, action, wealth and sex – many of these still resonating with masculinities performed today. If we are attentive to both the masculinities of the Bible and those of today, lessons can be learnt from their similarities and dissimilarities. It is in Scripture that we can learn about biblical masculinities as well as their particularly

Christian application to our thinking about modern masculinities, which includes their toxicities and crisis tendencies.
As Chris Greenough states: 'The Bible upholds the masculine
values of strength, dominance and power demonstrated by men
in the scripture that give rise to contemporary ideals of men.'[14]
For centuries of Western Christian history, the Bible has been
a cornerstone informing ethics, culture, politics and so on. It
is not far-fetched then to assume that the Bible has also hugely
influenced our modern understanding of masculinity. Though
the masculinities of the ancient world and the masculinities of
today may be distant in history and dissimilar in a multitude of
ways, they are not entirely unrelated.

Masculinity studies and theology

Naturally, Christians need to be attentive to what society seems
to require of men. After all, humanity is made in the image
of God and so what we learn about humanity might help us
reveal more about God, and vice versa. If the impact of such
culturally accepted understandings of masculinity result in dis-
proportionate mental health problems, deaths and suicide for
men, how can we as Christians help to ease the pain and contribute to changing the way we think? How can we stop the
violence in the world, perpetrated mostly by men? How can
we put an end to the victimization of those men who do not
live up to the insisted cultural standards? One of the best ways
to begin an exploration of these ideas is to start looking in
the rear-view or, perhaps more fittingly in discussion of gender
'queer-view',[15] mirror. To what extent is our Christian history
and mindset male? And, if we make a problem of this almost
unconscious masculinist thinking, what future masculinities
might we open ourselves up to?

As an example, one of the most contested concerns for
feminist theology is God the Father – not God's self but the
language of fatherhood that we may employ to describe God.
This can be used as a good case for the benefit of masculinity

studies too. In his brilliant book exploring the Lord's Prayer, Trystan Owain Hughes likens the debate on the use of 'Father' for God to a scene in the movie *Enter the Dragon* (1970): as Bruce Lee puts his finger up into the air, he chastises his student for focusing on the finger rather than the 'heavenly glory' in the sky to which he is pointing.[16] In the same vein, Hughes suggests that we ought to be wary of focusing more on the pointing finger of language to describe God than Godself. God's nature is, of course, greater than our human language could ever capture. But that is all we have: the human media of language, art, music, film and so on. To some extent we must use human language to describe God and must therefore be constrained by its limits. However, if we do this we need to be critical of our application of language so that we do not end up with its misuse and consequent misinterpretation of God. If we overuse the language of Father to the point where many assume that it is the only way to understand God, and that God really *is* a man, then we should be using alternative descriptions that are more expansive to our understanding of the divine. If our world is gendered (even if we know God's identity is not), then we must expect our limited understanding of God to be gendered too.

The problem that comes with this is the relationship between power and gender that has saturated both the ancient world and our modern world. As Chine McDonald highlights, when attributes such as whiteness and maleness are 'valued as so superior that the only acceptable and normative versions of God are as a white man', the scarily normalized language we use for God easily becomes 'problematic'.[17]

We need not look too far to see how masculine power portrayed in the Bible has caused damage when transplanted into modern Christian living. Ezekiel 16 for example, as well as several other similar passages in the prophetic literature of the Bible which have become known as 'pornoprophetic' material, talks of God the husband who strips his whoring wife Israel naked, before having her handed over to a gang to be stoned and cut to pieces. Here is just a snippet, but those who are feeling strong-stomached should take up their Bibles and read the chapter in its entirety.

> Therefore, I will gather all your lovers, with whom you took pleasure, all those you loved and all those you hated; I will gather them against you from all around, and will uncover your nakedness to them, so that they may see all your nakedness. I will judge you as women who commit adultery and shed blood are judged, and bring blood upon you in wrath and jealousy. I will deliver you into their hands, and they shall throw down your platform and break down your lofty places; they shall strip you of your clothes and take your beautiful objects and leave you naked and bare. They shall bring up a mob against you, and they shall stone you and cut you to pieces with their swords. (Ezek. 16.37–40)

Although this passage must undoubtedly be metaphorical, congealed with meaning rigidly attached to its time and culture, it tells of how the ancient world perceived men and their power over others. Francesca Stavrakopoulou is right to say that it cannot be ignored that

> Ezekiel's story is reflective of a patriarchal, masculinist culture, in which girls and women tended to be valued and defined in terms of their bodily configurations with men … Here, [God] is a predatory alpha male, whose sexual entitlement entirely shapes the identity and fate of this displaced and vulnerable young girl.[18]

It seems highly probable that an allegory that attempts to portray God in this way tells us more about the culture from which this text emerged, than about the nature of the God we worship. It informs us of how the ancient world perceived their God within their culturally and inescapably gendered setting – the God that we still believe in today. Evidently, there are problems with this that we should not avoid.

For example, this imagery in Ezekiel 16 would not be spiritually accommodating or comfortable for domestic abuse

13

survivors, to say the least. If they were to read this passage, I imagine they would see the face of the divine in the face of their abusers or, perhaps more scarily, the reverse. An illustration of this can be seen in Alice Walker's *The Color Purple*, where Celie, a young girl, confuses God with her abusive father.[19] She knows both God and her father are dominant masculine figures who exert power, so why would they not be the same person? The Bible has often been used as a justification for abuse, as Helen Paynter makes clear when she retells the story of an abuse victim in her book on this subject:

> Jenny knew her Bible well, but because of the way her husband had interpreted it to her, she could now only find in it themes which appeared to validate her treatment. Scripture had been weaponised against her. It had been shaped into something that could only hurt, not heal.[20]

As womanist biblical scholar Mitzi J. Smith points out, those in power often use their biblical interpretation to maintain their supremacy and exacerbate the marginalization of others. In the example of Ezekiel 16, this takes the form of maleness being attributed to the divine, becoming sacralized, so that such abusive interpretations of the Bible masquerade 'as divine mandates'.[21] We cannot overlook how often gender and power dynamics found in Scripture are still abused and weaponized against people to this day.

As we can see, because of its original contexts and subsequent interpretative traditions, the Bible's near-inseparability from manhood has only helped men justify their abusive behaviour in Christian contexts. If we know that this is the case, we know that a masculine God will have similar damage. Ezekiel 16 is only one example of many where a God who is a 'he' can be dangerous. If we are clear that God is not limited to any gender, then why has the Church become so obsessed with divine masculinity?

Furthermore, what is often left unspoken is the parallel imagery in the Bible for God as Mother.

You were unmindful of the Rock that bore you;
you forgot the God who gave you birth. (Deut. 32.18)

I will fall upon them like a bear robbed of her cubs,
and will tear open the covering of their heart (Hos. 13.8)

As a mother comforts her child,
so I will comfort you;
you shall be comforted in Jerusalem. (Isa. 66.13)

Jerusalem, Jerusalem, the city that kills the prophets and
stones those who are sent to it! How often have I desired
to gather your children together as a hen gathers her brood
under her wings, and you were not willing! (Luke 13.34)

These are only a few examples. Phyllis Trible devotes an entire
book to the feminine divine metaphor woven throughout the
Bible.[22] Christy Angelle Bauman advocates that women should
understand God through their bodies and, particularly, their
wombs.[23] And yet, in a sense, this has not been a new idea.
At some time between the fourteenth and fifteenth centuries,
Julian of Norwich wrote that it was only logical to see God as
Mother if we see God as Father.[24]

We have become fixated on God as Father even though it is
not our only option. A lack of openness to other metaphors of
understanding God could be dangerous, for if we restrict our
understanding of the divine, our receptiveness to revelation
might become limited. Gendered representation of God has
been situationally and contextually chosen by biblical authors
and theologians throughout Church history, and, in the same
way, we ought to be pastorally sensitive about the gendered
pronouns and imagery we use to present God, depending on
our context.

The preference for divine masculinity is particularly accentuated by the (biological) maleness of the incarnation of Jesus
Christ. When God entered our earthly realm, God chose to
be a man, though temporal in historical setting and context.

In other words, God became Jesus in first-century Palestine. If the incarnation happened once again but in the globalized (and yet ignorantly Eurocentric) twenty-first century, would he then return as a Middle Eastern Jewish man? I am undecided.

Scripture provides us with a beautiful insight into the gradual revelation of God. That revelation continues today, but in arguably less obvious ways. Scripture holds great importance and stands as an authoritative revelation of God. Importantly, though, it was a revelation given millennia ago as a diverse library of texts, with many authors addressing a variety of contexts and situations. God is so much greater than Scripture. We might learn more about God from engaging with fresh theological insights from others, our own life experiences, or the experiences of those around us. That is not to reduce the importance of the Bible, but to increase the awesomeness of God. This does not make scriptural texts redundant or irrelevant for today. In fact, the Bible still holds incredible cultural, social, and political influence in our world in a plethora of ways.[25] It does, however, mean that we must realize that many aspects of the texts will be culturally influenced by their origins. We must sensibly yet faithfully work with Scripture conscious of its background and original purpose.

The Bible is not a tool, but a gift. Rather, it is an entire *library* of abundant gifts from different authors, addressing a variety of situations and with a multitude of objectives. The Bible should not be (mis)used, abused, or manipulated for our own purposes or gain. It should, however, be heard. We should attentively listen to the stories present in the texts that are on offer to us. We are often too quick to jump into Scripture, picking our favourite parts and skipping over those bits we do not understand or appreciate. We read whatever is in the lectionary, without seeing what comes before or after the passage, often lacking time to spend meditating and praying with the texts. Even worse, we sometimes do not read the Bible at all but simply let those preaching or teaching tell us what it means through their own unavoidably biased lens – the passive engagement that the Reformation tried to move us away from in the printing of bibles in accessible languages. I iterate that we must listen to Scripture particularly because there are voices in these stories to which we have not paid enough attention, especially those of women, slaves and the oppressed, although there are brilliant scholars and authors who have helped to uncover these lost characters in recent decades.[26] Equally, there are some voices, largely those of men, which we hear all too frequently and could be forgiven for thinking they have little else to say to us. However, there may be more to unravel if we start listening in a different way.

We have all probably heard and talked about the hordes of men in the Bible, whether by focusing on the reign of David and the might of Samson in Sunday School or listening to inspiring sermons about the faithfulness of Paul and the twelve devoted men who loyally followed almost every footstep of Jesus. What academia has only just started doing is asking more intrusive questions about these characters and their own manhood. To me, in a Christian context, it seems that the best way to do this is by suggesting that the men of the Bible might not have been as great as we have been taught. Or, if they are still mighty and masculine, at least that their manhood might not be as stable as we once assumed. Particularly, what might it mean if we exposed, highlighted and explored the flaws of some of these men? What might we learn about our own masculinities today? Are there any similarities between the two? Breaking the illusion of the perfection of many biblical men will be a principle building block to our approach – not for the sake of it, but because that is what Scripture is already pleading with us to do.

It would be inadequate, however, to discuss these issues with only consequences and implications for men in mind. Patriarchy has affected men who have not lived up to the ideals that have been enforced, but its most damaging impact has been on the lives and voices of women. I hope that dismantling the idolizing of biblical men may also be uplifting for women. It means that our expectations of men will be altered and the male attitude to the rest of the world be reconsidered. Although there has been a focus on the damning impact that patriarchy and androcentrism have had on women, its simultaneous effect on men and the wider social issues this has caused have been ignored (by men themselves) for far too long.

Discussing gender should never be an isolated issue. These things affect everyone in society, whether visibly or not. The idealizing of masculinity results in the success of some men and the failure of others. It thus renders women necessarily inadequate. Simultaneously, those men who, for reasons of celibacy, sexuality, or mere uninterest, do not fit the heteronormative expectation of having a wife, are considered to be living unfulfilled lives. Further, if white masculinity is exalted, then people of colour are considered less masculine. If a man cannot perform ideally masculine tasks because of a disability, then particular bodies and body types are idealized. As will now be clear, gender is an issue entangled in so many other wider discussions. In turn, masculinity becomes an intersectional issue. The deeply ingrained systems of society that involve admiration of a particular masculinity need re-examination. Once we have done this, our long-held admirations for biblical men and our own understanding of masculinity can be reconsidered. Only then might we edge closer to God's kingdom, where no one but God is worshipped and glorified.

Bias and self-awareness

It is for this reason of intersectionality that I do not address this book to anyone in particular. Of course, these issues and themes have a primary impact and message for readers who are men. However, I suspect that there will be many other people who have picked up this book, for all manner of reasons, for which I am glad. Reassessing masculinity is a task for us all to engage with, though the responsibility for active change lies particularly with each and every man who will exhibit or has exhibited some level of toxicity in their behaviour. We all have experiences of men to bring to the table in these discussions and so, whoever we may be, our own personal background and stories are invaluable.

In the same vein, the personal impact that exploring gender can have means that a level of self-awareness is needed. Further, a deconstruction of the world around us is required in order to realize how much society forms who we are. We are constantly influenced by external factors. Conversations with others may convince us to change our opinions on a certain issue or inspire us to pick up a new hobby. Advertisements playing in the background on the television or radio often subconsciously persuade us to buy something new. Interviews and discussions on these sorts of media platforms will also affect our political and social viewpoints if we are persuaded by the speakers. Social media on our phones and laptops that we mindlessly consume as we scroll through our feeds each day will contain content that might reshape our opinions and attitudes, even if we do not realize it, with preconceptions and prejudices often being reinforced by the restrictiveness of the likeminded echo chambers we seem to find ourselves in. To some extent all these aspects continually sculpt our identity. Few of our desires, dreams, opinions and beliefs are solely our own configuration.

Gender is intrinsically linked to these things. If things are marketed as more suitable for men, then we start to attach certain attributes and items to particularly biological male bodies. More widely, we mark certain characteristics and gestures as masculine or feminine, just because we may have seen a comedian on the television, or even someone's Facebook post, that says so. As this escalates, external channels begin to tell us, whether consciously or not, what we should or should not like, think or desire, depending on our gender identity and even our genitalia. Once we realize that this socialized way of living can be changed, there are limitless ways in which we can inhabit God's earth.

The queer theorist Judith Butler calls for us all to 'trouble' gender once we realize how we are imprisoned by what society deems as feminine and masculine actions and interactions.[27]

This might be as simple as men liking the colour pink, or it could include men painting their nails, wearing dresses, growing out their hair, or using make-up. In 2020, Harry Styles caused a storm in the British media and celebrity circles by wearing a dress for a *Vogue* magazine shoot. It is exactly this sort of gender troubling that Butler encourages.

But Butler's advocacy is politically charged to change the way in which our entire societal system operates. Perhaps the thought of a man in a dress may be a bit far for some, but her wider aim should be considered. If we want to do something that we have been told is feminine, however our genitalia or body have been labelled, then we should be able to do it – whether that be painting our fingernails, getting a piercing, doing the dishes, dying our hair or taking up ballet! We should be comfortable acting in whatever way we wish, regardless of what society has deemed suitable for a man or a woman. The only way we can achieve this goal is to disturb our preconceptions of what gender is and how it affects our own lives, particularly when we might not even notice it.

This means acknowledging where we are coming from when we approach our perception of gender, particularly in relation to our own identity. In any case, an awareness of our own position and biases is important when we approach the Bible, but even more so when thinking about gender. We bring everything about ourselves to the reading of texts and that will almost unconsciously influence our interpretations and conclusions about what we are reading and even the world around us. In biblical hermeneutics, this is known as what is 'in front of the text'. Just like the liberation theologies we looked at earlier, our ideologies, experiences and contexts will determine what we consider to be the (or, more aptly, a) meaning of the text.

These factors will similarly impact our understanding of manhood. If someone lives their life identifying as a woman, their perception of masculinity (whether contemporary or biblical) may be different to a man's. Moreover, a gay man will understand masculinity differently to a straight man. A father will have an alternative perception of masculinity to that of someone without children. Someone who had an abusive father will understand what it means to be a man in an incredibly disparate way than if they had had a loving and cuddly one. A man who has been in prison for violent crimes will perceive manhood in a different way to one who protests for non-violence. These are only a glimpse of the numerous factors that might affect what we expect an ideal man to be. They all depend on our socialization.

To approach this subject with integrity, we have got to be honest with each other and ourselves about our own personal experiences and journeys. Part of the toxicity of masculinity is that men are afraid to recognize their own participation in the oppression of women and other men. It means that they shy away from gender and masculinity studies because they are too scared to confront the complexities of their own identity. It is exactly this problem that must be recognized and dealt with. The more we are honest about our own actions and attitudes as men, the more we can learn about the beneficial parts of our masculinity, the detrimental parts, and what needs to happen next.

As the author of this book I acknowledge my own biases and predispositions as I approach this subject matter. Such honesty and authenticity are incredibly important, even on an academic level, when exploring the subjects of gender and masculinity, which is why I have continually attempted to include and reflect upon personal experience throughout my writing.

Being brought up predominantly surrounded by girls and women may explain why in my adulthood I exhibit what are usually considered more feminine traits, including emotional openness, empathy and kindness. I have continued to be fairly unbothered by my gender portrayal, whether that comes from being slightly flamboyant, loving musicals, wearing dungarees, having a nose piercing, or not shying away from a cry. My life as a bisexual man (particularly while in a relationship with a woman) and being a member of the LGBTQ+ community while sometimes 'passing' as heteronormative will influence my view of masculinity. Similarly, the privilege of being white (with the power that whiteness brings, particularly in the Church)[28] will impact my understanding of being a man, having not experienced prejudice or oppression based on race. Because of this, I have made sure that in my writing I have drawn from scholarship and memoirs by writers of colour. Yet I am also aware that I will have picked up traits of toxic masculinity. I often call out male friends for their oblivious sexist and toxic behaviours, and I expect others to do the same for me. Personally, in the past these dangerous traits have chiefly exhibited themselves through a desire for control, a denial of mental health issues and a level of arrogance. Though there will be more that I will elaborate on throughout the chapters of this book, and undoubtedly others that I have not yet noticed, it is not self-destructive to recognize bad traits in our personalities, but healthy and constructive. These behaviours of toxic masculinity can thankfully be changed; they are not set in concrete in our biological make-up but are learnt, and so can be unlearnt.

As we reflect on our own gender performance throughout this book, we need to remember that part of our task is to work hard for the undoing of such indoctrination of unhealthy masculinity in ourselves and others. One of the first steps in this is simply acknowledging and apologizing for any hurt, damage or mistreatment caused, though this should never absolve guilt or diminish any moral responsibility. As Christians, we may find such repentance and forgiveness for our own actions and those of others more familiar.

In March 2021, Sarah Everard went missing while travelling home from a friend's house in London and was eventually discovered to have been murdered. Many took a sadly all-too-familiar approach to such stories, claiming that if Sarah had not been walking home alone at night in London it would not have happened. We see this 'victim blaming' so often in our society, where the fault attached to the abuse, rape or murder of a woman somehow lies with the victim themselves, rather than the perpetrator. For far too long we have expected women to make themselves safer, when we actually should have been tackling the problem of the men who consider it permissible to endanger women's lives. With such themes being regurgitated later that year in the news of the murder of Sabina Nessa, it has never been clearer that a prevalent attitude in which men's degradation of women often escalates into violent extremities of abuse, rape and murder needs to be immobilized and tackled urgently.

In the particular case of Sarah Everard, many people took to protests and social media to remind others of the dangers that men so regularly pose to women's safety, but in response they were met by the emerging trend *#NotAllMen*. The issue here is that those men who claim that not all men are at fault are the ones trying to find boastful pride in their innocence, declaring themselves exempt from any wider criticism of masculinity in general. They wash their hands of a widespread culture of which they will have inevitably been a part. Moreover, it begs the question of why such men feel so insecure that they must defend themselves – are they concealing their own sense of personal and/or collective guilt? As Natalie Collins states:

> Our discomfort at naming men as the majority perpetrators of violence both in the UK and globally is not because we are unaware of the facts, but because we all know men who are not violent. We feel uncomfortable with a portrayal of *all men* as bad. They say the last thing a fish notices is water; we are oblivious to the ubiquity of men's violence. Yet if we want to respond effectively we must not remain oblivious.[29]

As we shall see throughout this book, no man is spared from the chains of patriarchy and toxic masculinity. The onus is on every single man to change their behaviour and call out that of others. I do not aim in this book to present men as perfect, in fact quite the opposite. Whether we like it or not, we are socialized into a world where toxicity is the norm for masculinity, and so all men have at times exhibited it, whether consciously or unconsciously. Exceptionally few men could truthfully say that they have *never* passed up an opportunity to call out a friend, or even a stranger, who is misogynistically teasing, mocking, taunting, or sadly even abusing, women, often justified as 'just banter'. Realistically, those who say that they have not will have missed many opportunities that they had been unaware of, because of men's pure blindness to women's issues. There is a collective obligation for men to be part of the change towards gender equality, but that means criticizing our own masculinities and recognizing the problems within *all* of us, as individuals and as a collective culture.

I hope that this book will help in your exploratory journey through these pressing matters. It is on the premise of ubiquitous and undeniable toxic masculinity that our conversation is grounded. It is not emasculating to realize that the prevailing modern expressions of masculinity are flawed. Rather, it should be quite liberating, even if it must be uncomfortable at first. It just takes an initially painful process of deconstructive realization before that can happen – a process, I believe, that all men need to go through in order to live in true freedom and happiness. This is a journey of repentance and resurrection for those masculinities that harm us and others. By picking up this book, you are taking the first step.

Our objectives

The gender-criticism of academia has brought about progressive changes in the lives of many Christian women, particularly by the growth of accessible resources for how to read the Bible positively with an affirmation of the place, equality and ministry of women. In turn, this type of work has contributed greatly to understanding gender in the Bible and the Church more broadly. However, little progressive work has been done by Christian men towards liberating themselves. The books already available that are addressed to Christian men tend to look at what it takes to 'reclaim biblical masculinity', or act as instruction manuals on 'how to be the men that God intended'. The problem with the majority of these Christian endeavours

into what it means to be a man of God is that they are dangerously discriminatory and utterly sexist. With the usual biblical
quotations used for evidential backing, they argue for men to
be the heads of families, with particular control over matters
of finance and decision-making. They support the maleness of
ministry, regarding men as the only people able to lead worship and prayer as well as exercise authority. They claim that
strength, toughness and power are solely masculine attributes.

This book seeks to counter such thinking and to debunk the
myth of 'biblical manhood', something rooted in the comple-
mentarianism that has emerged particularly with American
conservative evangelicalism in the last century. The Council on
Biblical Manhood and Womanhood, founded by John Piper
among others, originated such thinking when it emerged in
1987 and continues to contribute to these narratives, in most
recent years with the Nashville Statement.[30] Scholarship in
very recent years has explicitly begun to bite back against this
modelling of manhood and womanhood in Christian settings,
particularly noting the work of Beth Alison Barr and Aimee
Byrd.[31]

I will argue frequently throughout this book that there is
no consistent 'biblical masculinity', nor a necessarily 'Christian
masculinity', because, as we shall see, the Bible is far too complex and multifaceted to portray just one way of being a man.
To suggest that there is an enaction of masculinity that is
intrinsically and undeniably Christian, whatever that might
mean, is to overlook the diversity of masculinities found in the
Christian Bible. The way in which a man should (and should
not) act in terms of gender is not a biblical, nor a doctrinal,
matter for Christianity. It has been wrong for Christian history to assume such a thing. God loves so many different types
of men in the Bible that it would be utterly impossible to pin
down one way that a man ought to be. I offer this book as
a work of applied and public theological and biblical study
that will contribute to the conversations and practices of the
Church and wider society in liberating masculinity from the
oppressive gender politics of the past.

Though there are other thinkers offering resources in this area, this book is, perhaps uniquely, designed to accommodate both academic and lay Christian readers who are interested in both the Bible and toxic masculinity, and how they intersect with our Christian faith. I hope the constructive questioning in this book will clear the ground of unthinking attitudes to masculine perfectionism and idolization and make space for new ideas to take root. We may not arrive at all the answers, but I hope that you will be encouraged to engage more critically with the biblical myths of masculinity that we so often take for granted.

I will draw from a variety of sources, including memoirs, stories, personal experiences, popular culture and scholarship in multiple disciplines. By doing so, I hope to communicate an accessible and faithful theological message grounded in academia, in which intellectual rigour is not lost. I hope that undergraduate and postgraduate university students (of any or no faith), as well as committed Christians, ministers and spiritual explorers, will find this book invigorating and informative. At the end of this book, you will find suggestions for further reading and resources to help you investigate further according to your degree of interest. This should produce a well-rounded approach to how we might tackle issues surrounding masculinity, creating a space for all to sit at the table of this discussion, making sure that intellectual engagement as well as pastoral concern are of equal importance.

This endeavour cannot be purely theoretical, however. By exploring this area, we are all helping to liberate ourselves from the chains of traditional and toxic masculinity. We are embarking on a political, social and theological pursuit of change. Implications are just as important as interpretations. In our Christian context, that means disturbing our possibly idyllic portraits of the men of the Bible and reconsidering them. If biblical men are not as perfect or homogenous as we may once have assumed, perhaps we can recognize that the men in our families and churches do not have to be either. This should not legitimize the toxic traits of men but provide a healthy way of engaging with them for change.

If we want to start undoing the damage that our constructions of manliness have done to so many people, of all genders,
then we might want to start reassessing our own faith and the
Bible that we hold so dear. The masculinities of the Bible and
those of today are starkly different in so many ways. At best,
there may be a common thread of characteristics between the
two cultures. At the least, we will be able to find topics and
themes that can be a springboard for our own discussing of
modern masculinity, based as it is on misconceptions of what
men should always be. These parallels will provide the space in
which we will operate.

Each chapter uses a particular man of the Bible as a focus
to look at a certain myth concerning both biblical and modern
concepts of masculinity, as well as other related issues. There
is an overwhelming plethora of men on offer for assessment
in the Bible, but I have chosen a small selection that have
the most potential for effective consideration; this is certainly not an exhaustive assessment of biblical masculinities,
but merely an introduction. We will go from Adam, Moses,
David, Jeremiah and Job to look then at Jesus, the disciples,
Paul, and eventually God. Each character will act as a vehi-
cle for assessing our own conceptions of masculinity. As we
travel through these discussions together, I want us to consider each man not only as a literary figure but also as a real
person – our same flesh and blood who walked this earth just
as we do. By doing this, we will have a much more authentic, emotive and consequential encounter with these biblical
characters, even if we may remain unconvinced of the actual
historicity of some of them. We will relate to them better as fellow humans, though distanced by time and culture, who faced
many similar struggles to our own. We will find toxic themes
of power, authority, control, homophobia/homoerotophobia,
violence, male-exclusivism, emotional suppression, mental
health stigma, sexual violence and the fear of nonconforming
masculinities, all of which will give food for reflection for both
modern and biblical masculinities.

So let us begin our voyage across the sea of masculinities

that awaits us. As we discover that biblical men do not always exhibit the perfect masculinity that we might have previously presumed, we will see that there is no perfect masculinity that God seeks from us. Christian men can begin to be liberated from the oppressive models of mythic masculinity that have been a cemented part of history. In doing so, we can begin to make reparations for the false way in which we have produced masculinity and the ripples, tides and tsunamis of violence that such gender coding has caused.

Notes

1 Gov.uk, 2020, 'Arrests', *Ethnicity Facts and Figures: Gov.uk*, 15 December, www.ethnicity-facts-figures.service.gov.uk/crime-justice-and-the-law/policing/number-of-arrests/latest#by-ethnicity-and-gender (accessed 3.7.2020).

2 Samaritans, 2019, 'Suicide statistics report', https://media.samaritans.org/documents/SamaritansSuicideStatsReport_2019_Full_report.pdf (accessed 3.7.2020).

3 Chris Hemmings, 2017, *Be A Man: How macho culture damages us and how to escape it*, London: Biteback Publishing, p. 20.

4 Natalie Collins, 2019, *Out of Control: Couples, Conflict and the Capacity for Change*, London: SPCK, p. 58.

5 Stephen D. Moore, 2003, '"O Man, Who Art Thou...?": Masculinity Studies and New Testament Studies', in Stephen D. Moore and Janice Capel Anderson (eds), *New Testament Masculinities*, Atlanta, GA: Society of Biblical Literature, 2003, pp. 1–22 (p. 1).

6 Elvis Onyedikachi Kawedo, 2021, 'Boys will not be boys: The toxic norms around masculinity we have to disband', *Indy100 Conversations*, 6 January, https://conversations.indy100.com/boys-will-be-boys-toxic-masculinity (accessed 7.9.2020).

7 R. W. Connell, 2005, *Masculinities*, 2nd edition, Cambridge: Polity Press.

8 Collins, *Out of Control*, pp. 242–3.

9 James W. Messerschmidt and Michael A. Messner, 2018, 'Hegemonic, Nonhegemonic, and "New" Masculinities', in James W. Messerschmidt et al. (eds), *Gender Reckonings: New Social Theory and Research*, New York: New York University Press, pp. 35–56 (pp. 48–9).

10 Judith Butler, 2006, *Gender Trouble: Feminism and the Subversion of Identity*, Abingdon: Routledge, pp. 34 and 187–93.

11 Gerard Loughlin, 1998, 'Refiguring Masculinity in Christ', in Michael A. Hayes, Wendy Porter and David Tombs (eds), *Religion and Sexuality*, Sheffield: Sheffield Academic Press, pp. 405–14 (p. 412).

12 Jack Urwin, 2016, *MAN UP: Surviving Modern Masculinity*, London: Icon Books Ltd, pp. 231–2.

13 Ovidiu Creangă, 2017, 'Introduction', in Ovidiu Creangă and Peter-Ben Smit (eds), *Biblical Masculinities Foregrounded*, Sheffield: Sheffield Phoenix Press, pp. 3–14 (p. 4).

14 Chris Greenough, 2021, *The Bible and Sexual Violence Against Men*, Abingdon: Routledge, p. 79.

15 Chris Greenough, 2020, *Queer Theologies: The Basics*, Abingdon: Routledge, p. 42.

16 Trystan Owain Hughes, 2017, *Living the Prayer: The everyday challenge of the Lord's Prayer*, Abingdon: BRF, p. 16.

17 Chine McDonald, 2021, *God Is Not a White Man (And other revelations)*, London: Hodder & Stoughton, p. 31.

18 Francesca Stavrakopoulou, 2021, *God: An Anatomy*, London: Pan MacMillan, p. 158.

19 Alice Walker, 2017, *The Color Purple*, London: Weidenfeld & Nicholson.

20 Helen Paynter, 2020b, *The Bible Doesn't Tell Me So: Why you don't have to submit to domestic abuse and coercive control*, Abingdon: BRF, p. 13.

21 Mitzi J. Smith, 2018, *Womanist Sass and Talk Back: Social (In) Justice, Intersectionality, and Biblical Interpretation*, Eugene, OR: Wipf and Stock Publishers, p. 4.

22 Phyllis Trible, 1978, *God and the Rhetoric of Sexuality*, Philadelphia, PA: Fortress Press.

23 Christy Angelle Bauman, 2019, *Theology of the Womb: Knowing God through the body of a woman*, Eugene, OR: Cascade Books.

24 Julian of Norwich, 2015, *Revelations of Divine Love*, trans. by Barry Windeatt, Oxford: Oxford University Press, p. 128.

25 For example, the Bible has been both an implicit and explicit force in contemporary British politics, from David Cameron and Theresa May to Jeremy Corbyn and Nigel Farage. See James Crossley, 2018, *Cults, Martyrs and Good Samaritans: Religion in Contemporary English Political Discourse*, London: Pluto Press. Not only this, but biblical images can be seen in popular culture to the extent that biblical literacy has become incredibly important just to navigate the modern world in which we live. See Katie Edwards (ed.), 2015, *Rethinking Biblical Literacy*, London: Bloomsbury Publishing. Finally, religion and the Bible even pervade our everyday use of language, whether we notice it or not. See Valerie Hobbs, 2021, *An Introduction to Religious Lan-*

guage: Exploring Theolinguistics in Contemporary Contexts, London: Bloomsbury Publishing.

26 In the case of women, for example, you can find academically informed but fictional autobiographies of many biblical women in Athalya Brenner, 2005, *I Am... Biblical Women Tell Their Own Stories*, Minneapolis, MN: Fortress Press. For an example of womanist midrash literature, see Wilda C. Gafney, 2017, *Womanist Midrash: A Reintro-duction to the Women of the Torah and the Throne*, Louisville, KY: Westminster John Knox Press, and Wilda C. Gafney, 2008, *Daughters of Miriam: Women Prophets in Ancient Israel*, Minneapolis, MN: Fortress Press.

27 Butler, *Gender Trouble*.

28 A. D. A. France-Williams, 2020, *Ghost Ship: Institutional Racism and the Church of England*, London: SCM Press, pp. 8–17.

29 Collins, *Out of Control*, pp. 64–5 (original italics).

30 For my response to the Nashville Statement, see Will Moore, 2017, 'Why the Church needs to reject the Nashville statement and embrace LGBT+ Christians', *Premier Christianity* blog, www.premier christianity.com/home/why-the-church-needs-to-reject-the-nashville-statement-and-embrace-lgbt-christians/3794.article (published 1.9.2017, accessed 2.11.2021).

31 Beth Alison Barr, 2021, *The Making of Biblical Womanhood: How the Subjugation of Women Became Gospel Truth*, Ada, MI: Brazos Press, and Aimee Byrd, 2020, *Recovering From Biblical Manhood and Womanhood: How the Church Needs to Rediscover Her Purpose*, Grand Rapids, MI: Zondervan.

2

Men Are Built Better: Adam

In the beginning

Where better to start our discussion than the very first book of the Bible and the earliest moments of the cosmos? The origin story of Christianity, as well as of Islam and Judaism, begins with God and the creation of the universe in the text of Genesis. Out of the formless void comes beauty: light, water, sky, land, plants, the sun, the moon and the stars, birds of the sky, creatures of the earth and humankind (Gen. 1). Each aspect of beauty is given a function, whether that be the presence or absence of light to create day and night or the abundance of plants yielding seed to provide food for humanity.

Recent scholarship on the Ancient Near East, such as the works of John Walton and Gordon Wenham, has understood the authors and original readers of the Genesis accounts to value order and function.[1] The act of creation is not the production or invention of something, as our modern minds might assume. For example, we might assume an object's creation is its first appearance as matter. To us, a table might only become a table once it has taken the final form of one, with legs and a top. Instead, in the ancient world, when something is 'created', it is given a function. There is no existence of something until it has a purpose or, as Greek philosophy would have called it, a *telos*. Once we realize this, the first account of creation in Genesis 1 has a much richer image of divine design to offer. God not only becomes the Artist of Life by sketching out characters and figures but also becomes the Author, by plotting out the living story arc in which they will participate and their purpose be realized. The possibilities are endless for the creative God who knows all that could, might and will happen for creation. God is in complete control of the order that surrounds us, while still giving creation its freedom to flourish.

Humanity is the pinnacle of God's creation, the last part of the divine jigsaw. It is in humanity that this beauty and order teems in its brilliance, because humanity is made in the *imago dei* (the 'image of God').

> So God created humankind in his image,
> in the image of God he created them;
> male and female he created them. (Gen. 1.27)

God breathes divine breath into human life. We are made from the very air of God's being. We exhibit the utmost excellence of God's creativity. Not only that, but we are tasked with the stewardship of the rest of creation, which undoubtedly includes maintaining its beauty and order. In a 2021 speech in the House of Lords, Archbishop of York Stephen Cottrell drew attention to the gradual move in the words of the Lord's Prayer from living 'in' earth to 'on' it, signifying our changed relationship as humans with creation. The theological implications of this mean that men (and for most of human history, it really has been men) have moved from being an equal part of creation, a puzzle piece in a bigger picture, to raping and raiding the goodness of the earth and all it offers. We see a masculinist dominance and abuse perpetrated against God's good creation.[2] Our actions need urgent attention.

At the same time as causing a climate crisis, we are also of God and have done equal amounts of damage to ourselves as human beings. Genesis 3, also known as The Fall, shows that humanity disobeyed a command and 'fell' from God – from God's perfection, from God's beauty and from God's order. Sin entered this world and has not left it. If we focus on moral and immoral actions, particularly pointing the finger of blame at people around us, then we start to distract ourselves from the point of this foundational teaching: we *all* fall short. Sin has itself become a dirty word to outsiders of the Church, and even to people inside Christian communities. As Jarel Robinson-Brown points out, we are quick to be taught about sin and its damning consequences sooner than we are to learn of God's abundant grace.[3] But all that such a stigmatized word like sin signifies is that humanity is imperfect: we are all prone to fall into the hands of temptation and do things that go against God's will for us.

It is not hard for us to justify this claim. As evidence, some only need to read the text of Genesis, written thousands of years ago, in which two people take a piece of fruit which was forbidden, even if it is much more likely to be allegorical than historical. But our world today offers so many more real and relevant illustrations – violent wars, slavery, deserted refugees, outrageous levels of poverty, oppressive regimes and environmental destruction. We can even see it on a more localized and personal level when those we trust fail to keep promises, or when we lose control and hurt others with our insensitive words or actions. From national acts of violence to the smallest mistakes in our day-to-day lives, it is obvious that humanity is not perfect. We continue to do wrong and damage ourselves. Of course, this does not mean that we cannot celebrate our humanity. We have achieved so much and any overwhelming focus on our imperfection can be detrimental to our mental and physical health. First and foremost, we should simply remember that we can never be perfect humans – but Jesus can be. We can always aspire to the righteousness of Christ.

But before humanity disobeyed God, there was perfection in creation. Some would argue that God's perfect design means that the creation of male and female is a key part of such beauty. This would mean that humanity is divinely fashioned in only two sexual categories, female and male. Further, they assume that they must therefore be feminine and masculine respectively, with a certain role for women and another for men because of this creational difference. What we tend to miss here is the leap made between sex and gender – both of which are highly debated. We have come to associate being masculine with male bodies and being feminine with female bodies. If we start to unpick this, we will see that this is not quite the case.

The difference between sex and gender

Sex is biological. The sex of a body is dependent on its genitalia and genetic coding. In the historically phallocentric Western world in which most of us live, there has been a binary classification: those who have a penis are male, those who do not are simply unimportant. We have attached power and authority to the male body. By doing this, certain attributes linked specifically to power have been associated with the biological male body, including authority, assertiveness, strongmindedness and control. Because this has happened for centuries, these ideas are embedded so deeply into our cultures that we subconsciously expect our men to be these things without recognizing it. But importantly, these characteristics have nothing to do with our biology; they are examples of learnt behaviour. As we have seen, Butler understands gender not as an identity (which many do argue for), but as a configuration of actions and interactions – a matter of performance. If this is the case, we have associated certain characteristics with masculinity or femininity, which themselves have been attached to a biological body, even though they are completely unrelated. In short, sex and gender are too often conflated when they are two separate and distinctly different things.

Both, however, are contested. Some argue that gender is a spectrum of masculinity and femininity in which one must be the opposite of the other. Others disagree because this still enforces some sort of binary where masculinity and femininity are the goal posts by which we define gender. For example, Joseph Gelfer suggests that although polarity is sometimes a 'fact' of nature, it is not always the case, and what is metaphorical polarity has been wrongly understood as literal.[4] But if gender is constructed and defined by us, then a spectrum of

34

masculinity and femininity is something that we have also created, even it is not necessarily 'true'. So gender might not be on any sort of scale. Sex, on the other hand, is much more widely accepted as binary – which means being male and female. Some say this is a fundamental and biological truth in the world that is unchangeable. To some extent this might be true. However, the simple binarity of sex that the media and other sources would have us believe is not quite the case. Society has built up a dualistic understanding of human bodies, when actually there can be an 'in-between'. First, there is a diversity of body types, with many sizes and variations of human sexual and biological components. As another example, there are a minority of people who are considered as intersex. These individuals may possess or lack certain biological attributes that would enable them to be defined as either (wholly) male or female. Here, there is biological ambiguity – or is it only ambiguous to us because we have been led to believe that there is only one binary way of understanding sex?

There are many views on sex and gender. This book is not the place to enter such debates in depth. However, one important guarantee I can offer is that sex and gender are distinctly different. Any conflation of the two shows a lack of understanding of contemporary gender studies as well as of basic biology. This is not intended to be some inflammatory proposition, it is simply an observable element of how humanity operates, backed by wide scholarly consensus. If men do not express emotion very often, how is it that now we talk more openly about men's mental health and many men have finally felt able to join the conversation? If women are not forthright or authoritative enough for leadership roles, how is it that, now that women have been enabled for success in society, they have become CEOs of businesses and bishops in the Church of England? The answer to these sorts of questions is simple: because they were always capable of doing such things, we have accepted the false and oppressive teaching that they never could. We have restrictively associated male and female with certain ways of acting that are utterly false, because our gender politics have infiltrated how we understand our own bodies. Once we start to unpick that, we realize that humanity can act in an unconstrained diversity of ways. In reality, masculinity and femininity are outdated concepts that have shifted substantially in recent decades. However, we do have to use them in order to discuss gender coherently in a world constructed around them.

But what does this mean in the light of the Genesis creation stories? Well, if God created humanity in beauty and order, what is the divine beauty and order of human gender and sex? Diversity, as we shall begin to discover.

It is widely agreed that Genesis contains two creation accounts. The first (which begins in Genesis 1) opens with a pre-existent, formless void, that God develops into substance as each element is given purpose. Notably, just like the other products of creation, humanity is given *one* function, not two separate ones:

> God blessed them, and God said to them, 'Be fruitful and multiply, and fill the earth and subdue it; and have dominion over the fish of the sea and over the birds of the air and over every living thing that moves upon the earth.' (Gen. 1.28)

They are told to have stewardship of the world, in which they should be fruitful and multiply. There is no instruction about how women or men should act differently. Even more, there is no sexual distinction of humanity in this account. God's ultimate creation of humanity and their purpose is of one species – not divided or segregated but considered as unified bodies acting together in accordance with God's will.

The second creation account (which follows from Gen. 2.5 onwards) is where theological discussion of gender and sex is much livelier. This myth is considered to be a couple of centuries older than the first creation story, which might give it a little more clout. It is in this narrative that we meet Eve and Adam. But, first, humanity is referred to in the singular. There is one (hu)man:

then the LORD God formed man from the dust of the ground, and breathed into his nostrils the breath of life; and the man became a living being. (Gen. 2.7)

Many have considered this to be some sort of sexless or androgynous being, the former meaning a being who is sexually undifferentiated and the latter as an amalgamation of maleness and femaleness. It seems there were certainly other Hebrew words available if the writer wanted to specify a particularly male human. Instead, the Hebrew *ha'adam* is much more generic of humanity.[5] Moreover, if there is only one human, and no mention of their sex, perhaps we should just assume that sexual distinction simply did not exist at this early point of creation.[6]

A division of the human does occur eventually, however. Many translations tell of the creation of Eve from the 'rib' of Adam.

So the LORD God caused a deep sleep to fall upon the man, and he slept; then he took one of his ribs and closed up its place with flesh. And the rib that the LORD God had taken from the man he made into a woman and brought her to the man. (Gen. 2.21–22)

This leaves Eve as almost a creational afterthought made from the wholeness of man. It is these sorts of ideas that position Eve in an inferior state to Adam, and thus women to men. But the imagery of division is helpful here in the sense of a literal halving or split. John Walton has pointed out that the Hebrew word usually translated 'rib' is much more commonly used to mean 'half' or 'side' in passages about objects such as the ark, tabernacle or altar.[7] God puts the human in some sort of anaesthetic sleep paralysis to create two distinctly and equally separate humans out of the initial sexually undifferentiated one. As Phyllis Trible puts it, we see God the Surgeon in these moments.[8]

Why does this happen? Why does the sexless human need

to become sexed? The writer of Genesis suggests that sexual union is the reason. Because the biologically distinct male and female are created together from the sexless being, their flesh will cling together (Gen. 2.24). If anything, this reading means that woman and man are united. They are created in one and have equal footing in the chronology of creation. Neither one lords over the other in their sexual difference. This does, of course, create difficulties for discussion about wider issues of human sexuality, particularly those surrounding LGBTQ+ people (which will be tackled in the next chapter). Perhaps, however, we might see this writing of the binaries of maleness and femaleness as two ends of a larger and much more whole spectrum, following the typical merisms seen in biblical litera-ture such as the way in which God creates day and night, as well as the heavens and the earth. To list creation dualistically is to put end markers in place, but that does not mean there is no in-between for the day and the night, the heavens and the earth, or even male and female.

It is also noteworthy that neither of the humans are 'ashamed' of their nakedness (Gen. 2.25). It is a natural part of their humanity. In today's world of perfect bodies in advertising and film, we have become obsessed with our own image. The bur-den of this shame and feeling of inadequacy has largely fallen on women, although men have had similar high standards to measure themselves against. The insistence on separate women and men's clothing, for example, has sexist undertones: men's clothing is fairly limited to jeans (with functional pockets!) and shirts, while women commonly wear dresses designed to accentuate certain parts of the female body. Men's fashion seems mostly designed with practicality in mind, whereas that of women has a prioritized the intention of looking attrac-tive and even sexually enticing, enforcing the male gaze that infects our culture. Further, many celebrities in film and tele-vision, as well as the models who display the clothes we buy, demonstrate the high standards of our culture. Pictures and posters of models with airbrushed skin and fit physiques tower over us as consumers, exalted as the norm. If we are not like those presented to us in culture and media, we are made to feel ashamed. Usually we are left wanting to change ourselves. Yet, here in Genesis, humanity has no shame for their biological circumstances. As we later learn, they do not even know yet that they are naked. They are not aware of any sort of sexual distinction between themselves in these moments. All they know is that they are human, joined in union, and are part of God's beautiful creation. Sex is neither an issue nor a defining category for them. Gender, and whether one should be masculine or feminine, is not even mentioned. Though this does not last for long, was this God's original intention for us?

The fall of genderless-ness

In Genesis 3 Eve and Adam start to act independently. They become individual agents of humanity. This distinctiveness in character starts to impact how we might perceive their gendered actions and interactions. God orders the sexless human not to eat the fruit from the tree but does not give this instruction to either Adam or Eve particularly. It is curious that the serpent first comes to tempt Eve. Is it because she is a woman? If so, is it because Eve is weaker and more susceptible than Adam? Or is it because Eve has more sway (and maybe authority) over him? Or is it because the ancient world expected, or perhaps sometimes even *wanted*, women to be the one blamed?

Nevertheless, in the biblical text Eve gives in to the temptation of the serpent. Readings of this narrative have historically been rather negative about Eve. She has become the criminal counterpart of humanity. She has been understood as the evil seductress who lures in Adam to take part in a deviant act against God. She became the one who tainted the perfectness of Adam, the dent in his pristine masculinity. She has been labelled the originator of sin for which the entirety of human history has suffered. She has been understood as the reason that there is suffering and death all around us today. Most importantly, she has become the blame. In turn, women have been scapegoated for centuries. As Katie Edwards says, many eras of art, literature and interpretation have portrayed Eve as 'the biblical bad girl whose predatory sexuality lured Adam into disobedience and out of Eden; a seductress whose powers of attraction were so potent that she caused the fall not only of Adam, but of the whole of humanity'.[9] As such, Christian understanding has placed women at a lower standing than men purely because it was thought that they all reflect Eve's deviance – women are the reason humanity is sinful, and so men are blameless. The irony of this convenience cannot go unnoticed. After all, 'patriarchy [was not] what God wanted; patriarchy was a result of *human* sin'.[10]

Of course, Eve's part in this fall of genderless-ness is not the entire story. She is certainly an active participant in this encounter with the serpent, in which she disobeys God, but Adam's part is a little more intriguing.

> So when the woman saw that the tree was good for food, and that it was a delight to the eyes, and that the tree was to be desired to make one wise, she took of its fruit and ate; and she also gave some to her husband, who was with her, and he ate. (Gen. 3.6)

So that is all he does: he eats. The fate of human history hangs on this entire moment and Adam – the man to whom so much of human history has given responsibility, authority and charge – does nothing. He does not verbally try to persuade Eve to change her ways, nor does he physically stop eating the fruit himself. In Nadia Bolz-Weber's words, 'he is unbelievably passive'.[11] As such, Adam is complicit and as much to blame; whether this passivity renders him even more at fault than Eve is an even further debate.

As we have seen, more traditional interpretations have considered the sexless being as Adam. This would mean that God only orders Adam not to eat from the tree, because at the point of instruction Eve has yet to be formed from Adam's rib. If this is so, then the onus is even more on Adam to make sure that this command from God is not disobeyed by him or his new partner. His complicity is therefore doubled in this particular interpretation.

I am more convinced by understanding the first human as a sexless being, rather than an Eve-less Adam. Regardless, both interpretations show that placing the blame entirely on Eve is flawed. Undoubtedly both Eve and Adam are at fault. The blame is not solely a female one, but a human one. The issue with reading this text is that it is 'irredeemably androcentric'[12] – it is most likely written by men and certainly focuses primarily on the male Adam and the masculine God. This works in our favour with our present discussion of masculinity, but it does provoke questions about how different the text might be if Eve's voice could be heard with more clarity.

God and the First Son

So far we have talked broadly about creation, sex and gender in Genesis, without isolated discussion of Adam's masculinity. I have implied that certain characteristics, such as power and dominion over women, are inappropriately assumed to be masculine because of the story of Adam and Eve. We can learn more about human masculinity from another relationship within the text, that between Adam and God.

There is often the assumption, which hopefully I have already debunked a little, that the Genesis creation accounts hold men in higher regard than women. If anything, this thinking, that men ruling over women (i.e. patriarchy) was divinely intended, only really came into being *after* humanity's wrongdoing, when it turned away from God (Gen. 3.16). But, either way, what is often missed is discerning where God fits within this dynamic. Throughout the Hebrew Bible (which is more often known as the Old Testament in Christian communities), God is commonly depicted as a superior (or hegemonic) masculine being to which all men should aspire. This is not to say that God has a male identity, for there are also many instances in which God is portrayed in feminine terms, as we have seen – it is precisely for this reason that I have avoided using gendered pronouns for God altogether.[13] But if a common image of the Bible is God as superiorly masculine, where does that leave other biblical men? Particularly, where does it leave the masculinity of Adam – the first man?

To answer this question, we have to work with the concepts of masculinity in the ancient world. Many of these ideas, such as the spurring on of men's violence and (often forced) sexual encounters, are damaging to women. They are similarly detrimental to men themselves because they set dangerous standards that encourage harmful behaviour. In other words, the analysis that follows does not mean that these attributes should really be understood as what a man should be. Rather, we are learning what the world of the Bible might have considered as manly or masculine.

First, God is in control. God has authority over all things that occur within the creation process. God is present from the very beginning, when there is only a formless void and darkness that covers the earth, transforming nothing into something. The ancient world associated masculinity with authority and power, which is naturally linked with control. If you had control over yourself and others, you had authority. If you achieved authority, you could then obtain power. As an example of this, we need only look at the final few chapters of Job, some of which we will look at in more detail in Chapter 5. Here God harks back to creation to tell Job of the power exerted in creating the skies, the waters, the foundations of the earth, and its inhabitants. Job answers rather cluelessly and embarrassed:

Therefore I have uttered what I did not understand,
things too wonderful for me, which I did not know.
(Job 42.3)

If any moment of the Bible exhibits the most extraordinary amount of command, which humanity cannot even begin to understand, then it is the opening chapters of Genesis in which God creates the entire universe.

A second common attribute of masculinity in the ancient world is progeny and the importance of continuing one's bloodline. There are many lengthy genealogies in the Bible in which figures are traced back through their heritage. Most notably, the Gospel of Luke follows Jesus' heritage all the way back to Adam and then God (Luke 3.38). This enables Jesus to be quite literally the Son of God and a rightful Messiah who is part of the royal line of King David. It also means that Adam too is a son of God, the first son. Therefore God begins creation as the ultimate Father. God is the beginning of all human heritage through which the divine breath of life runs. In a world where male ancestry is incredibly important for one's own status, God becomes the manliest Father as the initial procreator of the entire human race. Of course, there are obviously issues with this, such as God's advocacy of sexual reproduction despite being presented as a sexless being.[14]

Third, God's omniscience (or all-knowingness) is an obvious feature of Genesis 2 and 3. God unmistakably orders humanity not to access wisdom by consuming fruit from the tree. In this way, God is the gatekeeper of all knowledge and, in turn, the wisest figure within the Genesis narratives. Wisdom is a key attribute of masculinity in the ancient world. Literacy and knowledge made someone appear manly in the public sphere. An associated masculine quality would be public speaking and the extent to which it was persuasive. It seems that God achieves this in persuading the human audience of Eve and Adam to stay away from the forbidden fruit, for a short while at least.

These are only three examples of how God exhibits ancient masculine ideals. What is interesting, however, is that God's masculinity is challenged and then re-established in Genesis 3. This perfect order and authority that is built up over the first two chapters grinds to a halt. We can observe this by reassessing in reverse order the three attributes of ancient masculinity that we have discussed. Here I suggest, there is an attempted 'undoing' and subsequent 'redoing' of God's masculinity.

First, the serpent manages to change the minds of Eve and Adam. God's omniscience is challenged:

for God knows that when you eat of it your eyes will be opened, and you will be like God, knowing good and evil.' So when the woman saw that the tree was good for food, and that it was a delight to the eyes, and that the tree was to be desired to make one wise, she took of its fruit and ate; and she also gave some to her husband, who was with her, and he ate. (Gen 3.5–6)

The serpent is more persuasive than God. Because God's command is not followed, but the serpent's is, God becomes unmanned as the persuasive speaker.

Second, Eve and Adam notice their nakedness and thus their sexuality:

Then the eyes of both were opened, and they knew that they were naked; and they sewed fig leaves together and made loincloths for themselves. (Gen. 3.7)

In this moment, they lose their innocence, or perhaps their naivety, because they have gained knowledge and awareness of their nudity. Perhaps their shame is only induced because they become aware of their sexual differentiation, which is the root of the power dynamics that are to come. After all, it is from this grand cover-up that our 'complicated relationship with our genitals' has arisen.[15] Either way, not only is that divinely exclusive wisdom, of which God was the sole owner and gatekeeper, intercepted, but humanity gains awareness of their sexuality. As such, they must have become conscious that God the Father might not be the only father and that Adam might be able to become one himself. The detection of human sexuality threatens God's Fatherhood and progeny.

Lastly, in these moments God is faced with a loss of all the power and authority exemplified in the act of creation. The height of God's creation turns against their Maker. Humanity fights back. But God acts fast, nipping any threat in the bud. Eve and Adam are banished from the Garden and the risk to God's masculinity is eliminated. In these final moments, Adam (the primary participant of the couple in this 'man's world') who challenges the masculinity of God is declared un-masculine. God regulates him and punishes him for his actions. God remains in charge and thus the most masculine being. In this way, God's masculinity has been undone and redone.

In the ancient world masculinity was achieved almost like a competition. By challenging God's authority, Adam tries to become God and, therefore, just as masculine. If he cannot be God and have what God has, why would he want to worship God? And so off Adam goes to sulk beyond the safe borders of the Garden (Gen. 3.23–24). Nadia Bolz-Weber is right to say that the desire to be like God, found here in the First Man, 'has not stopped to this day'.[16] We see many parallels of this in modern society: the more masculine one acts (whether that be in violence, misogyny, crime, wealth, or fatherhood), the more one is accepted as a 'real' man. Men have been conditioned to have (or at least crave) power and success. We are told to want more and more.

I would argue that even today men still do this to the extent of challenging God like Adam did. As we watch church attendance plummet in the UK and across the West, the majority of the Western population do not wish to humble themselves before anything else. Individualism has meant that humans have worshipped themselves, as well as earthly obsessions such as money, vanity and power. If men cannot *be* God, why would they worship God? And so off men go to sulk beyond the borders of religion, faith and belief. Adam, and thus men, want to be in charge (and therefore, in biblical terms, the most masculine) and God will not let them.

We need only look at Jacob's wrestle with God for a similar illustration (Gen. 32.24–30). Jacob tries to wrestle with God but is struck on the hip as a reminder that we can never enter into conversation with God without the potential to be changed.[17] He may have come out of this one alive, but he was certainly not untouched. God will always overcome those who challenge him. But there is also some sort of blessing for those who dare to be so intimately engaged with God, which we will see more of when we observe the relationship between God and Moses in the next chapter.

Our findings in the creation accounts of Genesis have been varied. It may seem that we have talked more about God and Eve in a discussion about the masculinity of Adam. In one way, that is true. Yet, at the same time, masculinity should be observed in actions, interactions and relationships with others. If we realize that in Genesis Eve is not as subordinate or at fault as we once assumed, and that God is supremely masculine, then the masculinity of Adam becomes rather precarious.

Perhaps this has challenged some of your assumptions about men and their innate 'biological' masculinity. It seems that Eve was not made after Adam, but that female and male were created at the same time from a singular sexless being. Eve and Adam are made as equals. Further, Eve was not the evil seductress that caused the Fall but one of two human participants who failed to stop acting against God's will. Lastly, we have seen that Adam (and thus men more generally) are not called to be supremely masculine, particularly if that means yearning for power and authority, because these are characteristics that we should only attribute to God. We need to acknowledge that God will always be more powerful, wise and in control than we can ever try to be.

The implications

What, then, might this all mean for us today? My initial thought is a warning. Any attempt to translate some sort of masculine ideal from Genesis 1–3 into modern-day Christian thinking would be entirely inappropriate for three reasons.

First, there are many scholars who would argue that Eve does not come out as the weak one in these passages at all. They would argue that there is more complexity to these opening texts of the Bible than one might assume. I have offered just some of the ways in which that is certainly the case. To understand Adam and Eve's characteristics as being a model for Christian gender roles would be to underestimate the nuance and intricacy of the texts and their characterizations of Adam and Eve. Unfortunately, the interpretive history of the text has been very different, and the blame placed on Eve still echoes in modern culture today.[18]

Second, any person who claims to know the absolute truth of the Bible is someone of whom we might want to be wary. Of course, we all hold our views about what the Bible tells and teaches. We must, however, acknowledge that we can never be certain of our own interpretative accuracy. God is far beyond our understanding and this scripture is only a glimpse of that revelation. To say, 'This is how we should act because it is clearly how Adam and Eve did' is to claim a monopoly on biblical interpretation and truth, which is a dangerous stance to adopt. The question of a true meaning or interpretation of Scripture is a complicated one.

This leads to the third rebuttal of transplanting the interpretations of Scripture to today: this scripture is set within a time and context, no matter how much we may believe it is divinely inspired. That does not mean it cannot have meaning and truth for Christians today. It does, however, mean that any unwise translation of biblical teaching into modern Christian thinking, without considering its history and context, fails to do justice to the richness and beauty of Scripture. This is a conclusion that we will see repeatedly in our discussion.

To enforce a male-dominated hierarchy and theology because of Genesis 1–3 would not only be unappreciative of the Bible's literary complexity, as well as its ancient setting, but also damaging to those on the receiving end of such a teaching. These narratives were not devised to be a scientific account of biology, nor a blueprint for gender roles, but to be a myth from which readers could gain meaning.[19] To try to use them to convince others of the innate purpose of women and men is foolish use of the Bible. It just so happens that the ideologies of patriarchy and heteronormativity existent in the cultures from which the Bible emerged have also prevailed in the subsequent centuries of readership, predominantly in the systems in the West. We have seen a two-way transaction, whereby the culture of gender oppression in the ancient world seen in the Bible has not only influenced the perpetuation of the same ideologies in modern culture, but the contemporary world has also emphasized the patriarchy present in the Bible as an excuse to legitimize its own injustices. We have seen in the last century that such a vicious cycle has proved difficult to interrupt.

The principal idea communicated within these texts concerns the beauty of creation from which we have distanced ourselves. God gave everything order and function to make it so awesome. We see every day the ways in which humanity rips the gulf between us and God wider, pulling us further apart from this creational beauty. If anything, Genesis tells us of the perfection to which we should aspire; an Eden where everything in creation has its purpose as it lives under the loving care of God. After all, it is said that the Hebrew roots of the word Eden are thought to relate to 'enjoyment', 'delight', or 'pleasure'. We should aspire to live in a place where nature is celebrated, not abused. Where women and men live as one. Where no one tries to outdo the authority (and, with ancient eyes, the masculinity) of God. I sincerely hope that the world today is altering its path as we hurtle towards climate chaos, and I expect that the work of gender studies and feminism (as well as intersectional social justice movements concerning race, class, sexuality, etc.) means that we are journeying towards more equal relationships in society. We are certainly still a long way off from achieving a paradise like Eden.

In today's world, we have cultivated a masculinity that naturally assumes power. Men believe they are in charge because, for the most part of history and even still today, they have been. The creation accounts of Genesis tell us that no matter how much dominion Adam claims (whether that is over animals, plants, or wisdom itself), God remains the Creator and Ruler. Adam can try to acquire the knowledge and power of the divine, but there will be millennia-worth of repercussions. God does not want men fighting for masculine authority and control, but wants us to exist in a harmony and unity where we are in loving relationship with one another, regardless of sex or gender. It is God who breathes life into creation and gives it purpose, not men.

Notes

1 John Walton, 2015, *The Lost World of Adam and Eve: Genesis 2–3 and the Human Origins Debate*, Westmont, IL: InterVarsity Press; and Gordon Wenham, 2015, *Rethinking Genesis 1–11*, Eugene, OR: Cascade Books.

2 For more on the gendered dynamic between men and the earth, see Charlotte Trombin, 2021, '"Then the earth reeled and rocked; the foundations of the heavens trembled and quaked, because he was angry": Misogyny, the Bible, and Environmental Violence', paper presented at the 'From the Rising to the Setting Sun: Global Perspectives on Bible and Violence' conference. Centre for the Study of Bible and Violence, Bristol. Available at: www.youtube.com/watch?v=UN-fWX2TDpE&list=PLb-pzovmK3Erf2ETe4ZvQgW6Qiyk2b8f2&index=3 (accessed 4.10.2021).

3 Jarel Robinson-Brown, 2021, *Black, Gay, British, Christian, Queer: The Church and the Famine of Grace*, London: SCM Press, p. 37.

4 Joseph Gelfer, 2011, *The Masculinity Conspiracy*, London: Createspace, p. 44.

5 Walton, *The Lost World*, p. 58; and Phyllis Trible, 1978, *God and the Rhetoric of Sexuality*, Philadelphia, PA: Fortress Press, p. 80.

6 Walton, *The Lost World*, p. 58; Trible, *God and the Rhetoric*, p. 80.

7 Walton, *The Lost World*, pp. 77–8.

8 Trible, *God and the Rhetoric*, pp. 95–8.

9 Katie Edwards, 2012, *Admen and Eve: The Bible in Contemporary Advertising*, Sheffield: Sheffield Phoenix Press, p. 13.

10 Beth Alison Barr, 2021, *The Making of Biblical Womanhood: How the Subjugation of Women Became Gospel Truth*, Ada, MI: Brazos Press, p. 29 (emphasis added).

11 Nadia Bolz-Weber, 2019, *Shameless: A Sexual Reformation*, London: Canterbury Press, p. 132.

12 Edwards, *Admen and Eve*, p. 33.

13 Whether the ancient Israelites understood God as biologically male is a separate discussion, hence why I have made a conscious effort to label God as masculine (which concerns gender) rather than male (which concerns biology).

14 See Howard Eilberg-Schwartz, 1994, *God's Phallus: and other problems for men and monotheism*, Boston, MA: Beacon Press; and Will Moore, 2021, 'A Godly Man and a Manly God: Resolving the Tension of Divine Masculinities in the Bible', *Journal for Interdisciplinary Biblical Studies*, 2(2), pp. 71–94.

15 Francesca Stavrakopoulou, 2021, *God: An Anatomy*, London: Pan MacMillan, p. 94.

16 Bolz-Weber, *Shameless*, p. 132.

17 See Paynter, *God of Violence Yesterday, God of Love Today?*, p. 60, and Phyllis Trible, *Texts of Terror: Literary-feminist readings of biblical narratives* (London: SCM Press, 1984).

18 For discussion of the image of Eve as a temptress, a symbol of feminist liberation, and yet also a commodification of femininity in popular culture and modern advertising, see Edwards, *Admen and Eve*.

19 By using the term 'myth' here, I am not referring its colloquial use which implies the text's message or portrayal is untrue or ahistorical, although some may argue that that also may be the case. Rather, using the technical term 'myth' is to say that the story might be better understood metaphorically or allegorically as it contains deeper truths about human existence.

3

Men On Top: Moses

Bodies and intimacy

Imagine being best friends with God. 'What a Friend We Have in Jesus' goes the well-known hymn title by Joseph Scriver, and Christians commonly refer to Jesus as their friend. This understanding can be helpful: Jesus walks alongside us through our troubles, a companion who understands the burdens of humanity.[1] Simultaneously, however, the more we overstate Jesus as a friend, the more we cease to realize the mystery and awe that comes with a relationship with God.

Yet many of the characters of the Hebrew Bible were lucky enough to have intimate personal relationships with God. God interacted with them in all sorts of ways. One man, however, was luckier than the rest: Moses spoke 'face to face' with God 'as one speaks to a friend' (Ex. 33.11). He even managed to change God's mind:

> 'Now let me alone, so that my wrath may burn hot against them and I may consume them; and of you I will make a great nation.'
>
> But Moses implored the LORD his God, and said, 'O LORD, why does your wrath burn hot against your people, whom you brought out of the land of Egypt with great power and with a mighty hand?' ... And the LORD changed his mind about the disaster that he planned to bring on his people. (Ex. 32.10–11, 14)

In Christian theology, Jesus is understood to be the 'image of the invisible God' (Col. 1.15). If we, as Christians at least, wish to understand God in absolute fullness, we simply need to look at the person of Jesus. That does not mean, however, that the God of the Hebrew Bible did not reveal Godself and appear to others. So how did this take place and in what form? The technical term for the appearance of God is theophany. These appearances can be manifested in the still small voice to Elijah (1 Kings 19.11–13) as well as the thunder, lightning, fire and trumpets seen on Mount Sinai (Ex. 19.16–19). Other moments, however, are a little more anthropomorphic. In other words, God occasionally seems to have, or at least appear to have, a body – whether it is God 'walking in the garden at the time of the evening breeze' (Gen. 3.8), God's face shining upon those who are being blessed (Num. 6.24–26), God using the earth as a footstool (Isa. 66.1), or even God turning away from the indecency of those excreting outside camp (Deut. 23.12–14). These are only a few examples of a seemingly physical God. Francesca Stavrakopoulou argues that the body of God 'is nowhere denied in the Bible ... [but] is simply assumed.'[2] Though many of these examples lend themselves to a more metaphorical understanding, a sentence uttered by God in Exodus seems more convincing of the deity's corporeal nature:

> 'But', he said, 'you cannot see my face; for no one shall see me and live.' (Ex. 33.20)

God says no one may see God's face and survive it. Even if all the biblical references to God's body are metaphoric, this particular verse implies that there is a face of God even if no one is privileged enough to view it. In the ending verses of this chapter, however, God eventually grants Moses a look at God's self. Most translations of this passage offer something like this:

> And the LORD continued, 'See, there is a place by me where you shall stand on the rock; and while my glory passes by I will put you in a cleft of the rock, and I will cover you with

my hand until I have passed by; then I will take away my hand, and you shall see my back; but my face shall not be seen.' (Ex. 33.21–23)

What is remarkable, and also quite humorous, about this verse, as noted by many other writers and scholars and yet neglected by the majority of Bible translators,[3] is that the Hebrew word used here for back is commonly used to mean the rear or hind-quarters of an animal, and usually in reference to when they 'are to be cleaned of dung before [their] sacrifice'.[4] Whether metaphorical or not, perhaps God shows Moses the divine buttocks, as nakedly as that of an animal! Nonetheless, it is intriguing to ask whether Moses sees the literal corporeal body of the divine or just a glimpse of God's revealed self. Wherever we land with our conclusions, Moses shares an intimate experience with God which most other men of the Bible do not (with the exception of Jacob and his wrestle with God, mentioned in Chapter 2, where Jacob describes it in Gen. 32.30 as seeing 'God face to face'). This closeness between the pair is unparalleled in almost all other relationships in the Bible, until the people of first-century Palestine enter into intimate and physical relationships with the worldly person of Jesus who is the true and whole image of the invisible God.

Solving homoerotic tension

What does this close relationship between Moses and God mean for their masculinities? As you can imagine, in the ancient world an intimate relationship of men, which sometimes included the unveiling of a body, as depicted in Exodus between God and Moses, was suspicious. Masculinity, as we have seen, commonly revolves around power and status. In relationships between men, there was often an implicit or explicit competition of masculinity, which involved one man coming out on top (sometimes quite literally as what we might call a Top in matters of (usually exploitative) sexual intercourse). Subsequently, one participant would have been feminized, whether physically, sexually or socially. Men were and are always striving to assume power. If we look more widely, what happens to the men of the Bible and their status when they are faced with God?

God is always supremely masculine in the Hebrew Bible. As we have seen, Adam was unable to topple the masculinity of God. In any encounter with the divine, the human participant must be subordinate. In the ancient world, being subordinate or submissive was associated with being un-masculine, or feminine. If God's intimate relationship with Moses involved the revelation of the divine, then it is certain that Moses would have been the feminized participant in this encounter. This would be particularly accentuated if God chose to reveal a specifically male body,[5] heightening the divine masculinity even further. It is of interest to note, however, that the body would have been a concealed and therefore feminine space; for God to reveal a private body might have been considered a feminine action, too.

But why does one participant need to be feminized? Howard Eilberg-Schwartz addresses this issue closely in his provocatively titled book *God's Phallus*,[6] and I will outline this here alongside other scholarship. Ancient ideas of status and authority were very often related to penetration. Sex was rarely about desire, but about power. A hierarchy of status was built around who sexually penetrates and who is penetrated.[7] We have come to associate the active action of penetrating as masculine and the passive act of receiving penetration as feminine. We can assume then that the condemnation of male–male sexual encounters which was part of Israelite law was primarily because men should preserve their masculine status, which would be threatened in the act of being penetrated. As Francesca Stavrakopoulou outlines, 'penetrative sex between men of the *same* social status was unacceptable, for it improperly feminized the receptive partner by diminishing his masculinity',[8] adding that 'to be a penetrated male was to be downgraded, degraded and devoid of masculinity. To be penetrated was not only to be emasculated – it was to be like a woman.'[9] As you can imagine, any intimate relationships between men in the ancient world that did not involve competitions of status would have caused a suspicion of homoeroticism. This homoeroticism would have been intrinsically linked to power, because two men engaging closely, especially sexually, would mean one's masculinity was being challenged or reasserted. So to solve the issue and keep divine encounters in line with Israelite law, the text had to feminize one participant in order to make the other triumphantly masculine, and both to conform to gender stereotypes. As Linn Marie Tonstad states: 'Forbidding sex [and even intimacy] between men is not, then, really about sex between men, but about maintaining the boundaries of masculinity.'[10]

This fear of homoeroticism can be seen illustrated in Genesis 19 and Judges 19. Both chapters contain the threat of male rape and the offering of women as substitute victims. This shows that in the ancient world it was less dishonourable to rape a woman than to rape a man, because to rape a man was to attack his masculinity, take away his power and put him in the position of a woman. Rather, it would have been safer and much more 'proper' in the ancient world to rape someone already of low status, usually a woman, slave or a boy, rather than challenge another man's position. Such a dreadful moral perception of sexual violation, especially in the evaluation of particular types of rape as better or worse than others, may seem far away from our modern world and yet even today many rape myths are still perpetuated.

An example of the idea of feminization between men can be seen more clearly when the Bible talks of Israel. As discussed in the introduction to this book, Ezekiel 16 contains a troubling metaphor where God is the husband and Israel is the wife, with similar illustrations being drawn across the prophetic literature. Similarly, a traditional interpretation of the Song of Songs is for the male lover to be God/Jesus and the female lover to be Israel/Christ's Church. So 'deeply embedded in their religious DNA' was this that even Paul relayed this imagery of marrying Christ in his teachings (e.g., 2 Cor.

11.2).[11] But we know that Israel is a collective group of male believers engaging with a masculine God, in the same way that the Christian Church has been dominated for centuries by men worshipping their Father God. So the writers, according to Eilberg-Schwartz, are disguising this relationship in male/female heterosexual imagery in order to defuse the homoerotic dilemma lurking underneath these texts.[12] More than anything, what this does is place God in the dominant masculine position and humanity in the submissive feminine position, regardless of their actual biological or social identity. This imagery is the ultimate cover-up of a relationship between God and God's people, for the sake of heteronormativity and a fear of men being intimate in a challenge of power.

Some might say that this reading of the biblical understanding of God and the men of Israel is over-sexualized. Though these concerns are understandable, I do not think we can underestimate how much the perpetuation of status and masculinity through sexualized encounters permeated the ancient world. Any threat to masculinity would have been terrifying for a man, because it endangered their status, authority, reputation and privileges.

Homophobia and masculinity today

There is a similarly enduring unease in society today regarding penetration and its effect on one's masculinity. Men in our society wish to be dominant, including sexually. Men who wish to be penetrated themselves, and thereby become submissive, are seen to pose a threat to what society deems as masculine. We could think of this as one of Connell's crisis tendencies that I mentioned in Chapter 1. The sexual understanding of masculinity is shifting because we have always been told that men can only penetrate and should not be penetrated themselves. Rather than immediately entering a debate about whether these sorts of sexual interactions are right or wrong, though we will discuss some sexual ethics throughout the course of this book, we should first turn our attention to its impact on understanding masculinity.

LGBTQ+ people are the majority of those engaging in sex where a male is penetrated rather than the penetrator, although it is not uncommon for a man to be penetrated in some way in heterosexual relations even if it is taboo to discuss this. Because gay men (which I will use as an umbrella term for those men who are not heterosexual, consisting mostly of gay, bisexual and queer men) are very likely to be involved in male–male penetrative sex, they have been associated with effeminacy. This is largely because, seen through a heteronormative lens, one male in this sexual act must take the female role. Whereas heterosexuality is supposedly the quintessence of masculinity, homosexuality poses a risk because it means giving up one's masculinity for a feminine sexual position. Therefore, homophobia is essentially rooted in a similar fear of transgressing gender stereotypes and the boundaries of what we have been taught it means to be masculine.

As those of us who are LGBTQ+ may have experienced, homophobic bullying in schools begins with taunts of someone 'looking' or 'acting gay'. We know, however, that being gay is primarily about romantic and/or sexual desire. Because we have associated homosexual sex with effeminacy, anything or anyone that does not fit the masculine ideal is labelled 'gay', 'girly', 'camp' or 'sissy' – and these are the less expletive words often bandied about. Perhaps the more this happens, the more gay men feel compelled to fulfil the expectation to act in a feminine manner in matters of appearance and behaviour. When society considers gay men to be like women, they are then taught to act like them. This self-fulfilling prophecy may not be wrong in any way, for any man should be able to perform whatever masculinity they are comfortable with, but it does trouble many who think women and men should act and dress in specific, and apparently 'opposite', fashions.

However, as we have seen, toxic masculinity (and many men's protection of it) means that gay men are mocked and abused. It may begin with teasing at school, but it soon escalates into violent physical and verbal attacks. A 2018 Stonewall report found that 30 per cent of bisexual men did not feel able to be open about their sexuality with their friends.[13] In the previous year, another Stonewall report showed that three in every five gay men did not feel comfortable holding their partner's hand in public, and in that year one in five LGBTQ+ people experienced discrimination because of their sexuality or gender identity.[14]

We should not forget that, as Christians, we have had our own part to play in this tragic discrimination. In the same 2017 Stonewall report, almost three in ten LGBTQ+ people experienced discrimination in a place of worship because of their sexual and/or gender identity, and over a quarter of religious LGBTQ+ people acknowledged that their religious communities were not accepting of them.[15] Maybe that is because the Church of England still holds to its only teaching document on sexuality, which describes gay people as 'homophiles', questions whether some sort of 'gay gene' may be eliminated in the future,[16] and has told bisexuals that their sexuality is 'ambiguous' and that 'it inevitably involves being unfaithful'.[17] Or, as another example, that members of the Church of England are told that those in civil partnerships are seen as 'falling short of God's purposes for human beings'.[18] Or, simply, that some wings of the Church of England still believe today that 'gay sex is wrong'.[19] In recent years the movement for conversion therapy to be banned has taken the headlines. It should shock us to see Christian communities acting as some of the main perpetrators of conversion therapy, and to realize that they might even be exempt from any laws created against the crimes. I remember once sitting next to a gay friend of mine during the break in a Christian ethics lecture at university when one of the trainee Baptist ministers quizzed him on the broken-down relationship he had with his father, because she was adamant that this would be the reason for his homosexual orientation (and that it was entirely mendable). I wholly believe in the transformative power of Jesus, but there is a huge consensus that praying for the 'healing' of LGBTQ+ people is a misinformed, insulting and spiritually abusive thing to do.

Whether we are affirming supporters or fervent critics of equal marriage and LGBTQ+ equality, or are simply unsure about such deliberations, we all have a duty to apologise for the way in which the Church has treated members of the LGBTQ+ community. In my life, I have seen the wealth of opinions and (importantly) experiences on these issues that the Christian Church evidently holds: for example, attending an Anglican church under the leadership of a proudly transgender vicar; another where the priest told me that transgender rights were 'bonkers' while recommending so-called 'ex-gay' authors for me to read; participating in a public interfaith panel where I was accepted as a bisexual more willingly by people of other faiths than the fellow-Christian participants (with an associated audience member later calling me 'biologically incorrect'); and being part of an ecumenical Christian congregation designed specifically for and comprised of LGBTQ+ Christians excluded or excommunicated from their own churches for their sexual orientation and/or gender identity. We can mutually and lovingly disagree with one another on this matter unless LGBTQ+ people are hurt or abused. At that moment, there can be no other choice than to love – that is our only option as Christians. As Jarel Robinson-Brown says: 'To love ourselves to the extent that God loves us is the demand that grace makes upon as Christians', in the full knowledge and appreciation of people's God-given sexuality.[20] It is our chief commandment from Jesus, and discussions about human sexuality must be taken in the light of such a principle. And, seriously, I do want the Church to have a reformed, realistic and yet still regulated set of sexual ethics, but we must start with a baseline of treating each other with common decency as siblings of Christ.

There has been a popular slogan in the last few years from Christians and theologians on social media that 'bad theology kills'. This resonates as hurtfully true for LGBTQ+ people, who may feel unwanted and hurt by Christian communities and their teachings, so much so that it leads to mental health issues and eventual suicide. We must realize that we are called to love others, welcome them into our churches and nurture them in their faith, regardless of how they identify. We must end 'the famine of grace' that is so rife in our Christian communities.[21] The Church that is so obsessed with oppressive sexual and gender norms cannot continue its part in the oppression of LGBTQ+ people and must urgently change course.

Bisexuality and masculinity

It is of considerable interest in the light of masculinity studies that in the Stonewall surveys outlined above such a high proportion of bisexual men felt unable to tell their friends about their sexuality. As a bisexual man myself, I can certainly say that an in-between sexual identity sometimes feels like a 'balancing act' of an in-between sexual identity.[22] There is the opportunity to keep up heteronormative appearances by entering into a male–female relationship. If somebody does this, but still openly identifies as bisexual, they are choosing to risk their own masculinity. They give up the privilege and power that comes with straightness and accept the risk of prejudice. Of course, the bisexuality of someone is not intensified or diminished whether they are romantically or sexually involved with someone of the same gender or a different one. Someone who identifies as a bisexual man remains so whoever they are (or are not) in a relationship with.

This is not how most people perceive bisexual men, however. Moreover, this is how bisexual men are conditioned not to perceive themselves. Our society has come to work in (mostly false) binaries: men or women, masculine or feminine, black or white, light or dark, good or evil, and gay or straight. I resonate with Luke Turner, who for many years believed he could compartmentalize his bisexuality and 'shut away' the gay part, stopping the 'discomfort' that his sexuality caused him.[23] I for one have spent many hours of my past crying in prayer to be either gay or straight, anything but something 'in-between'. Despite this, Turner, like me, never felt like denying the existence of God: 'It might have been easier if, like so many others, I had rejected the entire system of belief, but I've never been able to – for in it I still found much to hold on to.'[24]

We all know that the world is much more complex than this and so can our sexuality be. As we recalled in Chapter 2 regarding creation, the truth is that our beauty is revealed in our complexity. Our diversity is God-given. Binaries try to simplify the difficult, making things even more problematic than they were initially. Where the problem for many lies, particularly with bisexuality I would argue, is that it cannot be boxed in. It is fluid and will not be categorized. The label itself is deceiving because bisexuality cannot really be categorized or generalized sufficiently. You will find that some bisexual men are only emotionally attracted to other men, but sexually attracted to women. Other bisexual men may be primarily sexually attracted to men, but emotionally to women. There will be some who are sexually *and* emotionally attracted to a variety of genders, whether evenly or not. The shapes and identities of bisexuals and their relationships are many. Even the Church fears this, because it becomes something that cannot be policed or controlled.

Homosexual men are classed by some as almost not being 'real' men, whereas bisexual men threaten the very essence of what it means to be a man. Bisexual men can linger in the realms of hegemonic, or normative, masculinity without conforming to it. They offer a new option for masculinity which endangers those who do not wish for manhood to change. One of the biggest examples of this is that, in our sex-obsessed culture, bisexual men are undefined in their sexual practices. Sometimes they are the penetrator and sometimes they are the penetrated, depending on who they are having sex with. They fluidly travel from masculine to feminine positions. Once again, this means bisexuality blurs the boundaries of masculinity and wider gender politics.

Society's perception of a man and his masculinity certainly does change depending on how they sexually identify. I have seen people's opinions of me alter whether I am currently dating a man or a woman. Not only that, but the way in which people interact with me changes. Some people bite their tongue before making a joke or a comment. And yet some continue to make a mockery of bisexuality and its 'greediness' (which, if it needs explanation, wrongly perpetuates the assumption that bisexual people need romance and sex with multiple people in order to be satisfied – we can be as faithful as anyone else).

Some people do ask questions, though, about my attraction to people of any gender. They are sensitively inquisitive about the things they do not understand. This is crucial. We cannot move forward as a Church, and as a society, until we freely and sensitively ask questions and have them answered. These topics are a matter of learning. We cannot progress until we are all educated thoroughly on the matters at hand, though the burden should not always be on those who are LGBTQ+.

The connection

Let me be clear, by making this connection I am in no way saying that there was an erotic or sexual relationship between Moses, or any of the men of the Bible, and God. Nor am I saying that any biblical men had homosexual encounters or feelings. There are passages that certainly might suggest this and there are writers who elaborate on these ideas at length, though such a debate is beyond the scope of this book. What I am suggesting here, however, is that there was an unease in ancient literature when a male was intimate with a masculine God because of the fear of homoeroticism and a challenge of masculine power. The human had to relinquish their masculinity and status in order to be feminized, which would solve this issue. So the masculinity of Moses might already be on a precarious footing because of the underlying homoeroticism in his intimate relationship with God, especially if God showed him the divine buttocks!

The threat that two men (human or divine) in an intimate relationship presented in the ancient world is not unlike the one that many people believe gay people create for modern masculinity. The homoerotophobia of the ancient world has developed into the homophobia of the modern one. Why? Because the idea of men being close, let alone romantically or sexually engaged, demands a reassessment of what it means to be a man. It threatens our boxed thinking of manhood, where a man can only be close with a woman.

If penetration was primarily a social performance in the ancient world in order to gain or maintain status, is it odd that we still have the same thinking today? The double standards by which promiscuous men are labelled 'lads' or 'studs', whereas women are called 'sluts' or 'slags', shows that there is still an element of social prowess to sexual performance. Further, the world is more sexualized than ever, with nudity and sex becoming a common sight in advertising, television, and film. On the whole, however, sex in contemporary society is something that happens behind closed doors. It is a matter for private relationships. We need to be wary when likening modern sexual practices of intimacy, and often love, to those of the ancient world that were primarily social performances of political masculine status. In this way, the Bible's concerns about male–male penetrative sex are not very applicable to discussions about homosexual relationships today. That does not mean that Christian discussion about human sexuality does not need to be had, but that we should approach the biblical texts with attentiveness to what they are really addressing, and questioning how they might relate to us today.

The competition for masculine authority

Aside from these matters, there is even more happening in the life events of Moses with regard to men and manhood. The first half of Exodus is underpinned with a competition of masculinity between Pharaoh and God, in which Moses is caught in the middle. In an academic chapter on this topic, Richard Purcell and Caralie Focht highlight how God and Pharaoh compete for the best masculine performance – and God, as always, wins.[25] They offer <u>four attributes of hegemonic mascu-linity that God enacts and Pharaoh</u> conversely fails. I will try to summarize them briefly here.

First, masculinity is measured by violence and triumph in warfare. Pharaoh fails to inflict violence on the Israelites as he intended, particularly seen in Moses escaping the slaughter of all Hebrew boys by being placed in a basket among the reeds (Ex. 2.2–3). God, however, defends the Israelites and attacks the Egyptians, seen best in the plague narratives (Ex. 7–12) and the crossing of the Red Sea (Ex. 14. 26–28).

A second attribute of ideal masculinity is a control over the sexuality of others. So the control Pharaoh tries to impose on male babies being killed is undermined by his midwives who fear God and instead act in God's favour, letting the boys live. God then grants the women children, having more control over sexuality than Pharaoh (Ex. 1.17, 20–21).

Third, the importance of family lineage is shown in the Israel-ite people, who grow from an oppressed group in Egypt to a liberated nation in the wilderness, continuing the family of God's elect people. Pharaoh, however, is emasculated by the killing of not only his firstborn son but all the firstborn sons in his care in Egypt (Ex. 11.4–7). The Egyptian people's heritage is dismantled.

Lastly, according to Purcell and Focht, masculinity involves the protection of those with lesser status. The Israelite people are under the protection of God throughout the Exodus narra-tive and are provided with sustenance, whereas Pharaoh is unable to stop God from essentially culling his Egyptian people.

In all these ways, Purcell and Focht show that God wins the competition of masculinity against Pharaoh. Divinity wins over humanity. God is the toughest 'man'. (That is not to say that God *is* a man, but that power and control were associated with masculinity, and God being so omnipotent would have consequentially made him masculine in the ancient world.)

The ten plagues offer another specific example of this. The worship of the Israelite God frightens the authority of Pharaoh. He will not give into the will of God, nor the will of Moses, because he clings on to his own arrogance and dictatorship. In the words of the Bible, Pharaoh continually 'hardened his heart' (e.g. Ex. 8.15, 32; 9.34). His obsession with power dissolves any compassion he might have left within him. And so a competition of masculine authority begins once again. Each time Pharaoh hardens his heart, God shows a mighty sign to change Pharaoh's ways. Yet, every time, it does not work.

The only instance in which Pharaoh finally gives in is when violence is inflicted on his own people. The slaughter of babies that Pharaoh attempted to inflict on the Israelites has been done unto himself. Only then does he concede. As you can probably tell, there is a common conclusion in the Bible concerning masculine power: human authority is no match for God's.

Pharaoh represents human power and authority that is inevitably fallible. This is not far off from our own view of the world around us. We commonly say that people can go mad with power; once someone assumes authority or power they cannot let go. They become fixated on remaining in their position or excelling even further up the ranks. For example, psychologist Peter Coleman says Vladimir Putin exhibits some sort of power psychosis.[26] By this, Coleman means that Putin has been in power for so long without check that he has become out of touch with the real world. Someone with power psychosis becomes arrogant in their authority, making decisions that might seem risky, not caring how that might impact other people's lives. This demonstrates the inconsistency and self-interest that usually comes with human authority. I am sure most of us could list a number of men who might be considered to have gone mad with power, but very few women – just another example of how contemporary cultural conceptions of masculinity have conditioned men to obsess over power and the status that comes with it, consequently barring women from these spaces and places of authority because of their coded gender politics.

This sort of leadership is not far distanced from Christianity at all. In his novel *The Good Man Jesus and the Scoundrel*

Christ, atheist Philip Pullman's Jesus says: 'As soon as men who believe they are doing God's will get hold of power ... the Devil enters into them.'[27] In 2020, during the increased awareness of the Black Lives Matter movement, Donald Trump stood in front of a church for a photoshoot while holding a Bible. In order to do so, protestors (and clergy from that very church, offering pastoral support and refreshments) were forced out of the area by smoke grenades and rubber bullets. While using violence to clear his path, Trump tried to legitimize his authority as President of the United States by holding holy Scripture in his hands.

By doing this, Trump implied that his leadership was in some way Christian. This can be disputed. First, as most people will be aware, the attitudes and actions of Trump were rarely Christian in their nature. That is not to make a judgement on his personal faith, but rather to critique his political and religious appearance. Disablism, misogyny, racism and transphobia are only a few of the prejudices he displayed during his presidency. The violent way in which he emptied the church courtyard of people for his own PR stunt showed his deficient care for others. Second, holding the Bible to elevate his own authority is undoubtedly a misuse of Christian Scripture. Later in the year, Trump labelled his presidential opponent Joe Biden as 'against God'. Religion became a way of affirming his authority and outlawing the authority of others who stood in his way. Trump was, as Kristen Kobes Du Mez says, 'the culmination of evangelicals' embrace of militant masculinity, an ideology that enshrines patriarchal authority and condones the callous display of power, at home and abroad'.[28] The power psychosis of Trump became presented as religiously legitimized and infallible by the right wing of American evangelicalism.

And, of course, nationalistic, white, evangelical American Christianity and Trumpism soon became widely synonomous. Weeks before the inauguration of Joe Biden as President of the United States in January 2021, protests claiming the election to be fraudulent erupted outside, and eventually inside, the Capitol Building. During concurrent protests for the same cause in Michigan, a cross was erected; it was surrounded by American flags, one bearing the words 'TRUMP 2020: NO MORE BULLSHIT', and others with biblical references. As a tall wooden cross soared among the protestors, it was clear that the symbol of Christianity had been appropriated for violent and domestic terrorist purposes that stood in sharp contradiction to the teachings of Jesus.

Trump, and indeed the arguably fascist movement he originated and further cultivated, endeavoured to make a claim to power that abused religious texts and authority for personal and ideological gain. Writing not many months before the Capitol Building events took place, Joshua Roose seemed to foretell such an uprising when he noted that the offhand rhetoric justifying political extremism from a demagogue like Trump, coupled with the perpetuation of a hyper-masculine militant form of evangelical Christianity, could certainly act as 'a call to arms'.[29] The events of the Capitol demonstrably proved this to be true. Roose is not wrong to liken the causes of these events to the similar emergence of what he calls 'ideological masculinity', that is, the reassertion of masculine domination in public life, in for example, the UK's Brexit referendum. The parallel rhetoric of Nigel Farage, among others, was similarly understood as a call to arms by those who believed in a truly English and Christian country, culminating in the murder of the pro-remain MP Jo Cox by a far-right neo-Nazi.

The Bible tells of the rise and fall of many leaders and kings; men obsessed with authority and power. Walter Brueggemann tells of the Pharaoh being the 'passive king' who is a model for the way in which the world works, never changing and always lacking in promise and hope.[30] Modern global politics seems to resonate with this still today. In contrast, God is the only constant in these many biblical stories of failing leadership, as guidance and direction is provided. As we have seen in Genesis and Exodus, God is always in authority and control, which makes God masculine in the eyes of an ancient reader. Pharaoh used his violent ways to assert his authority but failed, and many others in recent history – including Trump – have tried to achieve similar things. Perhaps in the same way, the Church ought to realize that it is part of maintaining this despairing status quo and has the capacity to be a false human kingdom itself. To be Christ-like, the Church needs to renounce its power, its status and indeed its privilege – whether that be of whiteness, maleness, straightness, or ability – in order to truly flourish as a people of God.

If Pharaoh and his manly authority are unmanned by God, where does this leave Moses? Well, as we have seen, Moses' intimate relationship with God means he must assume a subordinate (and un-masculine) position. He is, however, more masculine than Pharaoh. Throughout the Exodus narrative, Moses is God's right-hand man. Whereas Pharaoh fails to fulfil his duties, Moses follows God's orders and succeeds in being an authoritative (and masculine) leader who brings his people out of Egypt.

You may be familiar with the Moses of the film *The Ten Commandments* (1956), who parts the Red Sea with his arms stretched out into the sky while several women gasp in amazement and admiration. This Moses shows complete control and power over the water. In the Ancient Near East, water was typically seen as a symbol of chaos. If someone could tame water, they were considered powerful and thus masculine. Perfect examples of this include God showing off his masculine power in subduing the waters of creation in Genesis, as well as commanding the seas of The Flood. Moses manages to escape and defeat Pharaoh using his control over the water, but we should not forget that this power is granted by God. Moses is lucky that God uses him as a leader to employ such masculine authority. Human authority is fallible unless it has God's backing. As Milena Kirova says: 'Man cannot and above all must not attempt to imitate God unless God himself provides him with a magical staff, as is the case of Moses'.[31] Becoming an idolatrous figure for American evangelical Christians obsessed with nationalism, Trump tried to do just that, with no divine authority to do so.

Moses and the ladies

However, Moses does not owe all of his success solely to the character of God. It is interesting that he is continually saved by women. In the ancient world, women were lesser citizens than men. In Egypt, women were treated better than in most ancient societies, though this would have been nowhere near to what we might consider gender equality today. It is quite radical, then, that women were Moses' saviours. While Pharaoh asserts his masculinity in the violent killing of all Israelite boys, the women of Moses' family manage to save the little boy by placing him in the river in a basket.

> When she could hide him no longer she got a papyrus basket for him, and plastered it with bitumen and pitch; she put the child in it and placed it among the reeds on the bank of the river. (Ex. 2.3)

The Hebrew word for basket is also used to describe the ark that Noah builds for safety from The Flood. Both vessels float along the water to save their passengers from the worldly chaos around them. But Moses' vessel is fashioned and sent off by women, into the saving hands of more women. The basket takes the baby to the women of the Pharaoh's palace. At both ends of the stream are the women rescuers of Moses. The vessel of Israel's salvation is left in the hands of these women, just as the salvation of the world found in Jesus also hinges upon the hands of women, including Mary his mother and Mary Magdalene.

Without these women, Moses would not himself have been able to rescue the people of Israel. This happens not just twice, but three times.

> On the way, at a place where they spent the night, the LORD met him and tried to kill him. But Zipporah took a flint and cut off her son's foreskin, and touched Moses' feet with it, and said, 'Truly you are a bridegroom of blood to me!' So he

let him alone. It was then she said, 'A bridegroom of blood by circumcision.' (Ex. 4.24–26)

At face value, Moses seems to be the target of a murderous pursuit by God but is saved by his wife Zipporah. She manages to take a flint and circumcise her son, as well as Moses if we assume the reference to feet to be one of the common biblical innuendoes for genitals. This seems to please God as the hunt to kill Moses is abandoned once he and his son were circumcised. But why was God on a quest to kill anyway? Perhaps it was something to do with masculinity. In both ancient and modern Judaism, circumcision is a sign of someone's Jewishness. It is a symbol of obedience and faithfulness to God, reminding the circumcised man of Abraham's covenant with God, for him and his offspring, keeping allegiance to God and God's people (Gen. 17.10–14).

Perhaps, then, the uncircumcision of Moses and his son deemed them unworthy before God. As we have seen, penetration and thus the penis itself was an important symbol of masculine power. For an Israelite to mark their penis would have had an impact on their masculinity. It was likely to be a bodily mark of subordination before God. Without Zipporah rectifying the situation, Moses and his uncircumcised penis could have been considered a threat to God's masculinity. In these moments, Rhiannon Graybill suggests Moses embodies an oddly unique masculinity which she unsurprisingly calls Mosaic masculinity.[32] She says Moses' body is 'wounded, opened, vulnerable, [and] non-phallic'.[33] All of these open spaces and cavities described in Graybill's language signify un-masculine connotations or, more accurately, femaleness. Mosaic masculinity is not the ideal or hegemonic masculinity, but one that is subordinated to God in the vulnerability of circumcision. He relinquishes his own masculinity for the supreme masculinity of God, one that is hegemonic in the eyes of the ancient world.

Women seem to be a saving grace in Moses' life. In the ancient world and even contemporary society, women have commonly (but wrongly) been associated with weakness. Yet

Moses would not have survived without the help of these supposedly incapable women. He would not have gone on to be so intimate with God and save God's people. Women did not damage the masculinity of Moses but developed it to be suitable before God. There is a lesson to learn from this: women can help with the maturing of healthy masculinities rather than hinder it. In fact, I hope many women are reading this book so that they can help cultivate modern masculinity for the better today.

The implications

The life of Moses offers a lot of reflections for biblical masculinity and its impact for Christians today. First, both ancient and modern masculinities have a fear of male intimacy because it assumes a loss of male power, transgressing the boundaries of traditional gender stereotypes. In ancient Israelite religion, men had to be feminized to be considered close to God. Christians today understand God as beyond gender limitations because we are becoming less likely to associate masculinity with authority as the ancient Israelites did. If this is the case, we need not be concerned about the gender of God in relation to the gender of ourselves. Men can be close to a Fatherly God just as women, men and anyone else can be close to a Motherly or Parental God. The tension of homoeroticism should not be a worry in our relationships with God today because we have a much broader understanding of God beyond hegemonic masculinity.

Similarly, we ought to be less concerned about the intimacy of gay, bisexual and queer relations in society today. We have seen that the feminization of men was feared because it had connotations with penetration and power. To be penetrated was to lose one's masculinity. In a similar vein, modern men often disparage gay relationships because of the assumed act of penetration involved and thus the threat posed to masculinity. Bisexuality endangers hegemonic masculinity even more because the identity both conforms to heteronormativity and yet defies it, particularly in romantic and sexual practices. Regardless of these concerns, sex between males in the ancient world was understood in terms of social performance. As such, it should not be overly conflated with loving, faithful homosexual relationships today, which involve willing sexual intimacy. A societal unease still remains purely because there is an entirely untrue assumption that gay and bisexual men must lose their masculinity in some way in order to continue living with their sexual identity.

As this book has been outlining, however, modern masculinity has some unhealthy traits and this fear of gay men is one of them. I do not claim that this is an answer to debates on human sexuality for modern Christianity, but the fearmongering and abuse received by LGBTQ+ Christians is a result of toxic masculinity's phobia. Ancient understandings of sex and penetration were obviously much more complicated than I have outlined above, but I hope we have dipped our toes in far enough to see the similarities between the masculine fear of homosexuality today and homoeroticism in the ancient world. Yet, simultaneously, I hope that we may have noticed the seeming incompatability between the two for modern discussion.

Regarding the figure of Moses specifically, we can see that he submits to God as right-hand man. This does not negate his masculinity but actually uplifts it over the likes of Pharaoh. While obeying God causes feminization, in the Bible it also raises the masculinity of Moses above those who affront God. It is this complexity of masculinity, beyond binary or spectral nature, that we have noted.

Moses is saved by women multiple times, particularly in his circumcision which offers a visible sign of his obedience to God. Moses' service to God actually enables him to employ divine power, such as at the parting of the Red Sea (Ex. 14) and the transformation of a staff into a snake (Ex. 7.8–13). These are examples not of Moses' own power but of Moses being chosen as a channel for God to use. Whereas the Egyptians were led by Pharaoh and human authority, the Israelites were led by Moses as a vessel for God. The leaders of this world come and go, but the Kingdom of God never fails. If the ancient readers considered power and authority as masculine traits, then God was undoubtedly masculine. Human institutions, like the Egyptian monarchy, were unmanned by God in the Bible because they never did and never will parallel the power of the Kingdom of God.

Today, we should not cling to our own authority or the human authority of the world, not least because it is drenched in masculinity. We should instead look to the God who has created, redeemed and sustains all. A big issue with the masculinity that dominates our culture is that men fear losing the control, power and authority which they have the privilege of possessing simply by nature of being a man, whether that is physically, sexually or socially. Perhaps Christian men today need to surrender their own power, and the arrogance that comes with it, and cling to God instead – just as Moses did and Pharaoh feared.

Notes

1 This theology is something we will examine much more closely in Chapter 7 using the example of abuse and violence survivors.

2 Francesca Stavrakopoulou, 2021, *God: An Anatomy*, London: Pan MacMillan, p. 16.

3 It is incredibly important not to forget that every translation of the Bible we read has been translated by someone who has made conscious linguistic choices. We should remember how certain biases or prejudices may have affected the decision here, particularly if they are trying to present ancient texts as Holy Scripture.

4 Stavrakopoulou, *God*, p. 171.

5 Albeit tentatively, following the arguments of Howard Eilberg-Schwartz and Francesca Stavrakopoulou.

6 Howard Eilberg-Schwartz, 1994, *God's Phallus: and other problems for men and monotheism*, Boston, MA: Beacon Press), pp. 142–62.

7 Peter-Ben Smit, 2006, 'Jesus and the Ladies: Constructing and Deconstructing Johannine Macho-Christology', *The Bible and Critical Theory*, 2(3), pp. 31.1–15 (pp. 31.6–7). This source is particularly about the New Testament and the Greco-Roman world, but such a model of

penetrative hierarchy still holds relevance for the ancient world of the Hebrew Bible.

8 Stavrakopoulou, *God*, p. 116 (emphasis added).

9 Stavrakopoulou, *God*, p. 115.

10 Linn Marie Tonstad, 2018, *Queer Theology: Beyond Apologetics*, Eugene, OR: Wipf and Stock Publishers, p. 21.

11 Stavrakopoulou, *God*, p. 161.

12 Eilberg-Schwartz, *God's Phallus*, p. 99.

13 Stonewall, 'LGBT in Britain – Home and Communities', *Stonewall*, www.stonewall.org.uk/lgbt-britain-home-and-communities (accessed 5.8.2020).

14 Stonewall, 2017, 'LGBT in Britain – Hate Crime', available from www.stonewall.org.uk/lgbt-britain-hate-crime-and-discrimination (accessed 5.8.2020).

15 Stonewall, 'LGBT in Britain – Hate Crime'.

16 House of Bishops, 1991, *Issues in Human Sexuality: A Statement by the House of Bishops*, London: Church House Publishing, p. 32.

17 House of Bishops, *Issues*, p. 42.

18 House of Bishops, 2019, 'Civil Partnerships – for same sex and opposite sex couples', www.churchofengland.org/sites/default/files/2020-01/Civil%20Partnerships%20-%20Pastoral%20Guidance%202019.pdf (accessed 6.5.2021).

19 The Church of England Evangelical Council, 2020, 'The Beautiful Story', www.youtube.com/watch?v=VI8bb65vOiE&t=874s (accessed 6.5.2021).

20 Jarel Robinson-Brown, 2021, *Black, Gay, British, Christian, Queer: The Church and the Famine of Grace*, London: SCM Press, p. 29.

21 A term coined by Robinson-Brown in *Black, Gay, British, Christian, Queer*.

22 For more on my experience as a bisexual Christian and ordinand in the Church of England, see Will Moore, 2022b, 'Being Bisexual in Church – A Balancing Act', *Via Media News*, www.viamedia.news/2022/03/01/being-bisexual-in-church-a-balancing-act/ (accessed 1.3.22).

23 Luke Turner, 2019, *Out of the Woods*, London: Weidenfeld & Nicholson, pp. 97–8.

24 Turner, *Out of the Woods*, p. 102.

25 Richard Purcell and Caralie Focht, 2019, 'Competing Masculinities: YHWH versus Pharaoh in an Integrative Ideological Reading of Exodus 1–14', in Ovidiu Creangă (ed.), *Hebrew Masculinities Anew*, Sheffield: Sheffield Phoenix Press, pp. 83–104.

26 Peter Coleman, 2014, 'Mad With Power?', *HuffPost*, www.huffpost.com/entry/mad-with-power_b_5736728 (accessed 7.8.2020).

27 Philip Pullman, 2017, *The Good Man Jesus and the Scoundrel Christ*, Edinburgh: Canongate Books.

28 Kristen Kobes Du Mez, 2020, *Jesus and John Wayne: How White Evangelicals Corrupted a Faith and Fractured a Nation*, New York: Liveright Publishing Corporation, p. 3.

29 Joshua M. Roose, 2021, *The New Demagogues: Religion, Masculinity and the Populist Epoch*, Abingdon: Routledge, p. 13.

30 Walter Brueggemann, 2018, *The Prophetic Imagination*, 3rd edition, Minneapolis, MN: Fortress Press, p. 35.

31 Milena Kirova, 2020, *Performing Masculinity in the Hebrew Bible*, Sheffield: Sheffield Phoenix Press, p. 51.

32 Rhiannon Graybill, 2015, 'Masculinity, Materiality, and the Body of Moses', *Biblical Interpretation*, 23(4–5), pp. 518–40 (p. 539).

33 Graybill, 'Masculinity, Materiality', p. 539.

4

Violence Is Manly: David

Violent men

From the Romans of *Gladiator* and the swashbucklers of *The Pirates of the Caribbean* to the Jedis of *Star Wars* and Marvel's combat entourage *The Avengers*, modern film is swamped in male protagonists who use violence to make progress in the world. *Squid Game* (2021), Netflix's most successful show to date, centres solely around violence as a means of success, financial gain and survival. I grew up in the shadow of an accelerating film industry, with more brutality and gore as each year went by. Even in the innocence of Disney films we can find the centrality of violence. For example, in the original *Mulan* film (1998) the captain of the Chinese army performs the song 'I'll Make a Man Out of You', sung by Donny Osmond. The lyrics of this song are overflowing with militaristic hypermasculinity. When he is faced with the poorly-skilled warriors he has to train, Captain Li Shang asks whether he has accidentally been sent daughters instead of sons. In poetic lyricism, he then lists the characteristics of a manly warrior, including swiftness, force and mysteriousness. To train them up to be effective warriors, Li Shang is 'making men' out of them. Ironically, of course, Mulan is one of those being trained, who is a woman pretending to be – or crossdressing as – a man.

This physicality and violence of masculinity is championed in our society, most unnoticeably with children, whether it be through sports like mixed martial arts, wrestling, or boxing, or even just in the playground.[1] When I was growing up, my mum made me go to kung-fu lessons. I actually really enjoyed them, reaching national competition level at my peak (even if I was the only one on our team to come home without a medal!). Although I do not remember much of it now, the discipline and exercise of kung-fu were certainly good for me. If you asked my mum, however, she would tell you that she made me attend these sessions because I was getting too addicted to technology and would start getting angry when my gaming consoles were taken away as punishment for bad behaviour. Essentially, I participated in kung-fu lessons as some form of child anger management. Though whether it was needed, or if it worked, is a separate discussion, what is interesting to note is that this rarely happens with girls. It is almost assumed that boys need some sort of violent outlet. Boys and men are presumed to be uncontrollable in their rage and anger.[2] So whether it is how we are brought up or what we watch in films as children (or indeed adults), we are consciously and unconsciously being taught that you cannot have masculinity without violence, nor violence without masculinity.

This, of course, does not come without its consequences. At a personal and local level, such issues will include bullying, crime and assault. But there are larger and much wider concerns when men get into powerful positions, particularly in the world of national and international politics. Whether it is a fist, a gun, a sword, or an entire military army, men get their way by brutality and bloodshed. We tend to say that money makes the world go round, but violence seems to be a pretty big cog in its workings too.

The Bible is no different in that sense. In *The Da Vinci Code* (2006), Sir Leigh Teabing says, 'as long as there has been one true God, there has been killing in his name'. David Clines reckons that 'on average, there are more than six instances of violence on every page of the Hebrew Bible, including more than one of divine violence'.[3] Such a fact should not come as a surprise, for we are warned of this not long into the text of Genesis. Soon after the creation and fall of humanity, the author states that the world had fallen to sin and immorality.

Now the earth was corrupt in God's sight, and the earth was filled with violence. (Gen. 6.11)

In God's eyes, the good and pleasing world that was created had become nothing but a disappointment. As we know, God uses The Flood to try and remedy this situation. If we read this literally, it seems that God commands an act of divine genocide. This is only one example where violence can disturb us as readers of the Bible. The list of worrying passages goes on, from the conquest of Joshua (Josh. 1–2) to the civil war caused by the abuse and gang rape of the Levite's wife in Judges (Judg. 19–21) – we cannot avoid the matter of violence in the Bible, nor brush it under the carpet. Dealing with biblical violence as Christians is a big enough problem in itself, which there is not the space to deal with here. Thankfully there are scholars working in this field, with particular consideration for Christians and churches dealing with such Bible passages.[4]

For our discussion here, however, we do need to at least note the existence of biblical violence, as well as its association with masculinity. Violence pervades Scripture and it is usually something that is practised by men, although there are some exceptions (e.g. Judg. 4.21; 9.53–54).[5] Perhaps this masculine violence is a by-product of the text's setting, in which warfare was a common political mechanism and politics was a largely male affair. As René Girard says,

> To escape responsibility for violence we imagine it is enough to pledge never to be the first to do violence. But no one ever sees himself as casting the first stone. Even the most violent persons believe that they are always reacting to a violence committed in the first instance by someone else.[6]

There is always an explanation for violence, but whether we deem it worthy is another matter. Violence is used with political justification both in the Bible and throughout much of human history.

If we look at the Gospel of Matthew, we find Herod the Great reigning over the Herodian kingdom of Judea. However, when the Magi see signs of the *Christos* (or Messiah) coming, Herod panics. Will someone take his throne? Will he lose the power and authority that give him masculine status? This potential threat means that Herod has to find a resolution – which, of course, entails violence. The answer to Herod's problems is to order the Massacre of the Innocents as it has become known (Matt. 2.16–18). Herod instructs the murder of all boys under the age of two in the vicinity of Bethlehem in order to eliminate any potential political threat. He clings on to his authority so tightly that he is willing to slaughter babies to protect it. In this instance, violence is used by Herod as a way to maintain his own human power, authority and status – all of which, we now know, are intertwined with masculinity. This narrative in the Gospel of Matthew echoes the stories of Exodus which we have already examined, in which Pharaoh attempts to kill all the Israelite boys in order to stifle the growth of the Israelites. He does not want them to outgrow themselves in the land of Egypt under his governance because it might risk a revolt. So he uses violence to ensure the stability of his leadership.

This is not just a biblical matter. We have seen the political workings of violence in much of history. Henry VIII, for example, killed anyone who seemed a threat – whether that was his wife or a politician. The number of his executions is thought to be over 50,000. Moreover, and needing even less of an introduction, the last century saw one of the worst examples of human authority in Adolf Hitler. His desire for power resulted in the genocide of millions of Jews, disabled people, Romani Gypsies, homosexuals, intellectuals, political opponents and many others, in order to create an Aryan race. These people who were targeted represented an alternative, or perhaps even a challenge, to the ideal masculine power that Hitler tried to embody and impose on the world. He had a political vision that utilized violence for it to be achieved, creating one of the most abominable events of modern history, with tens of millions of people killed globally in the Second World War.

If we consider violence to be predominantly and historically a male act, and we are aware that the Church has been a mainly male enterprise, then we should expect the Church to have also had its fair share of violent input in the world's history. In recent decades the covering up of abuse within the Catholic Church began to attract global media attention. Between 2001 and 2010, the Church investigated cases of sex abuse concerning over 3,000 priests.[7] The Vatican concluded that this was an issue for the Church as much as for wider society. The last three Popes have addressed the issue and worked for more change, though the problem is still present. In the last couple of years, the Independent Inquiry into Child Sex Abuse (IICSA) revealed the extent to which the Church in its entirety, regardless of denomination, had been a place in which abusers existed and even went into hiding.

In earlier history, the Crusades became a war of religion with political motivations. The Church fought to retrieve the Holy Land from Islamic possession. A war only becomes a crusade when validated and often instructed by the Church, specifically the Pope, in order to combat something that is considered a threat to Christendom or the Christian world. This resulted in the deaths of millions of people. Not only this, but such a demonization of Islam provided much of the basis for modern day islamophobia in much of Western civilization, particularly in more conservative, as well as fundamentalist, Christian communities.

As brief further examples, the Crimean War in the late nineteenth century was initially caused by a dispute about Christian rights in the Holy Land. In more recent times, The Troubles in Ireland were sectarian in nature, partitioned by the nationalistic religious identities of Protestants and Catholics. Gathering up all this evidence, we should never forget the Church's history. Today, most Christians advocate for non-violence and world peace, yet we can see that in the past our beloved Church has been the cause of an unimaginable loss of lives. Even worse, the Church's violence has clearly been self-destructive – we hypocritically preach peace and yet have a history soaked in blood.

In the Bible, violence was not only political and sometimes

religious; it also seemed to have a social purpose. A valued characteristic of an ancient man was to be successful in war and combat. In order to be considered masculine, you had to have been a warfighting machine. This meant that violence sometimes had no more purpose than to elevate one's own authority or status, in much the same way as penetration was also principally a social performance, as discussed in Chapter 3. To beat another man in battle or warfare was to assume a more masculine position and 'unman' the opponent. Once the victor had proven their masculinity, their re-established manliness allowed them to obtain more power and authority. As a modern illustration, many readers may be familiar with the *Game of Thrones* series, in which men's braids represented their masculinity to the extent that they were cut off if the wearer suffered defeat in a battle but, on the other hand, had bells added for every person that they killed. Khal Drogo, the tribe leader, possessed the longest hair adorned with the most bells because of his military success.[8] In a similar way many cultures, including the ancient world, have associated manly status with violence.

Jack Urwin has noted the link between masculinity and the institution of the military,[9] which I would like to explore further here. He says that the two world wars have caused the biggest shift in what we conceive to be masculine behaviour. In the US and the UK there is to some extent a glorification of warfare. Many churches hang, or 'lay-up', decommissioned military flags until they disintegrate and fall, in order for them to decay respectfully. Nationally, and particularly as Christians, we annually remember those who have died in war on Remembrance Sunday in November. We regard those who have fought in wars as honourable as we wear our blood-red poppies. In recent years, however, there has been an introduction of a white poppy, not without its controversy. This alternative is similarly meant to signify a respect and remembrance for those who have died in war but is also allied with a commitment to promote peace. Further, it remembers those injured mentally and psychologically, as well as the forgotten victims of war such as mothers, children and animals. Those who wear the white poppy would suggest that in our traditional ways of remembrance we have venerated the act of war, or at least politicized it, rather than prioritizing the advancement of peace.

Similarly, we have honoured those men who actually fought in the war so much that the valour of violence has become some sort of masculine attribute. We are all probably familiar with the British Army, Royal Navy and Royal Air Force adverts that frequent our television screens. In them, the average man who finds himself watching should apparently be attracted to the pressure and suspense that violence brings. Why stay in the life of an office worker or a manual labourer when you could be risking your life and even have a sanctioned outlet for your anger?

Only in recent years have people who are not either heterosexual or cisgender men, including women, transgender people and queer men, been able to join the military forces. Naturally, then, it has until recently been a solely manly affair. Armed combat and violence have been intertwined with our expectations and stereotypes of masculinity. Though I have no issue with the remembrance of soldiers and victims of war in whatever way one may choose, the more we have glorified those men who have been to war and partaken in violence, without acknowledging that it should never happen again, the more we make it an attractive pursuit for men today. As we do this, we cement the idea that brutality and bloodshed must be an integral part of being a man. Is that healthy? I think not. Is that Christian? I really hope not. In speaking in this way, I do not intend to do a disservice to those men who have fought and even died in conflict. Many were called up to serve in these wars without choice, nor an opportunity to express their moral conscience. Rather, I suggest we have to re-evaluate the extent to which such activity is an especially masculine affair and how much it should be advocated for us now, post-war.

Warrior King

Warfare is ubiquitous in our modern world, but it was even more prevalent in the ancient world, where it served a political and social purpose similar to the other scenarios we have seen. In the Bible, wars were about securing land, gaining influence, taking control and building empires. Sometimes God was seen to advocate and even partake in these violent affairs. Once again, however, war in the Bible was a primarily masculine affair – although we should note that there are some astounding passages where women take the reins and are even relied on by other men in moments of war (Judg. 4.4–10).

In a chapter of his book *Interested Parties*, prolific biblical scholar David Clines talks about the masculinity of the biblical figure David.[10] This was one of the first endeavours at studying masculinity in the Bible. The first point that Clines makes about David is that he is a 'fighting male'. He notes that, in the biblical texts, David's body count is probably around 140,000 men. To make that understandable for us, such a number is not far off the estimated population of the city of Oxford. This means that the mighty King David, who most Christians consider to be the greatest king of Israel, happened to be personally responsible for the deaths of a staggering number of people. In the ancient world this would probably have been seen as a good thing. It would have given David status and credence as a monarch. Yet, with modern eyes, and acknowledging that our idea of masculinity might be shifting substantially in this area, such a barbaric number of fatalities is quite unsettling. Perhaps David is not as great as we once thought.

The violence of David begins in a rather unexpected place. The prophet Samuel chooses David as the one who has found favour in his sight. Yet, David is the youngest of eight sons.

> Samuel said to Jesse, 'Are all your sons here?' And he said, 'There remains yet the youngest, but he is keeping the sheep.' And Samuel said to Jesse, 'Send and bring him; for we will not sit down until he comes here.' He sent and brought him

in. Now he was ruddy, and had beautiful eyes, and was hand-some. The LORD said, 'Rise and anoint him; for this is the one.' (1 Sam. 16.11–12)

In the ancient world, David would have been considered the least important. Familial priority was always given to the eldest son. In the law of Deuteronomy, the firstborn son is entitled to receive double the amount of inheritance as that of his siblings (Deut. 21.15–17). Usually, the more sons there were, the more irrelevant the youngest one would become. This was particularly relevant for David, since his seven brothers indicated completeness in the typical numerical motif of the Hebrew Bible, so his identification as the eighth leaves him as the one 'without prospect, or to be nobody; this was the number of insignificance'.[11]

Age was an important factor in masculinity. Old men were considered wise and masculine (unless they lost any physical or sexual prowess), whereas young men were naive and foolish. So it is a subversive act for Samuel to find favour in David. This is emphasized further when David is chosen to fight Goliath, because he is only a shepherd whereas his brothers were soldiers who had already gone off to battle. In short, David was the most unlikely choice in this realm of ancient masculinity.

However, David trusts in God. As a youngest son and a shepherd, he is a lowly person, but he volunteers to take on the mighty Philistine Goliath.

And there came out from the camp of the Philistines a champion named Goliath, of Gath, whose height was six cubits and a span. He had a helmet of bronze on his head, and he was armoured with a coat of mail; the weight of the coat was five thousand shekels of bronze. He had greaves of bronze on his legs and a javelin of bronze slung between his shoulders. The shaft of his spear was like a weaver's beam, and his spear's head weighed six hundred shekels of iron; and his shield-bearer went before him. (1 Sam. 17.4–7)

The author of 1 Samuel purposely paints a tremendous picture. Goliath is supposed to terrify us. This monstrosity of a man seems unbeatable. And yet, with a faithful heart, David still tries. A helmet and some armour are slung on him before he enters battle, but he struggles to walk because he is not used to wearing such heavy equipment. So he removes them. Rather than arming himself with the usual signature masculine weaponry of a sword and shield, David then takes only a staff, a sling and some stones and faces Goliath with barely any help but God's.

David of course goes on to kill Goliath (1 Sam. 17.51). The little man beats the big man. To some extent, we have become a little desensitized to the shock of this narrative. In our gender-critical reading, the eighth son of Jesse, who is usually found tending the sheep, is victorious against a gigantic being who has been fighting since his youth. David the un-masculine unmans the hypermasculine giant that is Goliath. If we were to read this for the first time, or indeed saw it as ancient people, we would certainly be astounded.

The unmanning does not stop here, however. In the following chapter, King Saul is angered because of the parade of celebration taking place upon their return from battle.

> As they were coming home, when David returned from killing the Philistine, the women came out of all the towns of Israel, singing and dancing, to meet King Saul, with tambourines, with songs of joy, and with musical instruments. And the women sang to one another as they made merry,
> 'Saul has killed his thousands,
> and David his tens of thousands.' (1 Sam. 18.6–7)

As we have seen, violence is a masculine trait and masculinity meant status. Here, David is attributed with ten times the number of deaths than Saul's mere 1,000. This moment incites hatred from Saul. From here on in, he no longer praises David but wants him dead, because the lowly, un-masculine David has not only unmanned Goliath but even unmanned his own king. Yet more, on their arrival home Saul is shamed by the women of his city, no less.

Further, David later delivers 200 Philistine foreskins to Saul (1 Sam. 18.27). Although this may disgust us, it would have been a sign of manly fighting power to obtain these from the enemy.[12]

All of these events demonstrate how the man who held the ultimately authoritative masculine position of monarchy was ousted by the most un-masculine of men and then taunted by the even less masculine women. This would have been utterly embarrassing and emasculating for King Saul. Not only does David come out on top in terms of masculinity, of social status between humans, but also in the eyes of God because he later replaces Saul as king.

The ethics of sex and relationships

Leonard Cohen's famous hit 'Hallelujah' contains glimpses of biblical narrative within it. Not only is the throne and hair cutting of Samson from the Book of Judges mentioned, but also the characters of David and Bathsheba. His account of this latter story is rather romanticized compared to the original. As we will see, John Holdsworth is not wrong to suggest that the narrative of David and Bathsheba is rather like a scandalous, and even disturbing, article we might read today in a tabloid newspaper or a celebrity magazine.[13]

> It happened, late one afternoon, when David rose from his couch and was walking about on the roof of the king's house, that he saw from the roof a woman bathing; the woman was very beautiful. (2 Sam. 11.2)

As Sara Koenig informs us, the text has the possibility of interpreting Bathsheba as some sort of seductress who lures David away from his divine purpose.[14] This interpretation has taken historical precedence, though there is little credibility for this stance. Reading the text contextually, Bathsheba is actually lying in the bath in order to cleanse herself after her menstruation. Women were considered impure when they had menstruated and so were in need of some sort of ritual washing, as Levitical law tells us:

> When a woman has a discharge of blood that is her regular discharge from her body, she shall be in her impurity for seven days, and whoever touches her shall be unclean until the evening. (Lev. 15.19)

Why then was David watching her while she ritually bathed? Leonard Cohen's lyrics imply that Bathsheba was out on the roof for all to see. Suitable biblical translations actually describe David instead as looking on from the roof. It is much more apt for us to understand David as some sort of voyeur, driven by lust. While Bathsheba is ritually cleansing herself within the private space of the palace courtyard, the male gaze of David intercepts. He sees her naked and he wants her. As king, as he surely knows, he will not be denied this.

Following his almost paraphilic spying, David requests to know who this woman is. On receiving an answer (2 Sam. 11.3), David does not reply. Does he care about her name? Her family? Even worse, is he even slightly bothered that she is married? Evidently not, since he asks for someone to bring her to him immediately so that they can have sex. In the worryingly typical biblical fashion, it all happens rather quickly, without any explicit questioning or consent:

> So David sent messengers to fetch her, and she came to him, and he lay with her. (Now she was purifying herself after her period.) Then she returned to her house. (2 Sam. 11.4)

David is active in this encounter and Bathsheba is passive. The language implies that Bathsheba has no say and becomes nothing more than an object. He wants his way with her and so he gets it, regardless of Bathsheba's consent or marriage.

The history of interpretation may make it seem that David was seduced by some sort of evilly alluring femininity, but it is clear these events take place solely because David abuses his power to get what he wants. At the most, he commits an act of sexual violation and rape here, and those who wish to dampen such an interpretation must at least agree that he is knowingly initiating an affair with Bathsheba, who is already married. From this, we are able to draw links between the (over-)sexualization of women's bodies by men, affairs, grossly unfair sexual standards, and the abuse of the body, all within our modern world.

A 2015 YouGov poll found that 33% of British people have considered having an affair and 20% have actually gone through with it.[15] The findings discovered that most women cheated because of flattery or emotional deprivation in their relationship. Men similarly rationalized their affairs by the attractiveness of flattering and being flattered, but also indicated dissatisfactory sex lives. We exist in a highly sexualized culture. Bodily lust has become favoured over intimacy and relationship. While it is hard to escape the sexual nature of film and television in contemporary media, others actively choose to engage with it, particularly in the form of easily accessible pornography. It would be wrong, nor is it my intention, to shame those involved in the porn industry, as well as those who watch porn, especially with its propensity for addiction that many will have experienced. However, such wilful engagement with pornography and our wider hypersexualized culture does have dangerous repercussions that we should all be wary of.

Sexualized society sets high standards for sexual intercourse and its consequential pleasure. Throughout the mediums of television, film and pornography, you will find flawless bodies that are very unlike those of most people in the world. This rigid appreciation of specific body types is dangerous, with skinny, petite women and large muscular men, usually both white, considered to be the most desirable by the media. These sorts of idealizations result in standards that are unmet in everyday life. The psychological impact of pornography leads viewers, who are mostly men, to bring this world of fantasy into their ordinary lives; they will expect their relationships and the sex they have to be as rehearsed and perfected as that of the stars of the sexualized industries whose job it is to create such an illusion.

As JJ Bola notes, there are further and more troubling impacts caused by the misuse of pornography:

> More men than ever are watching pornography, while more boys are being exposed to pornography at a younger age, which is leading to sexual addictions, problems with intimacy, a desire for isolation and damaging relationships. Many young people are left to learn about sex and sex education through pornography, which seems to be where the issue stems from.[16]

> Furthermore, over the years, pornography has become increasingly violent and misogynistic ... The colloquial language men use to describe sex reflects this exacerbation of violence and misogyny in pornography ... The use of this language in order to refer to sex removes the intimacy of sex, and dehumanises the personal aspect of it, reducing sex to a mere action, physical and aggressive at its most reductive, and framed as something a man does to a woman, rather than a mutual engagement, and something the woman also enjoys.[17]

In this technological era, these problems begin at an early age. What starts as teenage girls taking photographs of their (partially or completely naked) bodies at the request or even pressure from similarly underage boys, who illegally store these images (which has become troublesomely normalized), grows into expectations, demands and assumptions made by young boys in school. Chris Hemmings points this out:

> So rampant is the lad culture within our schools that not only are young boys lifting skirts, pinching bums and regularly calling their female classmates 'slags' or 'bitches', but the girls I spoke to say they have become numbed to it all.

Take, for example, the testimony of one young girl I spoke to about this very issue. She's just fourteen years old and explained how, at her school, it was 'completely normal to get harassed'.[18]

Distressingly, these commonly unchallenged attitudes, particularly those rooted in access to pornography, develop into grown men who *still* expect, demand and assume the right to see, and even have contact with, women's bodies whenever they wish, just as David did with Bathsheba.

Pornography can be a toxic part of our culture that needs addressing, typified in the case of Conservative MP Neil Parish who was caught watching pornography in the House of Commons, exhibiting the toxic entitlement found in many men's perception of sexuality and pornography. More generally, however, the dispute is whether the toxicity is within pornography itself – for example, would wilfully watching two consenting adults who agree to being filmed for public viewership still be toxic? – or whether the issues are found more closely linked to the addictive consumption of such material, and how the enterprise of pornography has become abusively run. The industry itself has, after all, become a place where non-consensual and abusive sex has worryingly thrived.[19] Most people will be mindful of such issues already, considering that almost all boys and men have ventured into exploring pornography at some point in their lives. Perhaps one of the best ways to address these problems is by educating people, particularly young boys and men, on how to ethically and morally consume porn (if they should want to) and how this might relate to expectations of future relationships.

Another issue here is that not only do men get conditioned into this violent sexual pornography, but other viewers, including women, will buy into it. Perhaps it is then commonly expected by both participants in a sexual encounter for the man to be dehumanizing and aggressive in his approach, while the woman is passively objectified. The sexual and romantic intimacy gets lost within relationships – an issue that the Church

needs to place front and centre of its sexual ethics. Not only
this, but in this way sexual violence then becomes part of
normalized behaviour in our culture.[20]

Ultimately, these toxic expectations will lead to the dissatisfaction and destructiveness of men because they have been
taught distorted, unrealistic, unfair and even abusive standards. This will have many implications, including the unmet
self-expectations of men's own bodies leading to self-image
problems, and a rise in sexual violence (in order to force the
sex that they expect from women). Further, men may suspect that they can find something better elsewhere and have
affairs, rather than working hard to perfect the relationships
to which they have already committed. For clarity, someone
certainly should *not* remain in a relationship that is abusive
or harmful to their mental or physical health, nor should they
work at relationships and marriages that are clearly broken. As
Natalie Collins says, these sorts of issues are not the problem
of a relationship, but 'of an abusive person within the *context*
of a relationship'.[21] But perhaps there are some mutual loving
relationships that seem unfulfilled because they are measured
against the false standards fed to us by channels such as film,
television and media. In the real world, they could be unions of
love and flourishing, if men did not expect their partners to be
like celebrities, models and porn stars.

I hope this does not seem like a simplified sexual ethic.
Rather, I want to convey a generic observation of the world
around us. It is in these matters that the Church has been so
wrong before and remains so. There is no weight or credibility
in attacking the sexualized world around us while charging
ahead with an unrealistic so-called 'Christian' standard for
relationships, where cohabitation between two people is not
recommended unless they are married, and an active sex
life is a gift that should only be afforded to couples who are
ecclesiastically married. If anything, all we will do is damage
the trust people place in the Church as we instil guilt, shame
and degradation in their lives. This was not Jesus' approach
to these issues (see for example John 7.53–8.11), so neither

should it be ours. The Church's 'politics of sexual shame', and the theologies derived from it, have 'failed to acknowledge the original blessings of sexuality and human beings'.[22] So many Christians, including myself, have been brought to breakdown in tears in romantic encounters because of the guilt complex that the Church has made us associate with intimacy.

Of course, things like sex, pornography and affairs are temptations of the world that we will have all experienced to some degree. They are unavoidable. Again, there is no point in shaming one another if we have ever acted on those temptations, though we may judge our own actions as sinful. Whenever we have done those things, we often know immediately if it was an act against God's best will for us. This guilt is our own issue, and we will know when we feel the need for repentance. Christian faith is a discipline of living a Godly life, in which we will undoubtedly stumble and fall. But if we remain genuinely humble and repentant, we will always be forgiven for giving in to this world of temptation. Obviously, if other people are involved and have been hurt, part of this repentance is to try to make reparation to others and remedy our own wrongdoing.

What the Church needs to do is create a realistic and healthy sexual ethic that is aware of the happenings and surroundings of the world. Namely, the Church needs to begin listening to others: to those who are addicted to pornography; to those who have cheated; to those who have sex in monogamous, polyamorous and open relationships; to those who have non- or anti-normative sex; to those in LGBTQ+ relationships; to those who have had sex used as a weapon against them; and to those who do not have sex at all. Ironically, many of these people can be found within our churches already but they are silenced from telling their stories. The Church will get *nowhere* if it carries on sticking its fingers in its ears and marching ahead without an ounce of awareness of the world in which it situates itself, still claiming that it teaches infallible righteousness with regard to sexual ethics. Just as the Bible holds a varied multiplicity of portrayals of sex and sexual ethics, the Church should recognize that human experience holds such diversity too.

David might not have lived in the hypersexualized world in which we live today, though sex was certainly socially significant in other ways, but the ancient world still gave precedence to the male gaze.[23] In other words, women were objects for men's pleasure. Although I have entertained the idea of an affair, do not be fooled: David's unwanted sexualization of Bathsheba should much more accurately be classified as a disgusting act of sexual violation and even assault; namely, a consequence of the normalization of the male gaze and desire in the ancient world, where women were simply objects to be taken, used and abused by men. More than anything, this reading of the passage attempted to trace the arrogant sexual entitlement that men in the Bible and the modern world believe themselves to have, which not only causes destructive affairs but can also lead to harmful and atrocious acts of abuse and exploitation.

What is interesting is that, unlike the heteronormative relationship between Bathsheba and David, which is largely physically driven and exploitative, a queer reading of the relationship between David and Jonathan,[24] where their love for one another is greater than that which they have for women (2 Sam. 1.26), is, conversely, much more connected to emotion. The expected interaction between men and women in these sorts of biblical stories, exemplified by Bathsheba and David, involves toxic and abusive traits of masculinity; the queer hermeneutical alternative offers one of sensitivity and love. Such a counter-narrative reading has been suppressed and denied in order to maintain David's hypermasculinity, and thus his toxicity, which has been perpetuated in Jewish and Christian traditions and teachings ever since, even though the prophet Nathan explicitly disapproves of David's disastrous action against Uriah and Bathsheba (2 Sam. 12.7-14).

Worryingly, many men have maintained the same attitude of masculinity that can be seen in the Bible, where the normative traits of men include exploitation and violation of women, with no (accountable) understanding of women's bodies and the boundaries and consent around them. Pornography, and even television and film, tend to be shot from the perspective of men. Women are the sexualized focus of such videos. Today, the issue is that men walk away from their phones and computers with an unconscious expectation of the real world and real women (and men). Women may even be deceived into this expectation of relationships, too. These consequences may lead to dissatisfaction in relationships and subsequent affairs, and even to men feeling that they have the right to look at, touch and abuse women's bodies. Men's sexualized male gaze (both in person and through the camera lens) should unsettle us just as much as David's voyeurism and his invasive abuse of Bathsheba should.

Murdering mates

After David uses the body of a woman for his own pleasure, Bathsheba becomes pregnant (2 Sam. 11.5). It is only now that David panics about Bathsheba's husband, primarily because his masculinity is at risk. With women understood to be under the care (or, perhaps more accurately, as the property) of men, David has essentially committed some sort of theft. He takes Bathsheba without Uriah's permission and has sexual intercourse with her. With ancient eyes, this is violation of property, rights and custody.

David tries to tell Uriah to go home in the hope that the husband and wife will have sex. If that happens, David might get away with passing off the child as Uriah's rather than his. But Uriah is so faithful to his job that he will not leave his post, and sleeps at the entrance of the king's house (2 Sam. 11.9). This loyalty renders him as a masculine figure, especially because of his occupational association with war. David is scrambling around to save his masculinity while Uriah remains stable in his.

What else could David do to save this situation which will have catastrophic consequences for his masculine authority and reputation? Kill. For us, it seems rather absurd. In the ancient world, however, particularly for a man, violence would have been the most logical next step. Home-wrecking by taking and raping Bathsheba was not enough for David, he also wanted to kill her husband. David sends Uriah into the front of the battle, with an instruction for his fellow soldiers to fall back and leave Uriah to his death.

> In the morning David wrote a letter to Joab, and sent it by the hand of Uriah. In the letter he wrote, 'Set Uriah in the fore-front of the hardest fighting, and then draw back from him, so that he may be struck down and die.' (2 Sam. 11.14–15)

David kills one of his most loyal soldiers in order to protect his own masculinity. The voyeurism and control over Bathsheba's body seemed troubling enough, but these events add another layer of disturbance to the character of David. The situation only worsens, because as soon as Bathsheba has finished lamenting the death of her husband, David demands that she is brought to him and he weds her. Out of the bloodshed of her husband, she then gives birth to David's son within the much more licit arrangement of marriage.

And so, once again, interwoven with the themes of sex and authority, violence takes the forefront in David's masculinity. This time, however, it is much more personal. David does not kill thousands of unknown soldiers but one of his own trusted men. The former mass of statistics might be passed off by some as just a distanced body count, whereas this event can only be branded as a vicious murder. Both types of violence pose a threat to us today. With the impending potential of nuclear war in our lifetimes, in recent years toyed with by the likes of Donald Trump and Kim Jong-un, we are faced with the possibility of catastrophic destruction and death across the entire world. Coincidentally, the people threatening to press 'the big red button' and frolicking with the fate of the globe happen to be men. On a more localized level, in the year ending March 2020, the UK Office for National Statistics found a 10% increase in the number of homicides from the previous year.[25]

A report from the year before revealed that almost half of homicides that involved a woman as the victim were domestic (i.e. they were killed by a partner, ex-partner, or household member), whereas men were much more likely to be killed by a friend, acquaintance, or stranger.[26] It may seem shocking to us that David set out to murder someone close to him, but these homicide statistics show that those we know and those we do not both pose a threat to our lives. Clearly, death by violence is becoming more real and terrifying for each and every one of us on a national and personal level.

The implications

The mighty King David does not seem so mighty after all, favoured by God and yet undoubtedly flawed in his humanity and masculinity. He was the most unlikely son of Jesse to be selected, as the youngest and a shepherd but, unexpectedly, without any experience of warfare, David wins against the burly hypermasculine Goliath. His reputation consequently rockets from un-masculine shepherd to masculine king, but the power eventually goes to his head. David abuses his authority as he stands on the palace roof invading the privacy of Bathsheba ritually bathing. He craves her and so he takes her. When his masculinity comes under threat because of Uriah's reappearance, David quite literally kills off his friend-turned-rival in order to reclaim his manhood. Sadly, the possibility of a softer David who is in love with Jonathan, which might threaten his masculinity, has been ignored until queer readings in recent years have unravelled its potential for a liberative model of masculinity.

In previous chapters, biblical men have offered us insight into their own masculinities as part of their relationship with God. However, this chapter has been focused solely on the problematic dispositions of David himself. In our Christian communities we have often been led to believe that David is a flawless character, and yet his flaws are some of the worst in the Bible. His kingship is contaminated by an obsession for sex, violence and reputation preservation.

However, we can still learn lessons from David. Even if we are favoured by God, it does not make us void of wrongdoing. God not ceasing to love David should not be considered as a reward for his transgressions. Humanity can, and does, sin; we are unfortunately disposed to do so. Modern masculinity still craves sex and violence. Our sexualized culture provides a fictitious understanding of relationships where we always seem to crave more, rather than work hard on the upkeep of the relationships we are already blessed to have. Not only that, but a more general dissatisfaction with the world has resulted in men using violence in order to express it. For example, the 2011 England riots began with a political motivation after the shooting of Mark Duggan by police but ended as an outlet for violent characteristics. Across the country, riots, arsons and looting took place. It seemed that the original cause had been long forgotten. Where an opportunity for excused violence cropped up, men seized it.

As Christians, we know that any obsession with sex, violence or authority is wrong. It can become an addiction, and we know that addictions to earthly things become barriers to knowing God. Comedian and thinker Russell Brand has written extensively on his own journey of rehabilitation after various forms of addiction. He writes, 'you can never quench your spiritual craving through material means'.[27] Whether those material means are wealth, power, status, sex, violence, pornography, drugs, food or social media, none of them can provide what a profound nurturing of your spiritual well-being can. There will always be a void longing to be filled. If our treasure is found in earthly things, then our heart does not truly lie with God (cf. Matt. 6.21 and Luke 12.34).

It is evident that the dangerous characteristics of David's masculinity still largely reflect men in modern society. Perhaps, then, we need to realize the fault in society's tendency to associate masculinity with sex, violence and authority. Once we teach men that these are not necessary traits of being a man, we start to sever the toxicity from modern masculinity. By doing this as Christians, we can offer men the opportunity to follow God instead of the superficiality of earthly dependencies. As much as David has been used as a biblical exemplar for Christianity, perhaps it might be more fitting if we boldly use him as a teaching example of how men should *not* behave.

Notes

1 Chris Hemmings, 2017, *Be A Man: How macho culture damages us and how to escape it*, London: Biteback Publishing, pp. 113–14.

2 There are arguments for biological factors involved in this, but we are interested primarily in the extent of impact that social upbringing has here.

3 David Clines, 2019, 'The Ubiquitous Language of Violence in the Hebrew Bible', paper presented at the Joint Meeting of Oudtestamentisch Werkgezelschap, Society for Old Testament Studies, and Old Testament Society of South Africa. Groningen, The Netherlands. Available at: www.academia.edu/37260426/The_Ubiquitous_Language_of_Violence_in_the_Hebrew_Bible, cited in Chris Greenough, 2021, *The Bible and Sexual Violence Against Men*, Abingdon: Routledge, p. 2.

4 For a sensitive, accessible and informative resource on this topic, see Helen Paynter, 2019, *God of Violence Yesterday, God of Love Today? Wrestling honestly with the Old Testament*, Abingdon: BRF.

5 In the example of Judges 4, an interesting subversion takes place whereby the violence is performed by women whose femininity is accentuated while being masculinized in comparison to their male counterparts. See Will Moore, 2020, 'Militance, Motherhood, and Masculinisation: How is gender constructed in Judges 4 and 5?', in Helen Paynter and Michael Spalione (eds), *The Bible on Violence: A Thick Description*, Sheffield: Sheffield Phoenix Press, pp. 90–105.

6 René Girard, 2014, *The One by Whom Scandal Comes*, East Lansing, MI: Michigan State University Press, p. 18.

7 Aidan Lewis, 2010, 'Looking behind the Catholic sex abuse scandal', *BBC News*, 4 May, http://news.bbc.co.uk/1/hi/8654789.stm (accessed 2.9.2020).

8 Thank you to Olly Hearn for this illustration, as I confess to not having watched *Game of Thrones* myself!

9 Jack Urwin, *MAN UP: Surviving modern masculinity*, London: Icon Books Ltd, pp. 79–109.

10 David J. A. Clines, 1995, 'David the Man: The Construction of Masculinity in the Hebrew Bible', in *Interested Parties: The Ideology of*

Writers and Readers of the Hebrew Bible, Sheffield: Sheffield Academic Press, pp. 212–43.

11 Milena Kirova, 2020, *Performing Masculinity in the Hebrew Bible*, Sheffield: Sheffield Phoenix Press, p. 45.

12 Kirova, *Performing Masculinity*, p. 63.

13 John Holdsworth, 2010, *Lies, Sex and Politicians: Communicating the Old Testament in Contemporary Culture*, London: SCM Press, p. 15.

14 Sara M. Koenig, 2018, *Bathsheba Survives*, Columbia: University of South Carolina Press, pp. 1–2.

15 William Jordan, 2015, '1 in 5 British adults say they've had an affair', *YouGov*, https://yougov.co.uk/topics/lifestyle/articles-reports/2015/05/27/one-five-british-adults-admit-affair (accessed 4.9.2020).

16 JJ Bola, 2019, *Mask Off: Masculinity Redefined*, London: Pluto Press, p. 44.

17 Bola, *Mask Off*, p. 45.

18 Hemmings, *Be A Man*, p. 84.

19 Nicholas Kristof, 2020, 'The Children of Pornhub: Why does Canada allow this company to profit off videos of exploitation and assault?', *The New York Times*, www.nytimes.com/2020/12/04/opinion/sunday/pornhub-rape-trafficking.html (accessed 4.9.2020).

20 This can be understood as fostering a 'rape culture'. See Johanna Stiebert, 2020, *Rape Myths, The Bible, and #MeToo*, Abingdon: Routledge.

21 Natalie Collins, 2019, *Out of Control: Couples, Conflict and the Capacity for Change*, London: SPCK, p. 41 (original italics).

22 Robert E. Goss, 2002, *Queering Christ: Beyond Jesus Acted Up*, Eugene, OR: Wipf and Stock Publishers, p. xiii.

23 This term is a reference to the work of Laura Mulvey, who noticed the frequency of the male gaze in film. See Laura Mulvey, 1975, 'Visual Pleasure and Narrative Cinema', *Screen*, 16(3), pp. 6–18.

24 See, for example, Anthony Heacock, 2011, *Jonathan Loved David: Manly Love in the Bible and the Hermeneutics of Sex*, Sheffield: Sheffield Phoenix Press.

25 2020, 'Crime in England and Wales: year ending March 2020', *Office for National Statistics*, www.ons.gov.uk/peoplepopulationandcommunity/crimeandjustice/bulletins/crimeinenglandandwales/yearendingmarch2020 (accessed 23.9.2020).

26 2020, 'Homicide in England and Wales: year ending March 2019', *Office of National Statistics*, www.ons.gov.uk/peoplepopulationandcommunity/crimeandjustice/articles/homicideinenglandandwales/yearendingmarch2019 (accessed 23.9.2020).

27 Russell Brand, 2018, *Recovery: Freedom from our Addictions*, London: Bluebird, p. 134.

5

Men Know Best: Job

Bro-talk

When asked which biblical character I resonate with the most, or perhaps even my favourite figure in the Bible, I have tended to answer with Job. I certainly cannot resonate with his blameless righteousness, but I do identify with his courageous outbursts of questioning God. Stemming from his conversation with the Archbishop of Canterbury, Justin Welby, Guvna B writes of the need for us as modern Christians to be better at lamenting, saying that 'it is better to rage against [God] than to shut [God] out completely'.[1] Lamentation and passion are a necessary part of our faith in God, and therefore conversation with God. Job does that very well, as we shall see.

Aside from that, I feel sorry for Job. He lives his life to the full, being as good as he can be for God, and yet still ends up living a dismal life. He wonders why he is suffering, considering he has been acting with such moral goodness. Did he waste his time worrying about ethics and divine retribution? Surely God cannot be punishing him? No. It turns out that God (after Satan, or the Accuser, provokes God) was testing his faithfulness, trying his loyalty with the tests of life. This move from God is itself questionable and has sparked much debate, since Job's suffering involved some life-changing things. But even when Job finds out about the death of his children, he keeps his trust in the plans that God must have for him.

> Then Job arose, tore his robe, shaved his head, and fell on the ground and worshipped. He said, 'Naked I came from

my mother's womb, and naked shall I return there; the LORD gave, and the LORD has taken away; blessed be the name of the LORD.' (Job 1.20–21)

By doing this, Job yields himself to God. The tearing of his robe, the shaving of his head and his prostration on the ground exhibit complete submission in a time of grief. Though we know that, throughout much of the book Job does lament, question and strongly respond to the actions of God – and rightly so. There is a continuous tug-of-war between the two characters.

Until his father died, Guvna B had barely ever questioned God because his faith was the foundation of his entire life. He says:

> What right did God, in his almighty wisdom and power, have to take my dad away from me, from my mum, from all of those lives he'd touched? … That I was even questioning God concerned me. It was like questioning the purpose of my feet to walk, or my eyes to see. He was essential to my whole being, but at the same time, he had performed an act so utterly mystifying that I was not sure how I could find it in me to forgive him. This led me to wondering whether I would even be able to love God again.[2]

We are much more in tune with this reaction to grief than the particular one of Job outlined earlier. For us as modern Christians, God is usually on the receiving end of a torrent of questions, screams and wails. Job is presented here as an exemplar of faith, submitting himself before his Creator. I must emphasize that this is just one good example of a godly man in the ancient world of the Bible – acting in true masculine submission. Raging against God in lament was equally as common – a huge portion of the Psalms, for example, show us the wealth of human response to navigating the world and how we interact with God through our own experiences, both positive and negative. Whether Job's particular response in the passage above still holds relevance for how men should act today is a completely different matter. We will discuss processing emotions such as grief, and their relationship to mental health for us as modern Christians in later chapters.

As commendable as Job's attitude towards his anguish is, there is still something disturbing in this text: it is shrouded in the exclusivism of men, by which I mean that it can be assumed that the entire book is told from the perspective of a man, about a man called Job, who is in conversation with a masculine God, and then discusses his problems with his three friends who are men.

Once Job begins to suffer, he is troubled and confused. He is a righteous man, so why would God punish him? With no sufficient answer, and in a state of grief, Job's friends come to the rescue.

> Now when Job's three friends heard of all these troubles that had come upon him, each of them set out from his home – Eliphaz the Temanite, Bildad the Shuhite, and Zophar the Naamathite. They met together to go and console and comfort him. When they saw him from a distance, they did not recognize him, and they raised their voices and wept aloud; they tore their robes and threw dust in the air upon their heads. They sat with him on the ground for seven days and seven nights, and no one spoke a word to him, for they saw that his suffering was very great. (Job 2.11–13)

They sit alongside him and lament, like him taking off their clothes and placing ash upon their heads. They feel sympathy for his suffering and do not even speak. But this silence does not last for long...

After Job bursts into a curse on his own life, each friend takes a turn to speak their thoughts to Job, including the later surprise entrance of another friend, Elihu. Each of the men take between one and two chapters of poetry to explain their stance and what they think might be the cause of Job's suffering, with Job giving his own response every time. Each of them is certain that Job must have sinned in some way in order to have to endure affliction, with the ancient assumption of divine retribution, where those who are righteous prosper and those who are wicked suffer. Page after page of the Bible is taken up here with the rationales of these men. We shall return to this justification of suffering later in the following section.

Where's Job's wife?

But the most troubling aspect of this male-exclusivism is Job's reaction to the loss of all his children. Some readers will know the pain of such events, even if I can only imagine that sort of loss. But surely there is someone missing who would be stricken with grief by this news just as much, if not more, than Job? Job's wife, the mother of his children.

The first thing to note about her is that we do not know her name. The namelessness of so many women in the Bible should sadden us. We rarely hear their voices or their stories and, when we are privileged enough to hear them, often the author does not even give them the dignity of naming them. I often think of the appalling rape and murder of the so-called Levite's concubine in Judges 19.[3] Whether she was a historical figure or not, it is tragic that she is not even afforded a name in the text for us to remember her by. Perhaps the namelessness and anonymity of Job's wife in particular gives us as readers an opportunity to step into her shoes and imagine her outlook on these events. Perhaps it offers a wider representation for the place of women more generally in ancient society. Or perhaps the absence of identification here signifies a loss of personhood that the character experiences.[4] This final option is particularly convincing, in the light of Job's wife losing her very offspring, with Job not seeming to care about her at all.

Second, we should notice two opposing things about Job's wife: her presence and yet her absence. As a test of Job's loyalty, God and the Satan (or Accuser) instigate the death of his children to see if Job can survive without his family and the ones that he loves. Why, then, does his wife remain alive? Is she not worth being lost as a test for Job? Perhaps Job does not value or even love her enough for her death to mean anything to him. Nevertheless, this means she is present in the story, however much or little the text values her. After their children die and Job is inflicted with sores across his entire body, the wife remarks, 'Do you still persist in your integrity? Curse God and die' (Job 2.9). Interestingly, the Hebrew *barak* might mean 'curse' or it could alternatively be translated as 'bless'. These are certainly two rather different meanings. However, the fact that most translations you read will have chosen 'curse' shows how this woman has been commonly misunderstood. Job's wife has been frequently compared to Eve as some sort of temptress (the details of such a characterization we have already outlined in Chapter 2) who is trying to provoke Job to blemish his righteousness by saying these words.[5] If so, is she aligned with the evil character of the Satan? Is her presence in this narrative actually in order for her to act as a 'baddy'? I doubt it. I think the fault of such explanations lies instead with the centuries of misogynistic biblical interpretations.

And yet these words are still the only words Job's wife speaks and her only noticeable moment of presence. She is absent for much of the remainder of the narrative. So, paradoxically, her absence and presence are equally important to note. As we have seen, the rest of the discussion with Job is led by his male friends. As David Clines suggests, in the culture of the text and its author, 'weighty theological matters [were] the preserves of males, and … women [had] no place in such discussions'.[6] And when Job's wife does share her opinion, she is called 'foolish' (Job 2.10). She is cast to the outskirts of this narrative. Her presence seems to have been employed with an intention of provocation, but her absence sadly has no significance in the narrative. It is only in recent decades that feminist interpretations have endeavoured to create a voice for Job's wife, particularly in those narrative moments when she is not shown to be present.

This leads smoothly on to our third and final point of interest regarding the character of Job's wife. We do not see her grieve the loss of her children and neither, similarly, is she not described as rejoicing in the restoration of Job's life at the end of the text. It is important to note that the text seems to tell us that Job was given seven more sons and three more daughters in the divine reconstruction of his wrecked life. This suggests that God gives Job and his wife replacement children, rather than the restoration of the ones who had died. Well, no wonder Job's wife is not recorded with a voice here. For a mother to lose her children, and then be given extra ones in place of the ones she is still grieving for, is a distressing circumstance. Her trauma is not erased.[7] Regrettably worse, it is just not remembered or acknowledged. If she had been a part of the story here, I doubt whether it would have fitted with the joyful ending that is described. I suspect her silence was more pleasing for such an androcentric text. What does this brushing under the carpet of a woman's experience say about masculinity?

Men silencing women

History has silenced women for centuries. The more that women have been understood as property, the less they have been able to voice their thoughts, opinions and emotions. We need only look at the tradition that still lingers today whereby women take the name of their husband. This is derived from women becoming under the husband's care. They were considered an asset, just like any earnings they made or any land they owned. For many years, if women earned an income it would be considered the man's money. Or, commonly, the woman's salary would just not be considered part of the family accounts. If the reason for a wife taking her husband's surname was anything other than a matter of deep-seated sexism, then we would have seen the reverse occurring much more frequently.

Until the last century, sadly, to be a woman was to be silent. It is a growing concern that men still dominate conversation and debate today, particularly when these discussions primarily relate to the lives of women on topics such as abortion and women's rights. We all have a part to play in these conversations, but no one can share the stories, decisions and experiences of women better than themselves.

A prime example of women fighting to be heard was the suffrage movement in the early twentieth century. Emily Davison, a faithful Christian, is well known for her staunch protests, being arrested and force-fed in prison many times. More than that, however, she is mostly remembered for her death. Davison was hit by a horse owned by King George V at the Epsom Downs Derby in 1913. Her resultant death sparked a critical juncture in the fight for women's rights in the coming years, particularly bringing about the release of women protestors from prison and giving women who were over 30 years old and had sufficient education the right to vote. We must remember, however, that although this was a huge step forward for the suffrage movement, this progress still only benefitted white, middle-class women. In the spirit of intersectionality, these advances were only the beginning of a long and arduous journey in the struggle for gender equality, one which we still find ourselves on. Even more, the global war that ensued the following year gave women further credibility because they took on the roles and jobs traditionally thought to be reserved solely for men, such as munition work, farming, engineering, policing and firefighting. It is tragically important to note that in the case of Emily Davison it took the death of a woman for men to listen to women's voices enough to action change, and the deaths of many more men in the First World War for women to be given the opportunity to step up and show their worth.

Once again, Scripture is not detached from this issue, nor void of responsibility for it. The Bible is guilty of contributing to the gagging of women's sacred voices. The occasional prophetic and powerful songs of women in biblical texts (e.g. the Song of Miriam in Exodus 15.20–21; the Song of Hannah in 1 Samuel 2.1–10; and the similar Song of Mary in Luke 1.46–55) show that women always had something to say about the work of God in their own lives. Biblical authors just did not often afford them the space to express it in their texts.

In the biblical world, the voices of women were neither trusted nor appreciated. It is for this reason that it was remarkably revolutionary that those disciples of Jesus who were women were the first he appeared to (Matt. 28.9; Mark 16.9, although this was a later scribal ending; Luke 24.10; John 20.1). Their testimonies may not have been trusted by the ancient world around them, but they were obviously valued by Jesus.

On the other hand, St Paul, or at least one of his followers pseudonymously emulating similar teachings, tried to silence women:

> Let a woman learn in silence with full submission. I permit no woman to teach or to have authority over a man; she is to keep silent. For Adam was formed first, then Eve; and Adam was not deceived, but the woman was deceived and became a transgressor. (1 Tim. 2.11–14)

Although this passage is likely to be addressing particular circumstance, as we shall see more clearly in Chapter 9, these verses have been abused to suppress the contributions of women for centuries, not only in churches but also in families, work and public life. Passages like this have been used as weapons against women, perpetuating the idea that the Bible is a book by men for men. However, the voices of women are there, lying underneath the surface and between the lines, waiting to be listened to and heeded.

The excessive attention to the lives and opinions of men in the book of Job, in contrast to the supposedly foolish presence and yet grief-stricken absence of Job's wife, shows where the author of this ancient text places importance. It is regrettable that Job's wife is another addition to the list of lost biblical women. This is not dissimilar to the years of men-focused business meetings and boardrooms in modern society. As Chris Hemmings says:

> Men don't like a threat to their dominance. By hiring someone who is familiar to them, they feel more comfortable. It also helps to explain why so few women sit on the boards of companies, or why ethnic minorities are still grossly under-represented in many influential jobs.[8]

Men usually have an opinion on every issue on the planet apart from criticizing their own masculinities; they even ignorantly comment on the lives and experiences of women. As such, the voices of women have been ignored for far too long, solely because men have always refused to listen to others and pre-ferred their own voices instead, for fear of difference and for worship of the self-indulgent status quo. Our world, and our Church, is richer today for the opinions, experiences, intelli-gence, skills, talents and wisdom that women provide. I suspect the book of Job would also have been much better off includ-ing the figure of Job's wife much more substantially.

Gird up your loins!

> Then the LORD answered Job out of the whirlwind:
> 'Who is this that darkens counsel by words without
>   knowledge?
> Gird up your loins like a man,
> I will question you, and you shall declare to me.
> 'Where were you when I laid the foundation of the earth?
> Tell me, if you have understanding.
> Who determined its measurements – surely you know!
> Or who stretched the line upon it?
> On what were its bases sunk,
> or who laid its cornerstone
> when the morning stars sang together
> and all the heavenly beings shouted for joy? (Job 38.1–7)

This passage opens the final chapters of the book of Job, though God's speech goes on for many more pages than this. His erup-tion is in response to Job's accusation that God is unjust. Job cannot reason his own suffering, and neither can his several friends, so he demands an answer.

So, in response, God questions whether Job has had any part in the very creation of the earth and its ongoing sustenance. Job is shown the intricate details of God's design in the world, the formidable power that God holds, and the unfathomable knowledge that God possesses. Job thinks he should be able to understand the answers to the theodicy of suffering, but God refuses to let Job assume that the answers to such questions are capable of human rationality. As Moskala rightly says, the book of Job 'is not primarily about Job, but ... is first of all a revelation about our God'.[9] We learn about God's magnificence and marvellousness, not Job's, or indeed humanity's.

After launching into an elaborate tour of the universe, Job is left rather undignified. He loses any remaining masculinity to the magnitude of God's wisdom. To question the justice and character of the Almighty is quite a feat in itself, but Job does not get away with it lightly. I can only imagine how embarrassed and inadequate he felt.

> Then Job answered the LORD:
> 'I know that you can do all things,
> and that no purpose of yours can be thwarted.
> "Who is this that hides counsel without knowledge?"
> Therefore I have uttered what I did not understand,
> things too wonderful for me, which I did not know.
> "Hear, and I will speak;
> I will question you, and you declare to me."
> I had heard of you by the hearing of the ear,
> but now my eye sees you;
> therefore I despise myself,
> and repent in dust and ashes.' (Job 42.1–6)

The box-office success *Bruce Almighty* (2003) seems like a modern recapitulation of the themes, questions and narratives explored in of the book of Job. Bruce Nolan, a television news reporter played by Jim Carrey, is offered taking the place of God, beautifully played by Morgan Freeman, after he complains that God wasn't doing a good enough job. For a while, Bruce is ecstatic to harness such brilliant powers for his own benefit and amusement, from upgrading his car and wardrobe to scrambling the words on an autocue for his co-worker. But this all comes to a halt when he tries to use these divine gifts to fix his relationship with his girlfriend Grace. Unfortunately, as God had told him, he finds that he cannot meddle with a person's free will. Eventually, Bruce realizes that he is not cut out for such a big task, and he starts to understand why God might not be to blame for all the suffering and pain in the world. He relinquishes his powers and accepts whatever fate the world will pass upon him.

Both self-centred Bruce and overconfident Job have to relinquish the power they hold as men. To surrender to God, admitting defeat in understanding divine creation, redemption, guidance and intervention, is to surrender one's masculinity. In a similar vein, Guvna B found that he had to trust God even in the death of his father which turned his whole world upside down. We saw at the start of this chapter Guvna B questioning God, just like Job and Bruce did, in his time of grief. This did not draw him away from God, but brought him deeper into a relationship with him – knowing we will never fully understand what God has planned for us.

The closing speeches of God in the book of Job, recapitulated in the story of *Bruce Almighty* and familiar to many of us as modern-day Christians, offer us a clear message: we will never fully understand the workings of the universe. Why? Simply because we are not God. Just as we might ask a tailor how to make a sharp suit or an elegant dress, or a director how they produce a Hollywood blockbuster film, or a chef how to cook a delicious gourmet meal, we will never understand it fully unless we have done it ourselves. And, surprisingly, have any of us created the universe and sustained its intricate workings? I doubt whether I am too quick to assume that the answer to that question is no.

The implications

More than anything, I think that our brief analysis of Job should have taught us that men cannot provide all the answers to the problems that humanity faces. As much as many men think that they have the aptitude and intelligence to run this world themselves, this is simply not the case. The book of Job tells us that it is completely satisfactory for us to be lacking in knowledge, or to admit when we might be wrong.

First, the voices of women have an important contribution to make in our individual lives, our communities, our institutions and indeed our world politics. They have been ignored and forgotten for far too long. Not only do the experiences of women provide an entirely fresh perspective from the engrained male outlook that pervades our society and thinking, but their leadership could offer innovative and exciting ways to move forward in such turbulent times, where men are presenting us with more harm than resolution. Bluntly, men need to close their mouths and begin to open their ears.

Second, modern men have forgotten to listen to God. Not only have we too often overlooked the need for God in our lives, but we have also become deaf to hearing God's voice and guidance when we hunger for it. Perhaps this is one of the reasons why we have also ignored women's voices in the Church for so long, for God has been calling women to ministry much longer than the Church has recognized. Listening to the Spirit is integral to our Christian way of living. We must be in tune with God in order to find out the direction laid out for our lives. Only then can we be guided in the principles of love, peace and grace exhibited by Christ. As Christian men, we know that we cannot sufficiently live in happiness and holiness without living and loving in the ways that Christ teaches us.

Job, and Bruce for that matter, judged God's seemingly warped and unjust character and demanded answers. But as soon as they *truly* encountered God's self, and heard the divine voice, they submitted. They relinquished their arrogance and pride in order to let God continue to work out the purpose of their lives. Even if it frustrates us, the will of God for our lives may be beyond our comprehension. This does not mean that we cannot mourn, lament, grieve and rage against how we think God might be working out purpose in our lives – we are *called* to have that conversation with God, not just blindly accept what is in store for us.

But despite that, we must have faith in God, which means we must put our hope in Jesus for our journeys through life. We must let go of our egos and ambitions, and let God take our hand and lead us forward, whether we know the end destination or not. As the common Christian joke goes, 'if you want to make God laugh, tell God your plans'! Men will not know all the answers to the world's greatest problems, but we can be assured that God does.

Notes

1 Guvna B, 2021, *Unspoken: Toxic masculinity and how I faced the man within the man*, London: HarperCollins Christian Publishing, p. 137.

2 Guvna B, *Unspoken*, p. 127.

3 For a reparative reading of this text, that sees the woman with agency and a voice, see Helen Paynter, 2020a, *Telling Terror in Judges 19: Rape and Reparation for the Levite's Wife*, Abingdon: Routledge.

4 This option, and those preceding it, are outlined in a discussion of anonymity particularly in Judges 19, but are also applicable here. See Don Michael Hudson, 1994, 'Living in a Land of Epithets: Anonymity in Judges 19–21', *Journal for the Study of the Old Testament*, 19(62), pp. 49–66 (p. 59).

5 Katherine Dell, 2017, *Job: An Introduction and Study Guide. Where Shall Wisdom Be Found?*, 2nd edition, London/New York: Bloomsbury Publishing, p. 89.

6 David J. A. Clines, 1989, *Job 1–20*, WBC, Dallas, TX: Thomas Nelson, p. 1.

7 Isabelle Hamley, 2020, 'Patient Job, Angry Job: Speaking Faith in the Midst of Trauma', in Christopher C. H. Cook and Isabelle Hamley (eds), *The Bible and Mental Health: Towards a Biblical Theology of Mental Health*, London: SCM Press, pp. 85–95 (p. 94).

8 Chris Hemmings, 2017, *Be A Man: How macho culture damages us and how to escape it*, London: Biteback Publishing, p. 140.

9 Jiri Moskala, 2004, 'The God of Job and Our Adversary', *Journal of the Adventist Theological Society*, 15(1), pp. 104–17 (p. 104).

6

Boys Don't Cry: Jeremiah

Boys don't cry

I have woven fragments of honest personal experience through-out this book, primarily because I do not believe we can discuss masculinity without being transparent about our personal lives, even at an academic level. If you, the reader, can trust me as the author, then I hope you can trust yourselves to be hon-est about the experience of men and masculinity in your own lives. With a focus on expressing emotion, this chapter will inevitably be more personal than the others. Of course, our experiences are not the only ones on offer and so it is essential that we share and listen to the voices of one another, of which this chapter is only one contribution.

The band The Cure released a song in 1979 called 'Boys Don't Cry'. The lyrics speak of all the ways the singer could react after losing his lover, rather than crying. There is a suppression of emotion in this song particularly linked to masculinity, whereby tears are the very last response a man might want to enact in a social situation. Socialization happens incredibly unconsciously through mediums like film and music, and so young impressionable male listeners get taught not to cry in times of sadness because, according to this song, it is just not what boys do. Similarly, Guvna B tells of how he was con-ditioned to think that it was entirely factual that men do not cry, leading him to an absolute breaking point, bursting into overwhelming tears, as he had to process the unexpected death of his own father.[1] He says that he was always taught that an integral part of the traditionally masculine 'image' was for men to be 'holding it all together'.[2] The problem with this is that this 'image' is theatrically outward – there will always be much more going on underneath the surface level for men who seem to show no emotion. The normalization of the emotionally illiterate behaviour of family and friends who are men creates a model of masculinity that gives rise to young boys unable to process emotions like grief effectively and healthily. This perception, where emotion is seen as a weakness for men, is one of the most subtle and yet toxic aspects of modern masculinity. Almost unnoticeably we teach boys not to cry, but this has dangerous repercussions for many men later in life. Guvna B continues that 'suppressing our emotions, acting tough, and using aggression as a form of expression means that men, in particular, are completely ill-equipped to cope with all of the obstacles and challenges that life throws their way'.[3]

In his chapter on the emotional repression of modern men, Jack Urwin begins to talk about the significance of the colour of clothing which we have coded with gender.[4] We have come to associate pink with girls and blue with boys when we welcome new babies into the world, so much so that fashionable 'gender reveals' typically use these colours to demonstrate which sex the baby is to be. Some might say this is harmless but others might notice the subtle danger of it. The problem is not with the colours themselves, but the underlying coding of certain characteristics with a particular gender. In a similar way, emotional repression and suppression have been linked with masculinity. Men are taught not to cry, not to express themselves and to be stone-faced and strong. If boys are blindly taught to like the colour blue just because they are boys, then men can just as easily be influenced not to cry simply because they are men.

My experiences of masculinity and emotion

My own personal experiences of masculinity have mostly, understandably, stemmed from observing my dad navigate the world. He has always been a very insular person, not known for sharing many words or emotions. His confessions of 'I love you' have been few and far between in my lifetime. As a rather emotional boy and man myself, I have struggled to cope with this at times, though realizing that to some extent different personalities exhibit affection in different ways.

When my parents divorced during my late teenage years, my mum was the one to tell us the news. I had enough emotional intuition to be unsurprised by the announcement, having wondered for years when it might finally happen. When you are well-tuned to the emotions of those around you, it is often not hard to tell when the relationships of the people you are close to are breaking down. While my mum encouraged us to talk about our feelings with her about the divorce and the imminent rupture of stable family life, my dad hibernated. For the next few months before we sold our family home of nearly two decades, he spent most of his time silently painting the interior of the building, which presumably operated as his own mechanism for processing what was going on.

I have only ever seen my dad cry once in my life, when his best friend at work died suddenly in an electrocution accident. As I ambled in from school, I saw tears rolling down his cheek as my sister hugged him. Initially, I was perplexed merely at the sight of seeing my dad sad. When questioned about what had happened, he shrugged. He could not find the words, and my sister had to inform me. It was an odd situation, where it was just as difficult to process the death of a close family friend as it was to come to terms with my crying father. It was something I had never seen before, and well over ten years later I have not seen it often since.

Yet I remember an incident only a couple of years ago when I went to dinner with my partner's family for their parents' 25th wedding anniversary. Once we had got inside the pizza restaurant and sat down, my partner's dad just cried. I was a little baffled, but everyone else at the table seemed so undisturbed by the sight that it must have been familiar. After wiping away his tears and making a joke of it (as many men do!), he explained to us that the reason for his tears was simply because he felt privileged to have his family all around him: his wife, with their three children, and each of their partners, sitting around one table. He was so proud of what he had achieved that he could not do anything but cry. I really had not seen a dad do that before.

Personally, I have never felt too scared or embarrassed to share my emotions, being well-known for crying at almost anything really! Whether watching a film, sympathizing with friends and family, or observing my own turbulences through life, my usual first response is to shed a tear or two. As my university chaplains will probably still remember, I spent a lot of my time during my four years in Cardiff crying: in the chapel, on their office chairs and even on the floor. Reassuringly, they called it the 'spiritual gift of tears'. I am not ashamed of this. If anything, I have always been complimented on my emotional capacity, with interesting remarks such as 'You're not like other men'.

In a previous romantic relationship during my late teenage years, I formed an emotional dependency on my then-partner, because we were both in positions of bad mental health and difficult life circumstances. I grew to think that I could not cope without them, only realizing how perilous that was once we had broken up. Nevertheless, that partner had been supportive throughout a scary and tumultuous time of transition in my life. But, in hindsight, it was a mutually unhealthy relationship. Each of us projected our own unresolved issues onto the other, rather than dealing with them head on, causing strain on our own relationships with each other as well as with family and friends. Looking back, what felt like some of the best years of my life turned out to be considered some of the worst, and yet gave rise to the biggest period of self-reflection, growth and learning that I have had. It was only through the hurt done to me, as well as realizing how much capacity I, and all of us, sadly have to hurt others, that I recognized that we must begin to rewire the way we associate emotions with masculinity.

Retrospectively, I have realized that I had my own personal

problems at the time: co-dependence, paranoia, insecurity, a desire for control, a denial of my own mental health issues, working out my sexuality, and figuring out how my first teenage relationship to last more than a couple of months should function. Clearly, I was certainly not void of blame for the relationship's injuriousness. My own problem was not the suppression or repression of emotions that is commonly seen in modern men, but an inability to deal with the overwhelmingness of them. Whereas most men struggle because they are not taught how to recognize the emotions they feel, I had too many to know what to do with. While I was comfortable with emotional sharing, I was surrounded by men in my social circles who were not. Boys, and therefore men, are rarely equipped to navigate and manage their own emotional headspaces while growing up. Later in life, this can inadvertently cause damage to the partners and family of men. In this particular relationship, emotions became our weapons – we both used them to hurt each other, whether intentionally or not.

I recognize that some of my own traits could certainly be considered harmful. I think it is important that this is acknowledged from the outset. Since the beginning of this book, I have stated this: as a man, I inevitably embody toxic masculine characteristics. This is likely due to our defective process of socialization of modern boys and men, of which I will be far from the only victim. In essence, as a man I have been brought up to be toxic. On the whole, this will have happened unconsciously. It is not the direct fault of our parents, family or loved ones, even though they will have made such a substantial contribution to our socialization into the world.[5] Family settings normalize certain behaviour. As we grow up and become adults, our eyes our opened a little wider to other ways to live in the world.

It will have also been the larger influence of culture, media, education and religion, as examples, much of which will have been unconsciously filtered through our own life encounters and interactions. The vast and entangled webs of our own socializations are much more complex than we might assume

and are difficult to trace effectively. Yet these external socialization factors do not reduce the blame, responsibility or guilt
for any harm that has been done by us. Rather, they should
help identify some of the root causes of personal responsibility.
They enable change and bettering. It is only by putting our
finger on the pulse of the problem that we may be able to rectify
the cultural reproduction of toxic masculinity on a wider scale.
We must start with ourselves.

Perhaps if you are reading this and realized that you may
have done something wrong, then think not only about offering an apology, but also a strategy for you to change your
ways. Just as I am self-reflecting here, take some time to understand your own wrongdoings and how you might be able to
find solutions for them. As I will continue to urge throughout
this book, both the accidental and purposeful damage we cause
due to our inevitable toxic traits of masculinity are something
we, as men, must rectify. We will have *all* (and I do not say
that lightly) exhibited some elements of toxic masculinity in
our lifetimes – yes, even the best of men. I would like to suggest
that, at present, toxic traits seen in men are inevitable products
of our culture. I do not mean this in the sense that men cannot
be good, but that the way our society currently produces and
further manipulates our thinking around masculinity leaves no
holistically positive way for boys and men to be raised and
nurtured. This will result in everything from dangerous acts of
violence to comfortable complicity when wrong actions need
calling out.

Good intentions are meaningless in fixing this problem
unless they are followed up with decisive action. The way we
act as men, rightly or wrongly, impacts our own projections
of masculinity and how others perceive it. Until we start identifying our own issues, and actively making changes to them,
what culture says it means to be a man will never get better. It
provides cathartic self-therapy, which will inevitably result in
an awakened need for consideration and life reorientation. We
must begin with ourselves, and then broaden our reflection to
men and masculinities as a whole.

One of the results of my own self-reflection was the realization that the unhealthy relationship of which I write was painfully damaging in a two-way stream. I hurt this ex-partner, but they also hurt me. In my eyes, I had seen my partner as blamelessly perfect for the entirety of our relationship, but only in recent years have I recognized in hindsight that they had practised destructive traits, signifying that I was under a sort of traumatic attachment.[6] With such a large emotional capacity, the love that I felt for my partner of the time blinded me to admitting the damage they were doing back to me.

It is something that I am still coming to terms with nearly five years later, which shows the level of control that was exerted over me. The relationship with its lingering impact still enters my thoughts most weeks, days even, as I process what took place. I changed my opinions and values because they did not fit with my partner's expectations. I bit my tongue too many times because I knew that they would not agree with what I wanted to say. I watered down my faith because I was (quite literally) laughed at to my face for believing in the death and resurrection of Jesus Christ. I put the exploration of God's call on my life on hold for them, impeding the seeds of what has now led to training for ordination. I was lied to so much that I was never sure whether they were actually telling the truth or if I was going paranoidly mad. I lost friends because I was told that they were getting too close to me. I was made to believe that I did not need anyone else. And, when they finally broke up with me after threatening many times to do it, I was left alone: no friends, no security and no support. The first words I said to my family after the breakup were, 'I've got nothing.' It really was an astonishing eye-opener that, after the break-up, most of my friends and family revealed that they had never really warmed to, nor approved of, the partner I had, because of their controlling nature, and that my personality had considerably changed for the worse during our relationship; most of them just never had the courage to speak out, and I was never aware enough of what was truly going on to listen.

As Helen Paynter writes about these sorts of relationships,

'Forgiveness is not easy ... Forgiveness does not mean you have to make yourself available to be hurt again.'[7] It has taken me far too long to realize that a relationship actually should *not* involve hurt and pain, nor a level of narcissism where you forget who you truly are and become lost in someone else. I have finally reached some sense of forgiveness for some of the emotional and mental wounds inflicted on me in that relationship, as well as knowing my own fault for damage within it and seeking forgiveness for that.

I suspect the reasons why I acted in such unfavourable ways during the relationship, which I continue to learn from, are all linked to issues of toxic masculinity. Though we should recognize the damage we inflict on women and other men as men ourselves, that does not mean we ignore our own problems and personal damage, even if men have been taught to ignore their own well-being. As Lewis Howes says:

> Admitting that you are struggling and suffering is important. Recognizing what you are struggling with is just as critical. But understanding *why* you are struggling and *how* to overcome it, well, that's where the magic is.[8]

So, what was the problem (or, at least, my share of it) in this relationship? My mental health issues would not have helped my paranoia and jealousy, especially while I was working out my own sexuality. These difficulties would have also been fed by my desire for control, which caused some element of dependency on (and thus paranoia about) my partner. As my first serious relationship, in my late teens, I was working out what was 'proper' and 'improper' in relationships. These are only some of the issues I can highlight that were at work within this relationship, without going into the personal issues of my partner of the time too. If anything, it was a learning curve of relationships and indeed masculinity in my late teenage years (one that may perhaps be necessary for all those growing up, but could certainly be guided better if we taught boys and men more effectively how to function within relationships).

The damage done in that relationship was certainly due to the personalities involved and the circumstances we were in. Since then I have been in healthier and happier relationships. Though the events were distressing and have had a lasting impact on my life, this trauma has been part of the formation of who I am today, as well as being one of the initial reasons for moving into masculinity studies. Since then I have found a relationship of harmony and flourishing, with mutual respect and love, founded in God and yet entirely autonomous. Love *should* be liberating, not restrictive.

As Christians, we are devoted to repentance after sinning, seeking right after wrong, even believing in *resurrection* after death. We are not called to grovel in the wrongdoing of ourselves or others, even if some opt to do that, but to acknowledge our sins and the harm we have caused and work for improvement. Our Christian journey is one of the recurring death and resurrection of our very selves. We are invited to reconciliation with Jesus through one another and, in turn, we must always think better of ourselves and see better in our fellow humans. The darkness does not endure for ever and there is always light at the end of the tunnel. As a psalmist writes,

Weeping may linger for the night,
but joy comes with the morning. (Psalm 30.5b)

This does not mean ignoring or forgetting the damage that has been perpetrated by toxic men. It certainly does not mean that our anchor of redemption in the Christian faith should act as collusion with the violent and abusers,[9] nor as an absolution of guilt or responsibility. It does, however, mean acknowledging the wounds inflicted by toxic masculinity, learning from the scars and producing more preventative measures than just a plaster of excuses. Once again, 'boys will be boys' will not and *cannot* suffice any longer; until we socialize and educate boys and men to navigate relationships better, we cannot expect things to change.

There is evidently a difficult tension here between men acting as performers of toxic masculinity and yet being victims of society's perpetuation of such dangerous thinking about manhood. Men are simultaneously the preservers and yet some of the casualties of toxic masculinity. Such models of manhood do violence to others, but also unto themselves.

Back in Jack Urwin's book, he makes a series of logical steps, taking us from the coloured clothing of children that I outlined earlier to the damning number of suicides committed by men.[10] In the coded association of a colour with a gender we start to create expectations of what it means to be a man or a woman. These can be damaging when we start to expect men to repress their emotions because it might be deemed feminine or 'girly'. Once men start to conform to some sort of standard, those who do not or cannot meet those criteria feel abnormal – and therefore inadequate – in some way. It is no surprise that rates of depression and suicide in men are on the rise. We do not create enough space for all sorts of masculinities to survive and thrive.

I have always been an emotional man and it has never worried me that I might seem unmanly for it. But it could have easily been the case that because I did not often see men express emotion in my upbringing, I felt I should not either. It is in this way that boys and men commonly learn to bottle up their thoughts and feelings. If we do this, we fail to deal with our own problems which are then projected onto others, causing damage in relationships, whether they be familial, platonic or romantic.

The more men fear discussing their emotions, the more we inadvertently create a stigma around men's mental health, and suicide can be the result. For the sake of the lives of so many men we should pluck up the courage to talk about our mental health and emotional well-being much more sincerely and honestly. At this point, I must reiterate that there are helplines at the back of this book for those who need to take the first steps in speaking out.

In the words of Jack Urwin:

'boys don't cry' may seem insignificant, but it feeds into the idea that men should not express any emotion, and at its most extreme, this attitude is literally killing us. Just one less voice in the world telling a young man he's not allowed to cry and one more saying it's okay to talk about feelings can make a big difference. And if we can make these small changes, bit by bit, over time, it may just start saving lives.[11]

Miserable Jeremiah

So, what has this all got to do with the Bible? Part of an ideal ancient masculinity, seen both in the Ancient Near East of the Hebrew Bible and the Greco-Roman world of the New Testament, was self-control. One element of this was emotion. Those who displayed emotion were considered uncontrolled and, therefore, feminine (although there were some justifications of this as we shall see). This stigma around men expressing emotion is not so different from that surrounding modern masculinity.

I remember a vicar in Cardiff once opening a sermon on the prophet Jeremiah with: 'He's a bit of a miserable guy, really', commonly called the Weeping Prophet. To be honest, this has not given him a very good reputation. But when you look at the life of Jeremiah, you realize that his misery was understandable.

> But if you will not listen,
> my soul will weep in secret for your pride;
> my eyes will weep bitterly and run down with tears,
> because the LORD's flock has been taken captive.
> (Jer. 13.17)

> O LORD, you have enticed me,
> and I was enticed;
> you have overpowered me,
> and you have prevailed.

I have become a laughing-stock all day long;
everyone mocks me. (Jer. 20.7)

He was delivering God's message in the Babylonian exile, and
he was not listened to. His relatives and friends betrayed him
(Jer. 12.6; 20.10) and he was mocked by others in the stocks
(Jer. 20.2), even receiving death threats (Jer. 26.8). Because of
this, the writings of Jeremiah are some of the most personal
and expressive in the Bible. He is certainly not afraid to show
his emotions. As such, his book is some of the most biograph-
ical prophetic literature, arguably rendering Jeremiah one of
the prophets we know the most detail about.

Across this text, Jeremiah seems quite volatile. He tosses and
turns, changing emotion and behaviour on every other page.
He recognizes that God knew him before he walked the earth
and had consecrated him for his purpose (even if he argues
back a bit afterwards):

'Before I formed you in the womb I knew you,
and before you were born I consecrated you;
I appointed you a prophet to the nations.' (Jer. 1.5)

And yet later he wishes that he had never come out of the
womb and had been killed by God instead.

because he did not kill me in the womb;
so my mother would have been my grave,
and her womb for ever great.
Why did I come forth from the womb
to see toil and sorrow,
and spend my days in shame? (Jer. 20.17–18)

He goes from hearing God telling him that he is a person that
is created, known and loved by God, to self-hatred and almost
suicidal depression. A modern psychoanalytical reading might
even suggest that these confused feelings fulfil the traits of a
diagnosis of bipolar disorder, but perhaps that would be read-

ing modern science onto the text a little too much without more evidence. Nevertheless, he is certainly living with an incredible amount of distress and trauma, all in the name of God.

However, perhaps his feelings are rational. Jeremiah's calling to 'pluck up and to pull down, to destroy and to overthrow, to build and to plant' (Jer. 1.10) seems rather difficult. If he is tasked with simultaneously destroying and yet also building, it is inevitable that with such opposing missions he will seem erratic and changeable; his emotions *would* be all over the place. But, most importantly, at least he expresses them – something that both ancient and modern masculinity consider unmanly, unless the cause is reasonably justified.

But Jeremiah shares the tears of God in this work because each time the people reject the prophet, they reject the help of God.[12] Jeremiah's suffering and spirituality are intertwined here – he is pained by seeing people renounce the God whom he loves. But it is important to note that he is not afraid to share those agonizing emotions with the reader. His evangelism, as we might now call it, comes before anything else. He longs for the people to whom he speaks to know the God that he serves, even if that means surrendering any sort of reputation he might have as a man. Those of us involved in ministry may resonate with, and even aspire to, Jeremiah's selfless dedication to God's work here.

Further, if we draw similarities with our discussion of Moses in Chapter 3, Moses channelled God's power and had a raised masculinity because of this; perhaps by sharing in God's mourning for the people in the Babylonian exile Jeremiah is lifted in his spiritual status. However, it is clear here that Jeremiah is not particularly concerned for his status or position. He cares more about being in tune with God than any worldly labels of masculinity.

To conclude, I want to direct us to a few final talking points about Jeremiah that are relevant for our discussions about biblical and modern masculinity. The first happens only a couple of verses into the first chapter. God calls Jeremiah to his prophetic task, but he replies:

Ah, LORD God! Truly I do not know how to speak, for I am only a boy. (Jer. 1.6)

There are a few things that this could mean. Is he simply worried about his age? Perhaps he is young, naïve and immature. He might think he is just not of a mature and responsible age to fulfil the task God has given him. Feeling called to ordained ministry at a young age myself, I can certainly resonate with Jeremiah's words. But, of course, as we have seen with David in Chapter 4, in the ancient world age is a factor in how manly someone is perceived to be. If Jeremiah is indeed only a boy, and therefore rather young, then he cannot be much of a manly character. So might Jeremiah be saying to God, 'I am not manly enough'? Is this an issue of masculinity in his calling? Either way, God could not care less. If anything, God picks Jeremiah in unabashed recognition of this. No matter whether he is 'only a boy' or not, Jeremiah is affirmed as the one to fulfil God's prophetic mission. Just as with the least important son and shepherd David, God has picked the most unlikely figure to be an agent of mission. Jeremiah will be enabled merely because God is with him (Jer. 1.8).

Jeremiah is also single. He has no love interest or family members of notable importance. As Susanna Asikainen states, the fact that there was no word for 'bachelor' in the Hebrew Bible shows that Jeremiah was expected to be married to a wife (or several!) and have children.[13] This is obviously a matter of masculinity. In the ancient world an important part of being a man was sexual prowess, which also resulted in continuing one's name by means of reproduction. In addition, men were protectors of their family. Systems of corporate care, from families to tribes and clans, were a big part of the world of the Hebrew Bible. So it is certainly rather odd that Jeremiah does not have a wife or children – he is particularly unmanly. And yet God forbids him to do so:

The word of the LORD came to me: You shall not take a wife, nor shall you have sons or daughters in this place. (Jer. 16.1–2)

Nowhere else in the Bible does God do this, even if others like St Paul choose celibacy for themselves. Perhaps God *wants* Jeremiah to be an 'unmanly' prophet. Rather like the metaphor of God and Israel discussed in Chapter 3, as well as the relationship between God and Moses, it seems that Jeremiah is the wife of the divine instead of the husband of a woman. His sole devotion is to serve God, regardless of the implications that that might mean for his masculinity. What we have to be careful of, however, is understanding God as such a powerful masculine counterpart of our relationships that it becomes one of toxicity and control, rather than mutuality and reciprocity. Here, it is in biblical eyes that God is seen as masculine and Jeremiah as feminine – those associations of gender have shifted and will continue to do so.

Such devotion to God is not unlike that of many priests today, particularly in the Catholic Church, who feel called to choose a life of abstinence out of devotion to God's work on earth. Although this is certainly a matter for individual discernment, we can all learn from this dedication to the Christian faith. We are all called to devote ourselves to God, but in very different ways that are unique to us and that help our relationship with God to flourish.

The implications

I want to come full circle, back to where we began in this chapter: emotions. Ancient masculinity considered expressing emotion as unmanly. As such, Jeremiah – the Weeping Prophet – might have been understood as un-masculine. This is not so different from modern masculinity. Men in the twenty-first century have been conditioned to 'put a sock in it' when it comes to communicating emotions, being told to just 'man up', 'get some balls', or 'grow a pair', phrases which all show the socially embedded, and yet incongruous, connection between biological maleness and emotional aloofness. What has emotional behaviour got to do with masculinity? Well, nothing. Men can, and some do, express the same emotions as women. There is no biological stopper that differentiates how much men can cry compared to women. The problem is in the socialization process. We teach boys and men to keep their lips sealed, to act tough and to plough on. The problem comes when this causes serious difficulties for men's mental health, leading to issues such as depression, suicide and abusive behaviour towards others. Guvna B summarizes this well:

> Because men are human too: not *super*-human, not *semi*-human but *fully* human, meaning we have been wired with the same catalogue of emotions as women, it's just that, due to our conditioning, our emotions have been starved of food and sunlight, and so have become stunted, gnarled, misshapen; and they impede our full growth.[14]

I have spent pages sharing my own stories and emotions in this chapter, and I encourage you to reflect on perhaps doing the same. We must allow our grief, loss, anguish, angst, sadness and sorrow to unfold healthily. We must give emotion the space it needs in order for us to process it effectively. If not, it will eventually come out in the worst of circumstances.

As biblical examples, importantly, crying by prophets would have been somewhat justified in the ancient world. If they were lamenting God's judgement or wrath, or something just as legitimate, then crying and expressing emotion were seen as a justifiably prophetic action. As such, not only did God ask Jeremiah to be unmanly in his ban on marriage and procreation, but Jeremiah was also inevitably to be unmasculine as a prophet tasked with God's message. Crying for the importance of God, though, was appreciated – a bit like my spiritual gift of tears! Whether it saved Jeremiah's masculinity completely, however, is up for debate.

As we have seen time and time again, God is the most masculine in the context of the Bible and the ancient world, and everyone comes underneath that. As such, these obedient biblical men might be considered less masculine in the eyes of the ancient world, though exalted in the Kingdom of God. The figure of Jeremiah has been no different. If prophets were asked to be unmanly, all of us who are called to deliver God's message to the world as Christian people may also be called to defy stereotypes and norms of what it means to be a gendered person. We should worry about delivering God's message, not about the world's expectations of whether such work is considered manly or not.

Notes

1 Guvna B, 2021, *Unspoken: Toxic masculinity and how I faced the man within the man*, London: HarperCollins Christian Publishing, pp. 55–69.

2 Guvna B, *Unspoken*, p. 88.

3 Guvna B, *Unspoken*, p. 231.

4 Jack Urwin, 2016, *MAN UP: Surviving Modern Masculinity*, London: Icon Books Ltd, p. 39.

5 For more on parenting and toxic masculinity, see suggestions made in Natalie Collins, 2021, 'How can I teach my son to respect women?', *Woman Alive*, www.womanalive.co.uk/stories/view?articleid=3384 (accessed 6.4.2021).

6 Natalie Collins, 2019, *Out of Control: Couples, Conflict and the Capacity for Change*, London: SPCK, pp. 114–18.

7 Helen Paynter, 2020b, *The Bible Doesn't Tell Me So: Why you don't have to submit to domestic abuse and coercive control*, Abingdon: BRF, p. 78.

8 Lewis Howes, 2017, *The Mask of Masculinity: How men can embrace vulnerability, create strong relationships and live their fullest lives*, London: Hay House UK Ltd, pp. ix–x. Original italics.

9 Collins, *Out of Control*, p. 33.

10 Urwin, *MAN UP*, p. 59.

11 Urwin, *MAN UP*, p. 60.

12 Jill Firth, 2020, 'Spirituality from the Depths: Responding to Crushing Circumstances and Psychological and Spiritual Distress in Jeremiah', in Christopher C. H. Cook and Isabelle Hamley (eds),

The Bible and Mental Health: Towards a Biblical Theology of Mental Health, London: SCM Press, pp. 115–27 (p. 116).

13 Susanna Asikainen, 2020, 'The Masculinity of Jeremiah', *Biblical Interpretation*, 28(1), pp. 34–55 (pp. 40–1).

14 Guvna B, *Unspoken*, p. 233.

7

Men Are Unbeatable: Jesus

How many Jesuses?

I dare say that starting this chapter with such a subheading will be branded heretical. However, I do so brazenly for it has its justification. Many Christians are unaware that the Gospels, as well as other New Testament texts, paint very different pictures of Jesus. This does not mean that there are different historical Jesuses – I suspect that many readers will know and firmly believe that God became incarnate on this earth only once and in the form of the man Jesus Christ. However, we have to remember that the world's accounts, retellings, stories, films, music and art have multiplied the ways in which we can see Jesus, and even the Gospels themselves are simply depictions of the real thing. When we talk about Jesus, whose idea of Jesus are we talking about? As divinely inspired as they may be, the Gospels should come under scrutiny just like any other portrayal of Jesus.

A good illustration to underpin this discussion is to look at how Christian iconography has associated each Gospel with an emblem. This symbolism is rooted in Scripture, and you will find such images dotted around almost every church building. The prophet Ezekiel talks of four living creatures:

'As for the appearance of their faces: the four had the face of a human being, the face of a lion on the right side, the face of an ox on the left side, and the face of an eagle.' (Ezek. 1.10)

The Book of Revelation regurgitates this imagery, saying,

'Around the throne, and on each side of the throne, are four living creatures, full of eyes in front and behind: the first living creature like a lion, the second living creature like an ox, the third living creature with a face like a human face, and the fourth living creature like a flying eagle.' (Rev. 4.6–7)

These four beings have become known as the faces of the four Gospels, or the tetramorph.

Richard Burridge's well-known *Four Gospels, One Jesus?* is very helpful as introductory material in this area and I will outline some of his ideas as we try to understand the different Gospels' portrayal of Jesus and how they related to their respective symbols.[1]

The Gospel of Matthew has been traditionally associated with a man or angel. Burridge says that in the ancient world the human body indicated revelation and intelligence. More generally, the Gospel of Matthew is well-known for understanding Jesus primarily as a teacher with authority (e.g. Matt. 7.28–29). The text of Matthew is structured around five discourses or teachings, which includes the Sermon on the Mount. Some people understand these five blocks of discourse to mirror the Pentateuch (the first five books of the Bible: Genesis, Exodus, Leviticus, Numbers and Deuteronomy), traditionally associated with Moses, which identifies Jesus as the 'new' law. Whether he fulfils, supersedes, or cancels the law of the Hebrew Bible is a whole separate discussion.

Second, the Gospel of Mark is often depicted as a roaring lion. Burridge describes Mark as bounding on with the text, as the Greek *kai euthus* (or 'and immediately') continually moves Jesus' ministry on at a fast pace throughout the narrative (e.g. Mark 1.18, 2.12, 6.45, 8.10). This is one of the reasons why we commonly suggest Mark as the Gospel that new Christians (or at least those people who show an initial curiosity in the Christian faith) should read first, because it covers the basics most quickly and succinctly. Lions are also associated with royalty and power, which matches Mark's Jesus who exorcizes demons and performs astounding miracles.

The Gospel of Luke is usually symbolized by the ox. In the ancient world, according to Burridge, the ox was both a piece of powerful machinery for harvesting and agriculture, and a symbol of burden. We often associate the ox with lowliness, which accounts for Jesus' care for social outcasts such as the poor, sex workers, women, the hungry and tax collectors in this Gospel. The Beatitudes demonstrate this:

> Then he looked up at his disciples and said:
> 'Blessed are you who are poor,
> for yours is the kingdom of God.
> 'Blessed are you who are hungry now,
> for you will be filled.
> 'Blessed are you who weep now,
> for you will laugh.' (Luke 6.20–21)

Finally, the Gospel of John is not considered one of the Synoptic Gospels because it sees Jesus quite differently to its three literary counterparts. As an eagle, Burridge describes John's Gospel as soaring above the world. The Jesus of John's Gospel is an exalted and divine being.

> In the beginning was the Word, and the Word was with God, and the Word was God. He was in the beginning with God. All things came into being through him, and without him not one thing came into being. What has come into being in him was life, and the life was the light of all people. (John 1.1–4)

In the early Church, docetism (the belief that Jesus only seemed – in the Greek, *dokei* – to be human, rather than fully bearing the form of humanity) was rejected as a heresy. The Gospel of John was one of the leading texts that brought this heretical idea into consideration. You may be familiar with the language of Jesus' veiled flesh, sung in the carol 'Hark the Herald Angels Sing' ('Veiled in flesh the Godhead see'), which has a similar tone of docetism because it assumes Jesus was only hidden, rather than entirely embodied, in human form. Nevertheless, John's Jesus is the divine God who was, and is, and is to come.

So it is evident that each Gospel chooses to highlight a particular side of Jesus, whether that be Jesus the teacher, the miracle worker, the caretaker of outcasts, or the intensely divine. We must not forget that authors of any text make an intentional choice to portray their characters and story in a particular way. The same is true for the way in which the Gospels depict Jesus, and even his masculinity.

One Jesus, many masculinities

There has been lots of scholarly work on the masculinities of Jesus in the last decade within the academic sphere. I use the plural 'masculinities', rather than 'masculinity', because the Gospels showcase different parts of Jesus' masculinity just as they do with his other characteristics and behaviours, as discussed above. As the New Testament presents depict several Jesuses, so they depict several masculinities. In essence, each Gospel decides to portray Jesus in a particularly gendered light, whether that be traditionally and hegemonically masculine or not. In other words, they all have a gendered agenda. Most notably in the academic world, Susanna Asikainen and Colleen Conway have contributed heavily to the work of seeing Jesus in the Gospels through a gender-critical lens.[2] I will do my best to summarize their ideas in an accessible format, as well as give the occasional personal assessment and supplementary scholarship.[3]

The Gospel of Mark is largely considered to be the first Gospel to be written. It could be argued that because it is the earliest, it might be the most accurate. Of course, this is only an assumption and will be widely disputed. Nevertheless, Mark was most probably used as an initial source for the Gospels of Matthew and Luke and so it forms a foundation for how Jesus is understood across the three Synoptic Gospels.

Conway argues that we should understand Mark's Jesus primarily as a strong and ideal man. The titles used for him are very much related to divine as well as military figures. He commonly outmans opponents such as the scribes and pharisees because he showcases better (and thus more masculine) literacy and verbal skills (e.g. Mark 3.22–30). If we take the strong lion imagery that we have seen associated with Mark, it is understandable that Jesus can be seen as a masculine figure. He exorcizes demons from people and shows his authoritative power over spirits (e.g. Mark 5.8–13). If he is the one to rule over these entities, then he is not being ruled himself. This control over others rather than *being* controlled is essential to understanding an ideal ancient man.

Asikainen takes a rather different approach. She believes that Mark's Jesus is far away from the ideal man of the Greco-Roman world in which he is situated. For example, Jesus is commonly seen as lacking in self-control with regards to his emotions. He is angry on multiple occasions (e.g. Mark 1.41; 3.5). Further, Mark's Jesus teaches his disciples to be like servants and slaves (Mark 10.44). These are considered particularly un-masculine positions in society. What Asikainen suggests Jesus is doing is telling his followers to voluntarily give up their masculinity and become lesser citizens. As we will see, Jesus then does this himself when he is crucified. I would like to further suggest that perhaps Jesus is using his own masculinity here to instigate change, lowering the masculine to give rise to the un-masculine. Jesus is shifting what it means to be a man and disciple, which we will discuss in more detail in the next chapter. Nevertheless, we can see that even within the Gospel of Mark there are differing views on the masculinity of Jesus, according to Conway and Asikainen.

The Gospel of Matthew begins with a genealogy that roots Jesus in a royal line of men. As Conway notes, royalty is naturally associated with authority and therefore with masculinity. However, notice that some women are mentioned in this genealogy – namely Tamar, Rahab, Ruth and the wife of Uriah. Although there is much debate about the rationale for this, for which there is not the space here, I favour Sébastien Doane's reading: he argues that the rebuttal of hegemonic masculinity offered by the inclusion of women, for whatever reason, alongside their male counterparts who exhibit fundamentally flawed traits of masculinity, prepares us for the complexity of Jesus' own masculinity.[4] Perhaps the royal Matthean line is not as pure in its masculine authority and power as one might have assumed.

As we have seen, Matthew's Jesus is primarily a teacher. This exhibits persuasiveness in speaking and intelligence, both of which were very masculine traits in the ancient world. Conway notes that many of these teachings fit the masculine ideal, such as self-control (e.g. Matt. 5.39), justice and peace-making (e.g. Matt. 5.6–7, 9–10), and imitating the perfect divine Father (Matt. 5.48).

Yet at the same time the Jesus of Matthew teaches his disciples to become like un-masculine eunuchs and children.

His disciples said to him, 'If such is the case of a man with his wife, it is better not to marry.' But he said to them, 'Not everyone can accept this teaching, but only those to whom it is given. For there are eunuchs who have been so from birth, and there are eunuchs who have been made eunuchs by others, and there are eunuchs who have made themselves eunuchs for the sake of the kingdom of heaven. Let anyone accept this who can.'

Then little children were being brought to him in order that he might lay his hands on them and pray. The disciples spoke sternly to those who brought them; but Jesus said, 'Let the little children come to me, and do not stop them; for it is to such as these that the kingdom of heaven belongs.' And he laid his hands on them and went on his way. (Matt. 19.10–15)

Eunuchs were people who were either castrated (with their genitals being severed, crushed, or damaged in some way) or natural (most likely being celibate or simply lacking sexual interest). As we have seen time and time again, sex was an important part of ancient masculinity. If a eunuch could not or did not want to have sex, that left them un-masculine, particularly if they had had their male genitals removed. Eunuchs became a symbol of gender and sexual confusion. They defied what it meant to be a man. As such, they were often in close proximity with women as well as emperors because they were seen as no physical or sexual threat. This meant that they usually assumed quite high roles in the ancient world, like the Ethiopian eunuch whom Philip meets in Acts.

As for children, we have already established that the older a man was the more masculine they were considered to be, due to wisdom, emerging family lineage and life experience. Children, then, were at the bottom of the masculine hierarchy. Just like eunuchs and women, they were considered 'unmen', as Jonathan Walters puts it.[5] As Halvor Moxnes notes, when Matthew's Jesus welcomes eunuchs into the Kingdom of Heaven and tells disciples to come like children, he is telling them to give up their masculine social performance and come as they are – to trouble gender expectations.[6] This would have been radical, to say the least. As much as the Jesus of Matthew is a masculine teacher, he is also un-masculine in his teaching to be like unmen.

The Gospel of Luke is the most concerned with fitting Jesus into the Greco-Roman ideal of what it means to be a man. The genealogy of this Gospel identifies Jesus as a direct son of Adam and therefore of God (Luke 3.38). Jesus is the Son of the most masculine being that is God. Conway notes that Jesus is also commonly referred to as 'saviour'. This term was often used for Roman emperors who were sometimes considered divine in the Roman world both before and particularly after their death. Here, then, Luke is identifying Jesus as the highest human authority. Interestingly, Luke's Jesus teaches his disciples to be servants but not slaves who were considered even more un-masculine. On the whole, Luke's Jesus fits the imperial ideology of the time of what it meant to be a man.

Lastly, we have seen that the Gospel of John is principally concerned with Jesus being portrayed as fully God (as well as fully human, of course). This is similarly mirrored in the depiction of his masculinity. If Jesus is identified as the most masculine being that is God, which we know from the opening of John's Gospel (John 1.1), then his masculinity cannot be much more exalted than that. Whereas the Gospel of Luke says Jesus is the Son of God, John says Jesus truly *is* God. We also see the preparatory work of John the Baptist in this Gospel:

> '[T]he one who is coming after me; I am not worthy to untie the thong of his sandal.' This took place in Bethany across the Jordan where John was baptizing.
>
> The next day he saw Jesus coming towards him and declared, 'Here is the Lamb of God who takes away the sin of the world! This is he of whom I said, "After me comes a man who ranks ahead of me because he was before me."' (John 1.27–30)

Jesus' masculinity is uplifted in John the Baptist's relinquishing of his own. He recognizes himself as unworthy and lesser than Jesus who is to come.

Other aspects of John's hypermasculine Jesus outlined by Conway are self-control (e.g. Jesus' lack of romantic interest in John 4.1–42, paralleled in 20.1–2, 11–18) and an overwhelming lack of emotion. The only instance where this can be contested is Jesus' outbreak of anger in the temple, when he arms himself with a whip. However, this could be considered justified (and therefore masculine) anger because he was doing prophetic work, just like the crying of Jeremiah.

I hope I have managed to outline fairly briefly but sufficiently the different masculinities of Jesus in the Gospels, with a foundation of scholarship offered by Conway and Asikainen. Each Gospel has its own intention and audience, presenting a particular Jesus within their text. It does not mean that there are multiple Jesuses in reality, but that these texts want to describe Jesus in multiple particular ways for their own specific purposes.

Jesus in drag

As an illustration to help imagine this way in which Jesus is portrayed differently in each Gospel, I think it is valuable to imagine Jesus in drag. For clarification, I am not suggesting that Jesus cross-dressed in any way, nor that he was gender non-conforming, although there may be other material that puts forward such arguments. Rather, I argue that the way in which Jesus is presented by the Gospel writers can be visually and analogously understood as similar to the performance of drag.

RuPaul's Drag Race and related international counterparts have taken the world by storm in the last several years. The reality television show aims to find the next best drag superstar in a competition involving many challenges, runways and games. However, the performance of drag has its origins earlier than the last decade. For example, many of you will be familiar with the pantomime dame who never fails to make the audience laugh. Similar theatrical cross-dressing can be seen as far back as the plays of Shakespeare. Since women were not allowed to be actors, young men regularly had to dress up as women characters as part of the performance. Some scholars have identified the gender non-conformity of drag in even earlier history, such as the self-castration and feminine dress of the male-bodied galli priests in the Roman Republic and Empire.[7] It is worth mentioning, however, that drag has a much more profound recent history of social progress. Drag performers were part of the early political movements for LGBTQ+ equality, with a particular presence at significant protests such as the USA's Cooper Donuts riot and the Stonewall riots. It is still used as a form of protest today. For example, Melissa Wilcox writes about the Sisters of Perpetual Indulgence, a group of gay men who dress in parody of nuns and other religious leaders in order to make a statement of political activism against the religious intolerance of sexual and gender minorities.[8]

Drag performance itself involves the intentional confusion of gender. For example, a drag queen is someone who is usually male but who dresses and acts with feminine qualities. A drag king is vice versa. Gender becomes blended and ambiguous, with certain aspects of masculinity or femininity being accentuated while others are diminished. You will see drag queens with a beard but big breasts and drag kings with a suit and tie but eyeshadow and lipstick. To confuse things even further, there are hyper, faux, or bio kings and queens who perform as an incredibly exaggerated version of their biological gender. Through all this, we lose all sense of our fixed understandings of what it means to be a man or a woman and literally cannot label any of the performers in a gendered way. This is the pure objective of drag performance. It is in its very essence, as Terry Goldie says, 'always to some degree ridiculous'.[9] It turns stereotypical gender signifiers on their head, making them irrelevant and redundant. But, importantly, drag involves a 'transformation in being'.[10] It involves the subversions of the current constructions of what we consider to be gendered. One must transform in order to present oneself in a fresh and fantastic way.

So perhaps this might lend a hand in understanding the depictions of Jesus in the Bible. I am certainly not the first to suggest the notion of 'God, the Drag Queen',[11] with a Christ who owns an expansive wardrobe of dresses.[12] Where drag 'actively performs what is impossible' it should not shock us that many Christians associate this queer performance of drag with God and, indeed, Jesus.[13] The person of Christ in Scripture blurs the boundaries of what is conceivable, whether it be through the immaculate conception, transfiguration, miracles or resurrection. The laws of nature and expectations of social norms are all subverted. And, after all, if drag performance involves an entire transformation of self, as suggested above, then what can be more synonymous with this than the life-changing good news offered in Scripture through the person of Christ. With Jesus being transgressive for most of his earthly life, it seems quite fitting that a modern analogy of such antinormativity might utilize an act such as the queer performance of drag.

As we have seen, within each Gospel Jesus is portrayed in a different way. The Jesus of Mark could be seen as a militaristic, triumphantly masculine war figure, or equally as an un-ideal man, depending on the scholarship we listen to. The Gospel of Matthew has a Jesus who is a masculine teacher, but who teaches his disciples to be un-masculine eunuchs and children. Luke's Jesus is the most perfect example of imperial masculinity in so many ways, bearing a likeness to Roman emperors. The Jesus of the Gospel of John is the utmost divine being, one with the masculine God and in control of each and every situation that occurs in the narrative. These varying descriptions are only from the Gospels; it would take even more space, which we do not have, to consider the risen Christ robed in glory from the letters of Paul or the slain but redeeming Lamb of Revelation.

Which Jesus is the real Jesus then? Well, I think all of these texts are conveying aspects of Jesus that they wish to highlight. They want to show Jesus in a particular way. Or, in other words, they want to *show off* certain characteristics and behaviours of Jesus for their specific audience. This is not unlike the performers of drag whose personas are devised to accentuate certain aspects of their body or character. As such, perhaps Jesus is dressed up in drag: ambiguous in gender, cross-dressed by the Gospel writers, sometimes accentuating certain features and also occasionally concealing others – could we go as far as to suggest that the Gospel writers partake in the 'tucking' of Jesus' masculinity? Regardless, the portrayal of Jesus in each Gospel is a particularly gendered performance.

In his humanity, Jesus would have been limited to living in a certain way as we all are. But it is important to remember that as Christ, the transcendent divine who was at the very beginning of creation, Jesus is limitless. He can be all and none of the things described in the Gospels. These are only the ways in which we, and indeed the Gospel writers, can understand Jesus with our human imagination. As Gerard Loughlin writes, 'identities are destabilized in Christ' and Christ becomes 'multiple'.[14] This Jesus seems very much to fulfil the characteristics of performing drag, at least when looking primarily at the various portrayals of him in the Gospels.

I expect this notion may be very challenging to some, but I hope that it may also be quite a useful analogy to many. Anyway, what should theology be if it is not provocative? I would be concerned if the answer were that it should be safe or secure. Marcella Althaus-Reid, a famous queer theologian, made it her life's work to make theology *indecent*.[15] Proper theology should blow away the cobwebs, stir up the stagnant waters, and keep everyone on their toes. It is what Jesus did, after all. Perhaps this analogy has done the same. More than anything, this image serves to show how even the Gospel writers did not agree on some sort of Christian (in the most literal sense of the word, meaning being like Christ) masculinity.

The emasculating crucifixion

What is inescapable in all of these Gospels however, no matter how Jesus has been portrayed, is the crucifixion. The nadir of human (and particularly masculine) nature is violence, which takes its form in so many ways. The fact that humanity crucified God shows the extent to which we as humans will go to drive God away from ourselves. The violence seen in crucifixion, though set apart from us by millennia, is not some distant memory – similarities have been drawn between the cross and the lynching of African Americans in the late nineteenth century,[16] the violence still inflicted against women,[17] and even the violence found against animals in the slaughterhouse.[18]

But when we think specifically about Jesus' crucifixion, most of our mental images probably come from retellings depicted in film, television and artwork. In the victory achieved through the cross (in both death and resurrection), a skewed image of Jesus is now and again conjured in some contexts. In some artwork we worryingly see a Jesus who rips himself away from the restraints of the wooden cross, defeating death while baring muscular arms and six-pack abdominals. This hypermasculine imagery removes the social and physical injuriousness found at the crucifixion, in an attempt to preserve Jesus' masculinity for a hegemonic picture of the Bodybuilder Christ who cannot be defeated. Stephen D. Moore plays on this imagery in his book *God's Gym*, where the act of crucifixion is just another workout for this hench Jesus.[19] Moore notices that the phrase 'no pain, no gain – which also happens to be the supreme gym logion and the fundamental syllogism of bodybuilding philosophy' sums up the Passion narratives, for 'one subjects oneself to a murderous regime, as Jesus did, in order to emerge with a glorious body'.[20]

But, of course, there *was* pain, which cannot be erased or simply replaced by the image of a glorious, resurrected Christ. I have argued elsewhere that modern film depictions of the crucifixion have tended to either completely pacify the death of Jesus or, on the other hand, obsess over the blood and gore – even though the Gospels themselves barely describe what happened![21]

And when they had crucified him (Matt. 27.35)
And they crucified him (Mark 15.24)
They crucified Jesus there (Luke 23.33)
There they crucified him (John 19.18)

We hear fragments about the flogging and mocking of Jesus but are given no detail about the actual crucifixion. The meagre sentences and clauses stated above are all we are provided with.

Films that focus on the gore of Jesus' trial and execution are not remaining true to the Gospel accounts, even if they are staying closer to historical accuracy. This method I call the 'gorification' of the Gospel narratives, where violence becomes cinematically prioritized.[22] If you have seen Mel Gibson's *The Passion of the Christ* (2004) you will know what I mean! The gruesome nature of Jesus' death should certainly be appreciated, for it was far from an enjoyable public event to be present at, unlike our attendance at cinema screenings. However, if we obsess over the gore of the crucifixion of Jesus to cinematic extremes, I worry that we might focus too much on the gory to the detriment of the glory, though each is absolutely integral for the other, of course. There might have been a reason why the Gospels kept so silent about the details of the crucifixion in the first place.

As much as this event was excruciatingly violent physically, it was also socially injuring. The crucifixion was undoubtedly the most humiliating part of Jesus' life.[23] This form of execution was reserved for the likes of criminals and slaves and was considered the ghastliest practice in the Roman world. Not only does this mean that Jesus was killed alongside criminals and as someone of the lowest status, but also that he was essentially given a forgotten death. These victims were incredibly unimportant. We know this from Nicodemus and Joseph of Arimathea's eager wishes to collect Jesus' body, which needed Pilate's permission, because they wanted to give some respectability to the death of Jesus according to Jewish custom (John 19.38–40).

As we have seen, masculinity in the ancient world was always interrelated with many other issues, one of the most common being status. To gain status in society, one would have to act in a masculine manner. If you were seen to be effeminate in any way, it was likely that you would lose your social status. This sort of status was intrinsically linked to honour. Once again, the way in which you acted would gain you honour and, in turn, help you achieve status. So in this sense a moment like crucifixion would be one of the most damaging. As you can only imagine, being a man strung up high onto a wooden instrument, stripped completely naked by other men for all the public to see and violently tortured would have resulted in a total loss of any reputation. Jesus' death was full of shame. Being utterly dishonourable upon the cross, Jesus is feminized and becomes un-masculine. He looks nothing like the hypermasculine, muscular and invincible Bodybuilder Jesus. Instead, as he hangs helplessly, with his broken, bruised and vulnerable body exposed, Jesus embodies the antithesis of hegemonic masculinity.

Not only this, but we have to broaden our horizon a little to see the full extent of the social impact of the crucifixion.

This sort of practice was primarily understood as a deterrent. Some of the torture given to someone prior to crucifying them might have happened within an enclosed and private space, but the sufferer would have ultimately been hung up outside on a cross. This was a public event. It was supposed to scare criminals from committing crimes against the empire. This act of state terror was to deter any potential threats to imperial authority.[24] If you saw the Romans wounding a dying body and then dangling them from an instrument of torture for all to see, you would not be inclined to mess with them – and that was exactly the point. The Roman empire aspired to be the pinnacle of masculinity and power, and Jesus was seen as posing a threat to that. Once again, we see a competition between divine masculinity and human authority, just like that of Pharaoh and God. It might seem that Jesus loses this one, but his resurrection may tell a different story – perhaps Jesus is a beaten man, but simultaneously he remains unbeatable.

Jesus and #MeToo

We should not ignore the sexual undertones of the punishment of crucifixion. We have noted that many people across the globe who have experienced violence and trauma still resonate in some way with the cross today, and this also rings true for of sexual abuse victims and survivors. If you reconsider the description of crucifixion I have offered above, it might not be surprising that some scholars, the first and most notable being David Tombs,[25] have understood the torture and death of Jesus as a form of sexual humiliation, abuse and even violence.[26]

If, in modern society, someone was stripped naked against their will for dozens, if not hundreds, of people to see publicly, while their bare body was violently injured, and the sight was being twistedly enjoyed by the government of the time, we would not hesitate to label it as sexual humiliation and abuse. As this is what happened to Jesus, we should not be reluctant to identify Jesus as a victim of sexual abuse, though it might be an identification of paralleled analogy rather than exact equivalence. Though this interpretation may not be helpful, and perhaps even offensive, to some sexual violence survivors, others have found it hugely important and something that the Church must consider seriously.[27] Just as we would listen to a victim of such a horror today, we should be attentive to the experiences of Jesus in the final days of his life. Our conclusions may differ, but we must at least ponder on the body of Jesus and its sociality, both attacked here by the Roman empire, because it is the corporeality of Jesus that is so fundamental to the Easter story.

First and foremost, we most notice the centrality of Jesus' body, as well as its objectification and movement. Graham Ward says that the narrative of the Gospels 'propels' Jesus' body towards the cross, during which

> bodies touch other bodies – beginning with the kiss by Judas, moving through the slapping 'with the palm of his hand' by the Temple guard in the house of Caiaphas, to the scourging of the Roman soldiers and the nailing on the cross, and on finally to the piercing of the side with the lance – [which] are all sexually charged manifestation of desire in conflict.[28]

When we reach the latter components of the Passion narrative, if we look more closely at the historical details of crucifixion, it was likely that Jesus was flogged prior to his death. Depending on which Gospel is being read, we cannot be sure whether it was used as a preceding punishment before crucifixion, or as a lesser punishment by Pilate to try and appease the crowds and stop the crucifixion happening at all. We do see in the Gospels that Jesus was involuntarily stripped of his clothing, with his nudity being shameful in itself.[29] But if Jesus was then flogged naked, it is likely that his genitals and buttocks would have taken many hits by the whips and cords used by the Roman soldiers.[30] He would have been verbally abused, which would have been understood as an attack on one's identity and reputation.[31] Then, of course, Jesus was strung up high upon the cross, naked. This is unlike the films and art we commonly see that honour Jesus by dressing him with a white cloth to cover his groin area, arguably to retain some of his masculinity or for reasons of pornographic censorship. In the words of Chris Greenough, 'it reveals much more about religion, society, and culture that a penis is considered more taboo than a beaten, broken, and abused body'.[32] The covering we have come to see would not actually have existed in reality – Jesus' display of nudity would have been a central aspect of the, arguably pornographic, public viewing of the sexual humiliation taking place. He was then penetrated with nails in his hands (or perhaps, more likely, his wrists) and feet (or, again, most likely his ankles) and, suddenly, this identification of sexual humiliation and abuse escalates into sexual violence. While Jesus is vulnerable and naked, his body, which is handed over from person to person throughout the narrative, is physically and sexually violated.

Some readers may argue, as have some critics, that this might be too modern a view of crucifixion. They may say that to label these events as sexual violence is to use anachronistically terms from our culture and apply them to the ancient world. The issue with this criticism, however, is to misunderstand the extent to which the Roman empire knew what it was doing in its torture practices. Particularly, those who view this as an oversexualized angle on the crucifixion show little regard to the ubiquitous awareness of sex and gender in the ancient world. Even if it was not then labelled explicitly as sexual violence does not mean that it did not occur and that we cannot term it as such now.

Crucifixion was known for being the most physically barbaric of all punishments, but also the most embarrassing and humiliating. As David Tomb outlines, the sexual element of this torture was an integral aspect of the state terror performed by the Roman empire, seeking not only to kill but to 'reduce the victim to something less than human in the eyes of society'.[33] The ancient world was aware of the shame of nakedness. The Roman empire would have used this to their advantage. As Jayme Reaves and David Tombs have stated:

Punitive sexual violence can also be an especially effective way by which to humiliate and degrade a victim because its meaning is so densely encoded with social and cultural values around gender, identity, power and conquest. The use and meaning of sexual violence for this purpose is ... clear in Roman crucifixions.[34]

This has even more significance for the concern of masculinity. The Roman empire was built up by powerful (and power-hungry) men. Once again, we can see the theme of the battle of masculinities here. The empire's success was based on elevating their own status and destroying that of others. I reiterate here, as I have done elsewhere, that 'the physical and social violence of crucifixion undoubtedly impacts the victim's masculinity, particularly when we consider crucifixion as a display of power whereby bodily penetration is acted by men upon other (un)men'.[35]

The penetration of men by other men, even if it is performed with nails and other torture instruments, still has sexual undertones; an act of bodily penetration takes place.[36] Jesus becomes a helpless penetrated body under the dominance and power of the Roman empire. This, of course, is a much more symbolic understanding of Jesus as a victim of sexual violence, though there remains a possibility of literal truth in it. However, the historical fact of his nudity and flogging gives a concerning credibility to the voices of those who identify Jesus as someone who has experienced sexual abuse and violence. As Gerald West states:

Jesus is not a 'normal' male, and so he is stripped and abused by 'hegemonic' males. Among his disciples today are those who are stripped, abused and raped because dominant forms of masculinity are intent on exerting power over anomalous men.[37]

The wake of the #MeToo movement largely unmasked powerful men exploiting their power in the sexual manipulation and abuse of women. One of the most notable of these men was American film producer Harvey Weinstein, who was eventually sentenced to prison for his crimes. The #MeToo slogan that unified survivors of sexual abusers on social media in 2017, coined originally by Tarana Burke over a decade prior to its going viral globally, was not the end of this overdue exposing of sexual abusers but the beginning. The movement even had voices crying out much closer to home in Christian communities, blowing the whistle on many ministers and priests who had sexually abused women in churches. From there emerged #ChurchToo, devised by Emily Joy and Hannah Paasch on Twitter to show that the Church has not been exempt from these horrific events. For example, the famous Canadian American evangelist and pastor Ravi Zacharias was one of these Christian perpetrators of sexual abuse, with the evidence for such a claim only confirmed as 'credible' by Ravi Zacharias International Ministries in February 2021 after an investigation.

I was recently involved in a conversation on Twitter concerning the use of the Bible in situations of domestic abuse. One user criticized the way in which the Church of England had not yet appropriately recognized the men who had also experienced sexual abuse in churches. The Church of England safeguarding posters, circulated to all of its churches with the obligation for them to be made clearly visible in their buildings, offered a helpline for domestic abuse whose tagline stated it was to be used by women and young children. Where was the support from the Church of England for men who had been sexually abused? Had they been forgotten or ignored?

As we look at the way in which vulnerable women and men have been at the will of powerful abusers, we must be attentive to the fact that so was Jesus. The Roman empire was the height of imperial and militaristic masculinity. It used its power to hurt and abuse others, to the extent seen in the crucifixion of sexual violence and capital punishment. We should not be blind to the comparison here – sexual violence was just as prevalent in biblical times as it is today. The abuse of power for self-gratification, status and pure debauchery is not a modern phenomenon.[38] It has just sadly taken this long for those affected by it to speak out without fear of reactions of disbelief, mockery or contempt.

In a topic almost never wholly discussed before in theology, Chris Greenough's recent book *The Bible and Sexual Violence Against Men* brought the academic world up to speed with men as victims of sexual violence and its contemporary relevance to the study of the Bible.[39] It is not new to give suffering theological centrality,[40] but giving sexual abuse particular priority in theological and pastoral conversation may provide resonant comfort for those who identify with it. If Jesus can be understood as a victim of sexual violence, what does that mean for men who are survivors of sexual violence today and how can the Bible speak to them?

For the most part, men are statistically the perpetrators of sexual violence and abuse. Despite #NotAllMen coming to prominence in 2021, it is the collective culpability of all men that many people, largely women, do not feel safe around us. This abusiveness and violence are an aspect of the toxicity of masculinity that we have spent some of this book discussing: men have been afforded the power and status to think they have authority and control over women's bodies. These exist not only in brutal acts of rape and murder, but discreetly in smaller micro aggressions that can be just as impactful on a woman's life. However, men can be and are victims of sexual abuse themselves; it is a complete falsity to think otherwise. We are socialized in a society that tells us men cannot be raped, which puts men in danger of not realizing that they can be, and may have been, victims themselves.[41] In the light of our discussion of men being rather private about issues of emotion, mental health and personal experience, it is not surprising that there is a stigma around men also being sexual abuse victims. Just as we have been dispelling broader myths of masculinity in this book, Greenough uncovers the myths particularly surrounding sexual violence against men that we have become largely oblivious to, such as the assumption that women cannot be the perpetrators against men, that an act of sexual violence between two men must include some sort of homosexual desire, and that sexual violence must include penetration. All of these statements are wrong. And yet Greenough's book helps us realize that all of these myths are actually found within our own bibles.

In Chapter 3 we discussed how a fear of male intimacy exists in the Bible and quite similarly in contemporary culture. In the ancient world, this resulted in the feminization of Israel and the Israelites so that they could be close to their hyper-masculine God. In modern culture, we see the existence of homophobic abuse and violence as demonstrative proof of that fear. The same ideas are important for our present discussion of sexual violence against men. The verbal abuse experienced by gay and bisexual men is often associated with how they may subsequently be perceived as less manly and more like a woman for being sexually violated. Similarly, the stigma and shame attached to men as survivors of sexual abuse and violence involves the fear of feminization, physically and socially. Of course, the difference is that this sexual violence involves no sexual desire from the victim, nor do they need to be homosexual in order to become a victim of another man's sexually abusive actions.

Once an act of sexual violence is perpetrated against a man, he is thought to be feminized. That may be in the sense of a loss of control, authority or bodily autonomy. However, if penetration is involved, this feminization becomes much more real. The man who is penetrated involuntarily takes on the passive position, commonly associated with being a woman. In the world of the Bible, this was shameful. The stigma around men as sexual violence victims, as well as the incredibly problematic association with victimhood and femininity, shows that it is still the case in modern society today.

One of the most important ways to work towards reparations of this is to realize how hegemonic masculinity and its toxicity is hugely influential in these events. When we say that there is a way to be a 'real man' or not, those men who have been abused or assaulted commonly feel inadequate and ashamed. They feel that they have not met the standards that society measures them against, failing to defend themselves as their dignity is stripped away. Primarily, to fix this situation we need to stop setting toxic expectations for men. The damage of this can especially be seen in sexual violence against men because these instances do not involve consent. A man feels like he loses his masculinity without any say in what has happened to them.

What does this have to do with Jesus? Well, if we can identify Jesus as a victim (and perhaps more aptly termed a survivor, in light of the resurrection) of sexual abuse and violence, then many Christians who have experienced such hurt both inside and outside the setting of the Church could find comfort in a Christ who deeply knows what it is to experience this. The visibility of Jesus' penetrated male-body-in-pain, with his masculinity being 'undone', might show a potential way forward for modern masculinity.[42] Jesus shows a way in which vulnerability is an acceptable aspect of masculinity, rather than the perpetuation of the myth of masculine invincibility and impenetrability. Jesus' crucifixion of his own masculinity might be a model for how we can use the person of Christ to crucify toxic masculinity today (that said, having seen the barbarity of crucifixion, should we – even conceptually – crucify anything?).

We tend to forget the physicality and bodily nature of Jesus. We believe in a God who walked the earth, born of flesh, who endured the same sufferings each day as we do, and who knows our pain. But this Christology becomes so much deeper and personal for sexual abuse victims when we recognize that Jesus might have *really* understood their pain. His resurrection did not negate his bodily past, but he carried the wounds of his pain and despair with him as he rose again.[43] He, too, experienced sexual humiliation and even sexual violence at his crucifixion. His hurt is your hurt. His scars (whether visible, invisible, emotional, physical, mental or spiritual) are your scars. And, still, his love is your love.

As readers of the Gospels we are invited, as Michael Trainor says, 'to reconsider what is authentic discipleship in the experience of abuse, to encounter a God intimately involved in the human struggle and condition, and to engage the story of the abused Jesus'.[44] Some may be disturbed by this historical fact of Jesus' crucifixion. We need to be aware that some may be oblivious to the sexual violence happening in their own churches, and this reading may open their eyes to it. In turn, the victim Jesus, who may have been silenced for centuries, may help those who have been silenced in their own Christian communities, who are crying out to be heard. If we are not careful, we might find ourselves participating in blind ignorance. Though this reading may be controversial, it is at least worth the consideration that it is not only about #MeToo, or even #ChurchToo, but #MenToo and, perhaps, #JesusToo.

The implications

Jesus is commonly understood to be the perfect example of humanity. I do not disagree with that statement. I do, however, disagree that he is somehow the perfect *man*. As we have discussed throughout each chapter of this book, manhood is dependent on its setting. We cannot grade the manhood of Jesus in the New Testament, who is confined in some ways to the social setting of the ancient world, in comparison with the men of subsequent centuries and cultures, including our own. Once again, we can certainly say there is not a universally valid 'biblical' or 'Christian' manhood. That said, can Jesus be considered 'the ultimate non-toxic man', the exact opposite of the embodiment of toxic masculinity?[45] The follow-up question would, of course, be: which Jesus?[46] Depicted differently in each Gospel, let alone in various retellings in history since then that have infiltrated our subconscious image of Christ, can we ever make a clear categorization of the *real* Jesus?

To notice the cultural confinement of Jesus is not to say we should not listen to what he has to say. Of course, Jesus' teachings on morality and human living are guidelines which we should follow. They are, however, set in a particular situation. Similarly, whether Jesus acts in a manly or unmanly way is judged by ancient standards – the gendered agendas of the time. We cannot expect men of the twenty-first century to imitate the ancient world's idea of manhood. If we did so, we might find ourselves with very long beards, too many wives to count on one hand, and tearing our clothes apart far too often!

As I have argued before, the various portrayals of Jesus in the New Testament (and particularly the act of crucifixion) may create a potential problem for our understanding of God.[47] As Christians, we understand God to have three agents. Traditionally, this has been Father, Son and Holy Spirit, though more gender-neutral terms are now commonly used. So if we consider Father and Son in Trinitarian unity, in the crucifixion God simultaneously occupies two positions: the dominant and the subordinate. In other words, God is in control of the happenings of the cross as Father, but at the same time Jesus the Son surrenders as vulnerable and helpless, hung upon the cross and sexually abused. With ancient eyes, the God of control is masculine and the penetrated and wounded God in the suffering of crucifixion is un-masculine. We are left with a tension of divine masculinities in the Bible. How can we understand a Trinitarian God in this moment from a perspective of gender analysis and how does that impact our own understanding of masculinity?

As we have seen, some people tend to read the Bible as an instructive text on fixed gender roles. In other words, a man must be masculine and a woman must be feminine. I hope I have shed light in many of these chapters on the falsity of such thinking. Many men of the Bible are masculine but are quite often un-masculine too, particularly when they are faced with the quintessence of masculinity that is God. Similarly, many women of the Bible can be seen as manly, Deborah and Jael in Judges 4 and 5 being only one example of this.[48] In these chapters, the women take on power, control and authority, while the men become feminized by their inadequacy to fulfil their manly roles.

Similarly, we have seen that Jesus has been both masculine and un-masculine in the Gospels. Biblical gender is not as fixed as one might assume and neither should our thinking about contemporary gender be. In Jesus, we see that God can be the embodiment of subversiveness. God becomes inferior. God becomes abused. God becomes oppressed. God becomes crucified. God becomes un-masculine. God becomes everything that we would not expect to see, particularly after reading about the hypermasculine God in the Hebrew Bible.

In the New Testament though, if God is both feminine and masculine (much like the imagery of the Hebrew Bible), authoritative and vulnerable, perhaps even crucifier and crucified – where does that leave us? I believe it leads us to be exactly who we are meant to be. If, in the moment of crucifixion, God occupies both the top of the gender hierarchy and the very bottom, if we are to understand it in spectral terms, then we need not worry about our gender norms or stereotypes. If God is both man and 'unman', then we have no standard to aspire to. God is already occupying all the gendered positions.[49]

We are called to be who God made us to be – whatever that looks like and however that might be enacted. That means that gender should not matter to us, because the way we act out our performative gender does not matter to God. We can be as masculine as we like or as feminine, but God just does not care. To some, this might seem like a strong statement and a wild conclusion from the act of crucifixion. But if we look at this pinnacle moment of the Gospels with a gender-critical eye and an understanding of the ancient world, it seems to me that God does not want us to be a part of the human hierarchy of gender relations. God removes it for us in the act of the crucifixion. Power is broken and oppression is no more. The restoration of the resurrection shows us that glory comes after this, where a kingdom of equality reigns.

That does not mean we have to live our lives without being a man or a woman. It does not mean we cannot be masculine or feminine. What it does mean is that we need to be wary of the way we associate power with masculinity and vulnerability and victimhood with femininity, as if it were the norm. In this way, we need to make sure our understandings of manhood and womanhood, or indeed personhood in its entirety, do not lead to unhealthy relationships of power, and even abuse, between one another. Our gender identity should not affect how we treat ourselves and each other.

What we learn about masculinity from the life of Jesus is that status (which is intrinsically linked to gender in our fallen world today, as well as in the ancient world) does not matter; Jesus transcends the binaries and boundaries imposed upon him. The colourful and multidimensional Gospels shows us all the gendered ways in which Jesus can be understood, whether servant, Lord, or King. There is no limit to Christ. We might also find God in the kings and queens of this world, but we can find the core of God's essence much more visibly in the poor, the vulnerable, the criminals and the sexually abused. The crucifixion shows us that Jesus surrendered upon the cross in the most emasculating and vulnerable position. And yet he is still Lord. He is still Redeemer and Saviour of the world. The gender-bent and broken Jesus is still God.

Notes

1 Richard A. Burridge, 2013, *Four Gospels, One Jesus?: A symbolic reading*, 2nd edition, London: SPCK.

2 Susanna Asikainen, 2018, *Jesus and Other Men: Ideal Masculinities in the Synoptic Gospels*, Boston, MA: Brill; and Colleen M. Conway, 2008, *Behold the Man: Jesus and Greco-Roman Masculinity*, Oxford: Oxford University Press.

3 Some of these thoughts can also be found in W. Moore, 2021, 'A Godly Man and a Manly God: Resolving the Tension of Divine Masculinities in the Bible', *Journal for Interdisciplinary Biblical Studies*, 2(2), pp. 71–94.

4 Sébastien Doane, 2019, 'Masculinities of the Husbands in the Genealogy of Jesus (Matt. 1:2–16)', *Biblical Interpretation*, 27(1), pp. 91–106.

5 Jonathan Walters, 1991, '"No More Than a Boy": The shifting construction of masculinity from Ancient Greece to the Middle Ages',

Gender & History, 5(1), pp. 20–33; and Jonathan Walters, 1997, 'Invading the Roman Body: Manliness and Impenetrability in Roman Thought', in Judith P. Hallett and Marilyn B. Skinner (eds), *Roman Sexualities*, Princeton, NJ: Princeton University Press, pp. 29–43, cited in Stephen D. Moore, 2001, *God's Beauty Parlor and other queer spaces in and around the Bible*, Stanford, CA: Stanford University Press, p. 136.

6 Halvor Moxnes, 2004, 'Jesus in Gender Trouble', *CrossCurrents*, 54(3), pp. 31–46.

7 Chris Mowat, 2021, 'Don't be a drag, just be a priest: The clothing and identity of the galli of Cybele in the Roman Republic and Empire', *Gender & History*, 33(2), forthcoming.

8 Melissa M. Wilcox, 2018, *Queer Nuns: Religion, activism, and serious parody*, New York: New York University Press.

9 Terry Goldie, 2002, 'Dragging Out the Queen: Male Femaling and Male Feminism', in Nancy Tuana, William Cowling, Maurice Hamington, Greg Johnson and Terrance MacMullan (eds), *Revealing Male Bodies*, Bloomington, IN: Indiana University Press, pp. 125–45 (p. 130).

10 Steven P. Schacht, 2002, 'Turnabout: Gay Drag Queens and the Masculine Embodiment of the Feminine', in Nancy Tuana et al. (eds), *Revealing Male Bodies*, pp. 155–70 (p. 163).

11 Marcella Althaus-Reid, 2000, *Indecent Theology: Theological Perversions in Sex, Gender and Politics*, Abingdon: Routledge, p. 95.

12 Robert F. Goss, 2002, *Queering Christ: Beyond Jesus Acted Up*, Eugene, ON: Wipf and Stock Publishers, pp. 170–82.

13 Chris Greenough and Nina Kane, 2020, '"Blessed Is the Fruit": Drag Performance, Birthing and Religious Identity', in Mark Edward and Stephen Farrier (eds), *Contemporary Drag Practices and Performers: Drag in a Changing Scene Volume 1*, London: Bloomsbury Methuen Drama, p. 192.

14 Gerard Loughlin, 1998, 'Refiguring Masculinity in Christ', in Michael A. Hayes, Wendy Porter and David Tombs (eds), *Religion and Sexuality*, Sheffield: Sheffield Academic Press, p. 411.

15 Althaus-Reid, *Indecent Theology*.

16 James H. Cone, 2011, *The Cross and the Lynching Tree*, New York: Orbis Books.

17 Nicola Slee, 2021, 'The Crucified Christa: A Re-evaluation', in Jayme R. Reaves, David Tombs and Rocío Figueroa (eds), *When Did We See You Naked? Jesus as a Victim of Sexual Abuse*, London: SCM Press, pp. 210–29.

18 Charlotte Trombin, 2022, 'The Lamb on Your Plate: Finding the Crucified God in the Violence of the Slaughterhouse', in Michael

Spalione and Helen Paynter (eds), *In the Cross-Hairs: Bible and Violence in Focus*, Sheffield: Sheffield Phoenix Press, forthcoming.

19 Stephen D. Moore, 1996, *God's Gym: Divine Male Bodies of the Bible*, New York: Routledge, pp. 109–17.

20 S. D. Moore, *God's Gym*, pp. 102–3.

21 See Will Moore, 2022a, 'Gorifying the Gospels: the treatment of crucifixion violence in film', in Spalione and Paynter (eds), *In the Cross-Hairs*.

22 W. Moore, 'Gorifying the Gospels'.

23 To read more about the physical and social impact of crucifixion, see Martin Hengel, 1977, *Crucifixion: In the ancient world and the folly of the message of the cross*, Philadelphia, PA: Fortress Press.

24 David Tombs, 2021, 'Crucifixion and Sexual Abuse', in Reaves, Tombs and Figueroa (eds), *When Did We See You Naked?*, pp. 15–27 (pp. 16–17).

25 David Tombs, 1999, 'Crucifixion, State Terror and Sexual Abuse', *Union Seminary Quarterly Review*, 53(1–2), pp. 89–109.

26 For a wider diversity of scholarship on this emerging topic, see Reaves, Tombs and Figueroa (eds), *When Did We See You Naked?*

27 See a variety of views in 'Was Jesus Sexually Abused?', 1 April 2021, *The Church Times*, www.churchtimes.co.uk/articles/2021/1-april/features/features/was-jesus-sexually-abused (accessed 16.6.2021) and a survey taken with male survivors of sexual abuse by Rocío Figueroa and David Tombs, 2020, 'Recognising Jesus as a Victim of Sexual Abuse', *Religion and Gender*, 10(1), pp. 57–75.

28 Graham Ward, 2009, 'Bodies: The Displaced Body of Jesus Christ', in Björn Kronendorfer (ed.), *Men and Masculinities in Christianity and Judaism: A Critical Reader*, London: SCM Press, pp. 96–112 (pp. 103–4).

29 Chris Greenough, 2021, *The Bible and Sexual Violence Against Men*, Abingdon: Routledge, pp. 62–3.

30 Stephen Prince, 2006, 'Beholding Blood Sacrifice in The Passion of the Christ: How Real Is Movie Violence?', *Film Quarterly*, 59(4), pp. 11–22 (p. 16).

31 Michael Trainor, 2014, *The Body of Jesus and Sexual Abuse: How the Gospel Passion Narratives inform a Pastoral Response*, Australia: Morning Star Publishing, p. 255.

32 Greenough, *The Bible and Sexual Violence*, p. 76.

33 Tombs, 'Crucifixion and Sexual Abuse', p. 18.

34 Jayme R. Reaves and David Tombs, 2020, '#MeToo Jesus: Naming Jesus as a Victim of Sexual Abuse', in Helen Paynter and Michael Spalione (eds), *The Bible on Violence: A Thick Description*, Sheffield: Sheffield Phoenix Press, pp. 282–308 (p. 292).

35 W. Moore, 'A Godly Man', p. 84.

36 Although penetration is not a necessary component for an act to be considered sexually violent. Rather, sexual violence can be defined as any sexual act, comment or advance that is unwanted or forced.

37 Gerald O. West, 2021, 'Jesus, Joseph and Tamar Stripped: Trans-textual and Intertextual Resources for Engaging Sexual Violence Against Men', in Reaves, Tombs and Figueroa (eds), *When Did We See You Naked?*, pp. 110–28 (p. 122).

38 For more on #MeToo and the Bible's participation in the perpetuation and resilience of rape cultures today, see Johanna Stiebert, 2020, *Rape Myths, the Bible and #MeToo*, Abingdon: Routledge.

39 Greenough, *The Bible and Sexual Violence*.

40 One of the most prominent examples being Jürgen Moltmann, 2001, *The Crucified God*, 2nd edition, London: SCM Press.

41 Luke Turner, 2019, *Out of the Woods*, London: Weidenfeld & Nicholson, p.162.

42 Kent L. Brintnall, 2011, *Ecce Homo: The Male-Body-in-Pain as Redemptive Figure*, London: University of Chicago Press, p. 170.

43 Beth R. Crisp, 2021, 'Jesus: A Critical Companion in the Journey to Moving on from Sexual Abuse', in Reaves, Tombs and Figueroa (eds), *When Did We See You Naked?*, pp. 249–59 (p. 256).

44 Trainor, *The Body of Jesus*, p. 285.

45 Helen Paynter, 2020b, *The Bible Doesn't Tell Me So: Why you don't have to submit to domestic abuse and coercive control*, Abingdon: BRF, p. 119.

46 Thanks to Jayme Reaves for our conversation on this.

47 W. Moore, 'A Godly Man'.

48 For more on a gender analysis of these chapters, see W. Moore, 2020, 'Militance, Motherhood, and Masculinisation: how is gender constructed in Judges 4 and 5?', in Paynter and Spalione (eds), *The Bible on Violence*, pp. 90–105.

49 W. Moore, 'A Godly Man', pp. 87–8.

8

Men Don't Doubt: The Disciples

How to be a disciple of Jesus

In our world, where social media seems to be taken for granted and you can find out almost anything about anyone by looking online, the word 'following' has taken on quite a different meaning. Rather than following someone being an active and intentional act, it has become a nonchalant tap of a screen or click of a button. Do we transplant similar ideas to our following of Jesus? During seasons in the Christian calendar like Lent, we are reminded that discipleship involves deliberate and purposeful sacrifices in our lives, which should result in meaningful spiritual gains. As a previous chaplain of mine regularly preached, both the words disciple and discipline share their etymologies. Being a disciple is an ongoing journey but it is also always a *discipline* that we continue to learn too. It was this purposeful and even sacrificial discipleship that the first believers of Jesus took on in first-century Palestine.

In the last chapter, we briefly saw how in some of the Gospels Jesus taught his disciples to welcome, or perhaps even to be, gender-confusing eunuchs and to come to him like unmanly children. But the Gospels tell us that Jesus also appointed a particular and exclusively male group to be his first twelve disciples, at least the first who were named. Of course there were many disciples of Jesus, in the broader sense of the numbered twelve, who were women. As Weidemann uncovers, though teachings like the Sermon on the Mount seem to address particularly masculine issues of conduct and behaviour in the ancient world, which were inevitably gendered, this is not to say that the identity of discipleship, and the commission to teach and baptize all nations, was specifically and exclusively intended for men.[1] Jesus expected his disciples to permeate all spheres of the ancient world, including feminine ones.

Though there may have been twelve specific men picked as missionaries of Jesus' message, we are *all* disciples of Christ; there have been generations of us, of all genders, stretching back centuries. We can learn from the first-hand experiences of those original apostles about the trip-ups and tribulations of following in the Messiah's footsteps. To do this, we must particularly interrogate what it meant for the disciples to be men in the Greco-Roman world and what happened to their masculinity when they followed Jesus. In turn, we must ask what this might mean for us as Christians today. This short chapter will start to explore these ideas, as well as taking a closer look at two particular disciples: Simon Peter and Thomas. However, this only begins to scratch the surface of the many male disciples of Jesus. If we begin to unpick the regularly emerging themes of masculinity in being Jesus' disciple, whether 2,000 years ago or today, then a similar gender-critical lens can easily be applied to other New Testament characters.

Jesus' expectations of his followers did not follow the norms of ancient society. He wanted the world turned upside down, with power quelled and humility revered. These teachings run throughout the Gospels in various images and stories.

So the last will be first, and the first will be last. (Matt. 20.16)

'Which of the two did the will of his father?' They said, 'The first.' Jesus said to them, 'Truly I tell you, the tax-collectors and the prostitutes are going into the kingdom of God ahead of you.' (Matt. 21.31)

The Spirit of the Lord is upon me,
because he has anointed me
to bring good news to the poor.
He has sent me to proclaim release to the captives

and recovery of sight to the blind,
to let the oppressed go free (Luke 4.18)

In practical terms, we tend to take this as bringing about the
kingdom by looking out for those who are on the margins
of society. Even to the shock of his disciples (for example,
John 4.27), Jesus spent time with those society did not value,
whether that was different ethnicities, women, slaves, sinners,
sex-workers, tax collectors, the ill and diseased and so on. As
Christians we are rightly inclined to read these verses with
a renewed and impassioned desire to help the homeless, the
hungry, and those who find themselves furthest from the
reaches of support and community. But what does this kind of
thinking mean in terms of gender studies?

As we have seen, the Greco-Roman world worked in terms
of men and 'unmen',[2] whereby masculinity was part of a social
system that pervaded the everyday lives of its citizens. Those
who embodied the manliness of the time were at the top, while
others (including the likes of women and slaves) sank to the
bottom. These understandings of gender, intrinsically linked to
status and power, caused a stratification system not dissimilar
to the way our society stratifies by class, race, gender, sexuality, ability and so on. Humanity has always tended to judge one
another, whether because of appearance, social performance
or other factors. In the worst-case scenarios, these judgements
made by society as a whole have become stereotypes and the
resulting prejudices enable some types of people to succeed in
life while others' prospects are limited. Jesus' teachings offer
the opposite of this thinking. Those who are unnoticed or
unwanted in society are the ones who are treasured in the eyes
of God.

As we have outlined, it was the unmanly of the Greco-Roman
world that were at the bottom of the societal ladder, so were
Jesus' teachings for the last to be first an affirmation of those
who were unmanly? Further, in the light of our brief outlining
in Chapter 7 of Jesus' encouragement of eunuchs to be his followers and to come to him like children, was Jesus offering an

invitation and even recommendation for people to be unmanly if they were to become one of his followers? I think this is certainly worth consideration.

A familiar reading used in reference to our own Christian discipleship uses the image of carrying the cross.

> Then [Jesus] said to them all, 'If any want to become my followers, let them deny themselves and take up their cross daily and follow me.' (Luke 9.23)

What does it mean to take up one's cross? We have seen in the previous chapter that the cross was a sign of torture in the ancient world, acting as a deterrent for criminals and a reassertion of power for the Roman empire. The victims who carried their own instrument of torture as they approached their death were carrying something that itself conveyed incredible social shame. To carry a cross was not just to hold up the burden of its weight, nor to endure the eventual gruesome physical pain when crucified against it, but also to withstand the emasculation and dishonour that it also induced.

Considering everything we have learnt in the previous chapter about crucifixion in the ancient world, particularly in terms of masculinity, we could suggest that to take up one's cross and follow Jesus is to take up the burden of unmanliness and its associated disrepute. As Karen O'Donnell identifies, the first disciples would certainly have inherited the cultural and religious trauma witnessed and experienced in Jesus' torture, abuse and death, and so the shame and distress found at the crucifixion would undoubtedly have been carried into the early Church.[3] Taking up our crosses and following Jesus today means walking with him to the place where he surrendered any remaining masculine status he had as he died. Perhaps discipleship is intrinsically partnered with defying the gender norms of the world around us. The cross is the location where God's people are brought together regardless of circumstance, identity, geography, time and even gender, and are united in an act of self-offering sacrificial love that gives each and every one of us life.[4]

But let us take one step back. Before taking up our crosses, we are told that we must deny ourselves. In the many debates and panels that I have taken part in as a member of both the LGBTQ+ and Christian communities, the topic of identity has frequently arisen. Many are quick to say that we should always identify ourselves *only* with the name of Jesus, a label which cannot be superseded. I, for one, can agree with such a statement in all sincerity. But what many who make this remark tend to miss is that our Christ-ness, if you will, is fundamentally intertwined with the very essence of our being. Our label of identification with Christ does not need to, and cannot, stand alone. We are a reflection of God's image and Jesus has a transformative power that infiltrates our entire selves. To identify as a follower of Christ is to recognize that Jesus is with me in my bisexuality and in my masculinity (or even lack thereof), as well as many other parts of my life. If we understand these things to be necessary to our very nature as Christian beings, fundamental to the way in which we understand the world around us and indeed to the way in which the world understands us, and integral to our existence as God's creation, then we will not fail to appreciate that Christ is interwoven into that identity.

There are, of course, elements of our humanity and sinfulness that are *not* necessary to our Christian personhood and that attempt to tug us away from a holy and good life – it is for us to discern which is which. With God, we are continually transformed. However this transformation through the Living Christ should not separate us from who we once were, but '[lead] us into our authentic selves'.[5] As Stephen Cottrell says, self-denial will lead to a world freed of the shackles of hedonism and individualism, replaced by love and mutual giving, adding that 'God does want to change me, but not into someone else … God wants to change me into something of more lasting beauty: the person I am meant to be'.[6] Jarel Robinson-Brown also articulates this well, saying

God cannot redeem that which is *not* you because that person does not exist, and if individuals are being encouraged to be transformed to the point that they are no longer themselves, then grace becomes unworkable because God cannot bless who we pretend to be.[7]

If we focus on the instructional chronology of Luke 9.23, we ought to notice that the preceding instruction is to deny ourselves. Only then are we able to take up our crosses, bear the burdens of Christ and follow him to Calvary. Faith in Christ is an unending journey and during it discipleship means learning the discipline of walking alongside Jesus. But how do we actually achieve this? To deny ourselves begs the questions of our perception of the self and each other, as well as questioning *of what* we must deny ourselves. Is it our very identity, in order to have a clear allegiance to Christ? Yes, but not those elements of us that are inherently part of our creational goodness, for those parts we know to be intrinsic to our very being, reflective of the image of God, cannot be cut off.

In that case, then, what can be denied? With our gender-critical lens, I think one of those things can be the expectations of gender stereotypes, so often associated with status and power. Lewis Howes talks about the 'masks' of modern masculinity, whereby men pretend to be something they are not to hide insecurities.[8] These include the masks of stoicism, aggression, sexual conquest, invincibility, intellectual superiority and control. If we unmask our masculinity, we are free to be ourselves. This is part of our self-denial – it involves casting away the parts of our selves that are not true or authentic to God's design for us.

To deny ourselves is to rid ourselves of our egoistic and self-obsessed nature, and to take up our cross is to adopt the outlook of the socially denigrated crucifixion victim. It is to let go of the power and privilege that is not ours to keep, and bear the weight of the suffering cross alongside others who suffer much worse, for 'it will not do for some to carry crosses while others carry feathers'.[9] It is to put first the love, mutual giving and servanthood exhibited by Jesus. As suggested in the chorus of the popular hymn 'The Old Rugged Cross', we must give up the pride and successes of our lives in order to clutch onto the cross of Jesus, in the hope that they will one day be replaced with a crown. We must lower ourselves, bowing out of the world of competitive greed and popularity and falling into the place of the lowly. Particularly as men, we must remake our masculinities in light of the life of Christ. Our discipleship must be one of humility and 'unmanliness'. Perhaps as Christ endured the burden of the emasculating and dehumanising walk with the cross upon his shoulders, we must bear the brunt of defying the (inevitably gendered) expectations of the world by living out the gospel.

In sum, to deny ourselves does not mean the denial of our God-given parts, but to deny the world's expectations placed on us. What we deem as fitting in either of those categories is where our theology differs within the Church. But if our identity is truly in Christ, then the idealization of manliness, for example, should not be a concern. These gender stereotypes are crucified alongside the cross of Christ, where Jesus takes on the social crucifixion of his own status and honour. To deny ourselves and take up our own cross is to forget what the world places on us in terms of labels and expectations, and simply follow him. In other words, being a disciple always comes first, even to the detriment of status and reputation. The cross unifies humanity; it is the place where God's creation comes together in salvation and redemption, regardless of who we are, what we have done, and where we might find ourselves. To deny ourselves and take up our cross is to stand shoulder to shoulder, in all our diversity, united by Christ and his love.

That does not necessarily mean that we cannot identify in other ways and find identity in our hobbies, our friends, our careers, our sexualities or genders. However, we must have Christ at the centre of our very being and our outlook on the world must be adopted through this Christ-centred lens. If these identifications wrench us away from Jesus, then they are not life-giving and faith-giving parts of our Christian witness.

However, if they are essential to our very sense of faith and discipleship, then surely they are God-given.

In order to take up the cross, we must be ready to embrace the burden of social shame. If believing in Jesus and seeing the world with the hopeful expectation that Christianity gives brings about mockery and shame, tempting us to surrender any of these things, then we must recognize that we walk in the footsteps of Jesus to the cross. Part of our discipleship, for men, is to relinquish our masculinity and open up our lives to the transformative power of Jesus, wherever that may lead us. As Lewis Howes says:

> Stripped of the various masks of masculinity, we're free to be who we actually are. We can love. We can find our purpose. We can connect. We can actually work harder, do more, be better, and appreciate every step of the way.[10]

In essence, being a disciple is to focus our eyes on God, regardless of our own expectations, as well as the ones that society places on us. Now let us see how this works in practice in several case studies of biblical figures who were called by Jesus to follow him as disciples.

Simon Peter

Echoed in many children's worship songs, we will be familiar with the story in any of the three Synoptic Gospels of Simon Peter (and his brother Andrew) being called as the first disciples.

> As Jesus passed along the Sea of Galilee, he saw Simon and his brother Andrew casting a net into the lake – for they were fishermen. And Jesus said to them, 'Follow me and I will make you fish for people.' And immediately they left their nets and followed him. As he went a little farther, he saw James son of Zebedee and his brother John, who were in their boat mending the nets. Immediately he called them; and

they left their father Zebedee in the boat with the hired men, and followed him. (Mark 1.16-20)

In a world where economics centred itself around the trade of goods such as grain, oil, wine and fish, Simon Peter and his brother are so convinced by Jesus' call that they do not bat an eyelid but instead leave immediately. They abandon the financial security and stability of their work, something that was a huge part of the independence that brought status in the ancient world. Moreover, they leave their father behind. It seems their fishing work was a family business, where the male relatives all went out during the day to earn their keep. Simon Peter and Andrew are committing a double blow against their masculinity here. Not only are they leaving behind the financial security that gave them the manly role of breadwinner and family protector, but they also leave their father. They create a rupture in the line of the family business, pursuing Jesus instead.

Here we see a clear example of the relinquishing by Simon Peter of all the things pertaining to being a man in the ancient world, in order to be a disciple of Jesus. And it does not end there. One of the most important things to note is that the twelve disciples were all men, we can assume mostly single and devoted solely to Jesus. In an ancient world where progeny and family lineage were so important, for these men to gather together as a collective group, rather than have families of their own with wife and children, was to renounce another part of their masculine status.

However, if we look a little more closely, we might find that something more subversive is going on. In Chapter 3, we briefly touched upon the issue of the anthropomorphism of God in the Bible and how many scholars have questioned the physicality of God in the Hebrew Bible. On the whole, we could probably suggest that God is presented as a sexless being in the Bible. But if God is the ultimately masculine being to which religious men of should aspire, then an issue occurs.

As Eilberg-Schwartz questions, 'How can men, who are expected to procreate and reproduce the lineage of their fathers, be made in the image of a sexless God?'.[11] What we can notice, however, is that both God in the Hebrew Bible and Jesus in the New Testament seem to still be reproductive, although their means of performance of this are notably subversive. Instead of reproducing in biological terms, we see God and Jesus both amassing followers and growing their 'family line' in that way, if you will.[12] By doing this, we see the ancient model of masculinity conformed to and yet flipped on its head.

Why is this relevant to our discussion? Well, in Simon Peter's calling to follow Jesus, he is to become the first disciple. Or, to use our paradigm above, Simon Peter becomes the first 'son' of the new Jesus family. As we have seen, the importance and masculine status of sons decreases for each new youngest son that is born, and so Simon Peter is in the top position of this emerging family unit, fathered by Jesus. Later on, in the book of Acts, we see him continue the family line further by leading the early Christian movement in its spreading across the region and establishing itself. The irony of all this is that reproduction is happening within the almost entirely male domain of the early Church. We might ask whether Simon Peter actually benefits from the patriarchal systems of the world in which he is situated through this reproduction, regardless of whether it is biological or not. Or, as a follower of Christ, is Simon Peter living out a subversive masculinity by turning the expectations of reproduction on their head? This might lead us to suggest that Simon Peter enacts a type of hybrid masculinity, whereby he appears to be going against the grain of the gendered world but actually profits from its structures. After all, whatever a man's view on masculinity, he always benefits from a world that is built to privilege him.[13]

Finally, in our case study of Simon Peter as part of our discussion of masculinity, we turn our attention to his denial and doubt. As Jesus invites Simon Peter to walk on water, fear starts to take hold. As he sees the wind, he begins to sink, but Jesus saves him.

Jesus immediately reached out his hand and caught him, saying to him, 'You of little faith, why did you doubt?' (Matt. 14.31)

Simon Peter, unfortunately, does not do well in shaking off this reputation for having little faith. Simon Peter is also known as one of the disciples who fell asleep in the Garden of Gethsemane. Might his failure to stay awake in solidarity with Jesus be seen as an unmanly trait? Even more, is Simon Peter's violent outrage, which results in the cutting off of someone's ear (John 18.10), an act of embarrassment and even an attempt at compensation for his loss of masculinity? After all, Jesus always taught a way of peace. Guvna B talks about how Jesus' instruction to turn the other cheek in moments of violence (Matt. 5.39) might be considered 'mazza', or madness, that disrupts the norms of today's world.[14] It might be this subversive masculinity, countering traditionally masculine violence with peace, that we are called to as disciples.

Moreover, we are all incredibly familiar with the (in)famous denial of Simon Peter during the Passion narrative of the Gospels (Matt. 26.33–35; Mark 14.29–31; Luke 22.33–34). Three times he is asked by strangers if he knows the man who is about to be crucified, and each time Simon Peter refuses any knowledge of that man who is Jesus. Doubt and denial are recurring attributes of this disciple. We are not unfamiliar with this tumultuous road of faith ourselves – would we be inclined to reject Jesus as Lord as he was strung up on a cross like a criminal? Would we deny any association with him? We can always hope that we would not, but I think Simon Peter is much more similar to us than we would like to think.

And yet Simon Peter becomes the 'rock' or *petros* of the Church. Alongside Paul and, of course, Jesus himself, Peter is one of the founding figures of what we now know as Christianity. We might say that he is one of the most unlikely choices; the disciple who is known to doubt and hold little faith is given the responsibility of leading the Church in the years following Jesus' death, resurrection and ascension. Just like with David, the most unexpected is chosen for a mighty mission. By doing this, Jesus upholds the consistent message we have seen: that (at least, traditional) masculinity is not exalted in his kingdom. In God's new world, Simon Peter, the most unlikely of people, is made first in the lineage of the Christly line of the Church and is established as its foundation. Once again, the ideals of gender are turned right on their head in the eyes of God's topsy-turvy kingdom!

Touching Thomas

Finally, I would like to discuss briefly the figure of Thomas in relation to masculinity. He is commonly known by Christians as Doubting Thomas, due to his immediate denial of the risen Christ unless he can see proof. Famously recorded in the Gospel of John, Thomas says,

> 'Unless I see the mark of the nails in his hands, and put my finger in the mark of the nails and my hand in his side, I will not believe.' (John 20.25)

The intriguing thing about this is that, although Thomas did indeed doubt the resurrected return of Christ, he was one of the first to declare the resurrected Jesus as Lord. If anything, Thomas becomes one of the most faithful followers of Jesus by recognizing him as the risen Messiah. But, as usual, we can see something of ourselves in the disciples. Only a few decades ago, we too would surely have said 'I will not believe it until I see it', though in this technological era of screens, photoshopping and holograms, I think even we would now say 'I will not believe it until I *touch* it'. Just like Thomas, we also would surely require proof if we were told that Jesus had resurrected.

But importantly, Thomas' doubt leads him to the sensuality of touch. It is the significantly spiritual action of placing his fingers in the marks on Jesus' body left by the Roman empire that converts Thomas' doubt to verified faith. Perhaps we can call him, for our purposes, Touching Thomas. The physical and sensual experience of Jesus' wounds are integral for Thomas to believe in Christ. Many of us will resonate with this. Sometimes nothing is as spiritually nourishing as feeling the presence of the Spirit, whether that be when we are participating in the Eucharist, praying together, or singing hymns and worship songs as a congregation of worshippers. There is nothing quite like *feeling* God in our lives. But for Thomas this was on another level, being able to touch and quite literally feel the wounds of Jesus, proving that Jesus really had died and yet resurrected. Thomas' scepticism, and indeed his touch, were essential components in the revelation of Christ's glory among his disciples.

An untraditional and queerer interpretation might be beneficial here. Though the Gospel of John does not reveal whether Thomas does actually put his fingers in Jesus' wounds, I want to entertain the interpretation seen in centuries of Christian art that he did go through with it. As we have already seen, in this chapter and the previous one with regard to the crucifixion, the penetration of the body in the ancient world was damaging not only physically but also socially. This was mainly because it meant that the boundaries of the male body were violated by other men. In other words, Jesus' wounds were a mark of the attack on masculinity that he had experienced at the hands of the manly power that was the Roman empire, and yet they were a sign of survival. This resurrected body has not been healed – at least not in the traditional sense – of the trauma inflicted on the person and body of Jesus, the marks of the past still lingered. Rather, these wounds of physical and social rupture made the resurrected body *whole*.

In this way, we must reassess Jesus' invitation for Thomas to touch his wounds. We could suggest that Jesus is actually encouraging Thomas to experience the penetration that Jesus felt himself. The sense of touch is one that we use so often, reminding us of the true materiality of the world and the physicality of one another. For many of us, it is the foundation of our sense of what is true and untrue in the world. We do not really believe things until we touch or feel them in some way. And when multiple people touch the same thing, there is a shared experience with that subject. It is for this reason that I am captivated by church buildings. Unless there have been major renovations, generations of Christians have used the same altar, pews and baptismal fonts in churches. The oldest parts of the buildings, the stone walls themselves, are soaked in centuries of Christian prayer. To be physically present in churches is to share in the history of Christian experience in such buildings. In a similar way, by placing his fingers in Jesus' wounds, Touching Thomas, as we can now call him, relived the events of the crucifixion and could truly understand Jesus' social and physical penetration. He entered into the trauma that Jesus experienced and perhaps even recognizes that it must be carried into Christian discipleship.

However, there is a further point here. Jesus invites Thomas 'into' his wounds (John 20.27, NIV) or 'in his side' (John 20.27, NRSV), which leads us to assume that the gashes are still open rather than healed up in closure. The wounds are a site of damage – bringing with them a sense of gender ambiguity, and yet proudly presented by Jesus. His physical penetration, and visible loss of masculinity, are apparent for all to see. This openness of Jesus' body identifies his wounds as a queer space – it is ambiguous, exposed, indefinite and unstable. In medieval literature, this imagery was even explored with vulvic and vaginal comparisons (erotically intensified through the physical and tactile interactions with these pages, by touch and other sensory contact as part of devotional practice).[15] Yet this imagery of a queer and open wounded site is furthered when we realize that Thomas not only feels the marks of penetration inflicted on Jesus, but in placing his fingers inside these wounds Thomas is *repenetrating* Jesus. The male intimacy that occurs is another infiltration of bodily boundaries. But with consent here, masculinity is not necessarily being attacked, but instead negotiated. Jesus, and indeed Thomas, readily act in an unmanly way as they share in a spiritual moment that leads to the declaration of Jesus as Lord.

Once again, we see an example of a relinquishing and even reshaping of what it means to be a man in the close following and devotion to Jesus in the ancient world. Touching Thomas broke bodily boundaries of masculinity in order to experience Jesus in the most real corporeal sense, regardless of what the ancient world's reactions to his actions might have been.

The implications

What then did it mean to be a male disciple of Jesus in the Greco-Roman world? Through the lives of Jesus' followers, and particularly Simon Peter and Thomas, we have learnt that discipleship meant relinquishing their own masculine status and devoting the entirety of their lives, and even selves, to following Christ. It is not dissimilar to the discipleship, in the loosest sense of the word, of all those characters, found throughout the Bible, that we have assessed in this book so far. After all, discipleship is, as Dietrich Bonhoeffer famously argued, a 'costly' undertaking that involves breaking away from the 'ties of life'.[16] Each biblical man we have looked at so far, whether it be from the Hebrew Bible or the New Testament, has had to compromise, surrender or concede their masculinity in some way to God. Perhaps this is just part and parcel of following something much higher and greater than ourselves.

Although we have distinguished similarities between the masculinities of the Bible and those of modern society, we must recognize that this discipleship might look a little bit different for us in today's different context and time period. What we have learnt in this chapter does, however, still give us a message of resurrecting ourselves in Christ. If we are men obsessed with our reputation, status, money, security or stability, to the detriment of our faith in Christ, then we ought to reassess our priorities. To be a disciple in this modern age is to place Jesus at the centre of everything we do. To do so alters the way in which we navigate the world, transforming our outlook into a wholly Christian one. We must seek peace in a world of vio-

lence, creation in a world of destruction, reconciliation in a
world of conflict, justice in a world of inequality, and love in
a world of hate.

More than anything, as disciples we must keep our eyes on
the cross. It is empty, for Christ has risen, and yet it still held up
the body of our broken and abused Messiah. Perhaps it is still
marked with the nails that were driven into it, or the stains of
the spattered blood can still be seen across the beams. It is not
unlike the person of Christ himself, whose wounds were left in
his resurrected form as an indicator of where he had been and
what he had experienced. The cross is not void of its past. We
too will have our own visible signs in following Christ. Some
have given up jobs to pursue their calling, others may have
found themselves living an entirely different life to the one that
they did before recognizing Christ as Lord and Saviour. As
his disciples Jesus transforms and changes our lives, but that
does not mean that the marks of what we have relinquished
and renounced are not still visible. Just as Simon Peter left his
family and occupation and Thomas willingly repenetrated the
wounds of Jesus, we must be ready to give up things in our
life for Christ. Discipleship will have its obstacles and we must
discern what and where they are and remove them if we can.

The cross is a symbol of loss and yet gain, death and yet
life, despair and yet hope. Perhaps this could be the same for
masculinity for us as disciples. We are called to take up our
crosses. Imagine if, in our faith, we could crucify the toxic masks
and stereotypes that we impose on men on the cross. By doing
this, the symbol of the cross can become a place of renewal and
endless possibility. Our discipleship can become unrestricted,
unbounded by gender confinements of supposedly 'manly' and
'unmanly', focusing only on the gospel of Christ and how we
might live that out in our own lives. It is only through Jesus'
brokenness that he finds wholeness, and disciples are called
to walk in the same footsteps. We can 'through rupture, into
fragmentation, find ourselves – by losing ourselves – anew'.[17]

Notes

1 Hans-Ulrich Weidemann, 2017, 'Being a Male Disciple of Jesus according to Matthew's Antitheses', in Ovidiu Creangă and Peter-Ben Smit (eds), *Biblical Masculinities Foregrounded*, Sheffield: Sheffield Phoenix Press, pp. 107–55.

2 Jonathan Walters, 1991, 'No More Than a Boy' and 1997, 'Invading the Roman Body', cited in Stephen D. Moore, 2001, *God's Beauty Parlor and other queer spaces in and around the Bible*, Palo Alto, CA: Stanford University Press, p. 136.

3 Karen O'Donnell, 2021, 'Surviving Trauma at the Foot of the Cross', in Jayme R. Reaves, David Tombs and Rocío Figueroa (eds), *When Did We See You Naked? Jesus as a Victim of Sexual Abuse*, London: SCM Press, pp. 260–77 (p. 264).

4 Karen O'Donnell, 2018, *Broken Bodies: The Eucharist, Mary, and the Body in Trauma Theology*, London: SCM Press.

5 Jarel Robinson-Brown, 2021, *Black, Gay, British, Christian, Queer: The Church and the Famine of Grace*, London: SCM Press, p. 40.

6 Stephen Cottrell, 2021, *Dear England: Finding Hope, Taking Heart and Changing the World*, London: Hodder & Stoughton, p. 122.

7 Robinson-Brown, *Black, Gay, British, Christian, Queer*, p. 111.

8 Lewis Howes, 2017, *The Mask of Masculinity: How men can embrace vulnerability, create strong relationships and live their fullest lives*, London: Hay House UK Ltd, pp. 8–10.

9 Robinson-Brown, *Black, Gay, British, Christian, Queer*, p. 113.

10 Howes, *The Mask of Masculinity*, p. 12.

11 Howard Eilberg-Schwartz, 1994, *God's Phallus: and other problems for men and monotheism*, Boston, MA: Beacon Press, p. 199.

12 Will Moore, 2021, 'A Godly Man and a Manly God: Resolving the Tension of Divine Masculinities in the Bible', *Journal for Interdisciplinary Biblical Studies*, 2(2), pp. 79 and 88.

13 Thanks to Lottie Trombin for this thought.

14 Guvna B, 2021, *Unspoken: Toxic masculinity and how I faced the man within the man*, London: HarperCollins Christian Publishing, p. 174.

15 Sophie Sexon, 2021, 'Gender-Querying Christ's Wounds: A Non-Binary Interpretation of Christ's Body in Late Medieval Imagery', in Alicia Spencer-Hall and Blake Gutt (eds), *Trans and Genderqueer Subjects in Medieval Hagiography*, Amsterdam: Amsterdam University Press, pp. 133–53.

16 Dietrich Bonhoeffer, 1959, *The Cost of Discipleship*, London: SCM Press, p. 84.

17 Kent Brintnall, 2011, *Ecce Homo: The Male-Body-in-Pain as Redemptive Figure*, London: University of Chicago Press, p. 197.

9

Bottle It Up: Paul

Teachings on gender

At the beginning of this book, we used the opening chapters of Genesis as a springboard for discussion, asking preliminary questions about the definitions of gender and sex. As we established, the prevailing traditional interpretations of these creation accounts have been some of the most influential in the preservation of patriarchal, and indeed misogynistic, structures across the global, and especially Western, Church.

Second to these texts, however, has to be the epistles of St Paul. They have been incredibly divisive in their interpretations with regards to the place of women in both the Church and wider society. This has manifested itself in a fairly binary way: on one side, many consider Paul to be someone who liberally subverted gender norms of the time by elevating the rights and privileges of women; whereas there are others who see Paul as justifiably ordering society with male headship and female subordination.[1] Paul, as you can imagine, and much like all of the other characters we have assessed in this book, is substantially more complex than this – nothing, or no one, can ever be so binary.

Writing to a breadth of communities across Asia Minor and the Mediterranean, Paul addressed his letters to churches in the likes of Galatia, Corinth and Thessalonica to name a few, though some of the works attributed to him in our Bibles may actually be pseudepigraphic. These disputed texts (namely Ephesians, 1 Timothy, 2 Timothy, Titus and perhaps even Colossians and 2 Thessalonians) may have been written by followers of Paul, proposing similar ideas in honour of him and accrediting the writings to their teacher. This would have been common practice in the ancient world, though it may seem odd to us in our world of copyright! If this is the case for any of these letters, it does not mean that they become obsolete or redundant. They still offer a message that was delivered to early Christian communities and might speak to us today.

I outline this initially because one of the reflex reactions to Paul's teachings on gender is to say that Paul did not actually write some of them and so they have no lasting validity. Although this is worth consideration, it does not dismiss the text's message or meaning. As I have said, it still communicates something about the emerging early Christian movement, whether written by Paul himself or one of his later followers. It still, of course, has meaning for us as Christians today as well.

Far more importantly, however, I wish to emphasize the geographic scale and social diversity of the communities to whom Paul wrote. In each of his letters, he addresses particular situations, contexts and problems. Remember: we are only reading *his* letters, not the replies he undoubtedly received. We are eavesdropping on just one side of this ancient conversation. It would be risky for us to assume definitively anything that is going on behind the scenes solely from Paul's words. I do not intend this chapter to be an in-depth exegesis of Paul's writings, but instead to simply touch upon the main hermeneutical lenses of circumstance and situation that we must adopt when reading Pauline material.

So what are some of the basics that Paul has to tell us about gender and masculinity in his world that we can briefly explore? First of all, as we have done throughout our discussion, we must initially look at personal circumstance and the resultant biases. Here, this means looking at Paul himself. We must notice the maleness of Paul's environment, theology and sense of self as the author. Paul was considered the *paterfamilias*, or male head, of the early Christian communities. He assumed a position of father to the early followers of Christ, which obviously had masculine connotations. Yet it seems that although

Paul was powerful in his writing and perhaps in his position, his bodily presence was not overly commanding:

> For they say, 'His letters are weighty and strong, but his bodily presence is weak, and his speech contemptible.' (2 Cor. 10.10)

As we have seen, masculinity was a social enactment, but this also manifested itself in bodily performance. This usually took the form of certain behaviours or characteristics, such as a manly appearance, violent actions or sexual potency. If many noted Paul's insubstantial physicality, as we see in this passage from 2 Corinthians, then perhaps he was not considered very masculine. Maybe his formidable theological writing compensated for such inadequacy. Interestingly, it has been noted that the similarly phallocentric attitude imported into much of evangelical Christianity today has also caused many Christian men to feel that they do not, quite literally, 'measure up', which gives them a failed sense of masculinity.[2] Perhaps, like Paul, many conservative evangelical Christian subcultures live out and teach some sense of 'traditional' masculinity in compensation for their own insecurity.

Perhaps Paul performed his masculinity in other, more subversive ways. David Clines has argued that Paul fulfils masculine ideals through five means: strength, violence, powerful and persuasive speech, male bonding and being womanless.[3] Yet I find the ways in which Paul fulfils these typical criteria of ancient masculinity quite destabilising. Paul's strength is not recorded in physical or muscular terms as one might expect. For example, in Chapter 4, we saw the number of deaths David had been responsible for in militaristic wars. But for Paul, this is found in his faithful, spiritual strength established in Christ. In a similar vein, Paul's violence is not similar to David's murders, but is seen rather in the description in his letters of the militaristic imagery of the ancient world. However, he uses this metaphorically to describe adorning oneself with the armour of faith in Christ.

Although Clines sees these descriptions as an adequate preservation of Paul's masculinity in the ancient world, these creative interpretations of strength and violence seem to me to prove that Paul was using some form of gender mimicry here, seemingly conforming to the gendered masculine expectations around him while simultaneously turning them on their head. The other factors of Paul's masculinity outlined by Clines do conform to traditional expectations, however. Clines concludes that Paul's masculinity seems 'pretty normal',[4] though I do not know if this still holds after the criticisms above which suggest that Paul offers subversive masculine traits in terms of strength and violence.

Nevertheless, I would like to draw on the fourth of Clines' criteria for a manly Paul, in particular depth: male bonding. Clines draws on Paul's homosocial relationships with the likes of Barnabas, Silas and Timothy seen in the book of Acts and various Pauline letters, but I wish to take a queerer perspective. Similar to the male exclusivism seen in the book of Job in Chapter 5, Stephen Moore notes the 'male sanctum' of Pauline theology, where there are 'no females' but 'only males acting upon other males: God, Jesus, Paul'.[5] Moore goes on from this to show that the imagery of submission between each of these agents present in the phallocentric sex-gender system of the ancient world is used by Paul to model the ideal relationship between humanity and God.

However, Paul's traditional masculinity can certainly be called into question by his surprising use of maternal imagery in his writings.[6] Here are only two examples:

My little children, for whom I am again in the pain of child-birth until Christ is formed in you... (Gal. 4.19)

But we were gentle among you, like a nurse tenderly caring for her own children. (1 Thess. 2.7b)

However, even if this dampens the masculinity of Paul and shows him as fairly unconcerned about his own gender presentation, there are still obvious issues here. As Alicia Myers points out, although when presenting himself in a feminine way Paul

> relativizes his own masculinity, as well as Roman-era masculinity more generally, [he] does not do so in a way that makes room for real female bodies. Rather, it blurs female bodies and even risks hiding them behind undeniably male ones who birth and nurse in their place.[7]

Is Paul actually making manliness the centre of his thinking by attributing feminine imagery to a male body? By doing this, is he taking part in the obstruction and even censorship of women's bodies and presence?

Further, Pauline texts, both disputed and undisputed, are frequently used to justify women's oppression, particularly in the Church. Here are some examples:

> But I want you to understand that Christ is the head of every man, and the husband is the head of his wife, and God is the head of Christ. Any man who prays or prophesies with something on his head disgraces his head, but any woman who prays or prophesies with her head unveiled disgraces her head ... Indeed, man was not made from woman, but woman from man. Neither was man created for the sake of woman, but woman for the sake of man. (1 Cor. 11.3–9)

> As in all the churches of the saints, women should be silent in the churches. For they are not permitted to speak, but should be subordinate, as the law also says. If there is anything they desire to know, let them ask their husbands at home. For it is shameful for a woman to speak in church. (1 Cor. 14.33–35)

> Wives, be subject to your husbands as you are to the Lord. For the husband is the head of the wife just as Christ is the head of the church, the body of which he is the Saviour. Just as the church is subject to Christ, so also wives ought to be, in everything, to their husbands. (Eph. 5.22–24)

Wives, be subject to your husbands, as is fitting in the Lord. Husbands, love your wives and never treat them harshly. (Col. 3.18–19)

Let a woman learn in silence with full submission. I permit no woman to teach or to have authority over a man; she is to keep silent. For Adam was formed first, then Eve... (1 Tim. 2.11–13)

I think it is important that these verses are written out in full. If we are not careful, our familiarity with these passages normalizes and thus desensitizes their (ab)use for misogynistic ends. In these passages women are silenced. They are told to submit. They are told they cannot teach. They are told not to have authority. They are told that they were simply an afterthought in creation.[8] Fundamentally, women are told that they are *less*. And, sadly, we have been told that this is because Paul says so – yet does this tell us more about the centuries of mistakes made by Christians in their use of Pauline literature against women, rather than what Paul thought, and particularly what world Jesus might have envisaged as possible?[9]

Although it is thought that women were actually a large part of the ministry of the early Church, but that their leadership roles were diminished in the subsequent centuries,[10] this apparent absence and even depreciation of femininity and womanhood in its own right (without Paul appropriating such imagery) is reflected in the practical instructions of Paul's writing. Sadly, women are still told such things today by members of our churches. For example, in 2015 the consecration of the first woman bishop of the Church of England, Libby Lane, was interrupted by a protestor who rejected the Archbishop of York's invitation for affirmation, arguing that such a thing was 'not in the Bible'. Thankfully, by God's grace, things are changing. The number of women being ordained, holding incumbent's status and joining the episcopate is on the increase in the Church of England.[11] But the Pauline texts we have mentioned are among the most cited in these sorts of debates, which still continue in many churches and Christian communities.

Significantly, we must remember that these verses were speaking to particular circumstances – Paul would not be talking about these gender dynamics, nor be writing to these communities at all, unless there was a specific issue to address.[12] Once again, we cannot understand these passages fully with only one part of the correspondence in front of us. Similarly, how can we enforce these teachings as gender roles today if we only have one side of the story? If a letter of disapproval or dislike was written about us and sent to local communities far and wide, would we not wish for someone to hear our side of the story before it got passed around and treated as fact?

However, our spotlight remains on masculinity and so I want to draw our attention to the relational aspect of these passages. Many of these verses are situated within wider narratives about gendered people more generally. We return to this imagery of women and men as the other halves of each other, or even as the opposite ends of the gender spectrum, which perhaps reflects the merism seen in Genesis. Women are not just told to be submissive but to be submissive *to their husbands*. I agree with Stephen Moore here that much of this imagery and metaphor is to reflect the exemplary relationship between humanity and God – one of submission.[13] It is used as a model of humility and respect, unfortunately yet inevitably gendered by the (abusive) patriarchal setting in which Paul is communicating. In this way, gender should not be centralized as a fundamental factor in its understanding. Rather, it is the model of relationship that is important.

As Aimee Byrd points out, women are not the only ones who are taught to submit in biblical texts – it is often expected of men too, as imitators of Christ.[14] As such, we should remember that the headship of God, not man, is the most valuable message here. To portray this, Paul uses the relationship of (inescapably gendered) submission found in marriage within the ancient world. The way that we approach God has changed substantially since the time of the Bible and so has our definition and practice of marriage. By saying this, I am not necessarily talking about issues of marriages that are not between one man and one woman. Rather, I am addressing the dynamics in marital relationships, where women have much more autonomy and influence now than they would have had in the ancient world. Some might say that this shift in understanding marriage is precisely a problem in itself, but I doubt many would want to revert to the contractual agreements of marriage from the ancient world. The marriage metaphor is a contextually moving picture, as is humanity's relationship with God as it waxes and wanes in understanding, love and faithfulness. Perhaps the loving reciprocal relationships of marriage today between all sorts of people similarly reflect God and humanity's relationship. Further, Paul addresses many of his teachings not only to men, but to women, children and slaves. As Beth Alison Barr points out, when we read – for example – Colossians 3.18–19 or Ephesians 5.21–33, our focus as modern Christians is naturally drawn to wives being subjected to husbands, whereas there is a radical teaching here that men should also be loving and compassionate to their wives.[15] In Barr's words, 'Paul's purpose [was not] to emphasise male authority.'[16]

Our perceptions, and what we search for in Scripture, has substantially shifted over time. We are no longer attuned to the nature of what Paul is trying to say and the metaphors he tries to use. We owe Paul so much, and yet still have a lot that we could learn from him. His work formed the foundations of the global Church we see today. His theology is essential not only to our contemporary understanding of God and Jesus, but to the millennia of Christian thinking that have proceeded from him and preceded us. Essentially, without Paul there is no Christianity, as a religious organization at least.[17] But I do think that he might be rolling in his saintly grave to know that some are still following his writings on gender to the letter in twenty-first-century Britain. What might have been offhand comments to pacify a fractious situation in a particular church community have now become dangerously gendered issues of doctrine for many Christians.

Paul was most likely trying to construct ethical guidelines for the emerging church communities that he dealt with directly, not attempting to assemble a divinely authoritative lawbook for the rest of Christian history. He was using metaphors and imagery especially relevant only for those to whom he was writing. What is crucial here is that Paul is *always* in submission to Jesus and God throughout his life and writings. He is *not* the male headship he teaches about when in relationship with God and Jesus, because the divine always pull rank. With such rich theology about grace, faith and ethnic inclusion, I doubt that gender was a priority for Paul. It only became a concern when it threatened the harmony of some of the early Christian communities. His instructions addressing squabbles in church communities about the place of women should not be widely applied across time and cultures; we have seen the damage of such interpretations being put into action. As we have observed time and time again, context is key. If we dispose of Paul's writings in their entirety, just because of some circumstantial, even blasé and extemporaneous, comments concerning gender relations, we will lose much of Paul's beautiful insight into the revelation and nature of God. We should be incredibly wary of the trap into which we could fall that leads us to think that Paul is either liberal or conservative in terms of gender – the picture is much denser, with so many other factors at play.

Mental health

Not unlike Jeremiah, the writings of the apostle Paul tend to dwell on moments of pessimism. Though he is prone to rejoicing in God's provision and power, namely in the incarnation of Jesus, Paul's focus on eschatology, salvation and spirituality could be seen to portray him as having a dislike of the body and physicality. In other words, Paul's values lie so much with heavenly glory that it might be to the detriment of our own bodies. Whether this is true is not our focus. What I do want to concentrate on, however, are Paul's comments concerning his own emotional and mental well-being. A psychological and psychiatric approach to Paul's writings (both the disputed and undisputed epistles of Paul, because I am more interested in the general theme of mental health emerging in this Scripture than who actually wrote about it) might uncover some interesting ways to understand Paul's well-being, as well as providing a discussion about modern masculinity and how we approach mental health as men today.

Once again, we find ourselves discussing a man with an unfathomable mission ahead of him, commissioned by God. We consider Paul as one of the most important figures in the Church, spreading the Christian message in the first century much farther from where Jesus originated it. This will have undoubtedly had an impact on his well-being – it was not an easy job! We only need a glimpse of some passages that point towards this:

> Wretched man that I am! Who will rescue me from this body of death? (Rom. 7.24)

> While he was making this defence, Festus exclaimed, 'You are out of your mind, Paul! Too much learning is driving you insane!' (Acts 26.24)

> We do not want you to be unaware, brothers and sisters, of the affliction we experienced in Asia; for we were so utterly, unbearably crushed that we despaired of life itself. Indeed, we felt that we had received the sentence of death so that we would rely not on ourselves but on God who raises the dead. (2 Cor. 1.8–9)

At times, Paul's task leads him to unbearable depression, and even insanity. If one of our friends, relatives, congregation members, or even our ministers and clergy felt like this, saying they felt so 'crushed that [they] despaired of life itself', we would be extremely concerned. If our first response might be to suggest seeing a therapist, counsellor or doctor, then we ought also to be at least attentive to the distress of Paul. He commits his whole life to God, just like Jeremiah, regardless of the toll that it will have on him. Travelling from community to community, town to town, Paul must have been worn out – physically, emotionally, spiritually and indeed mentally. Not only that, but he also certainly showed anguish when he found followers of this very early form of Christianity not following his teachings.

Importantly, though, we do get to read about his troubles. Paul freely communicated in his letters the emotions he felt and the situations that distressed him. He was honest with his recipients about his own shortcomings and theirs. Imagine if Christian ministers told their congregations today how they felt about their work and ministry. There would probably be a lot of groaning, moaning, blaming and exhaustion... I doubt it would go down well with their congregants and parishioners! It is commendable then that Paul is willing to share his own journey of faith and emotions with his fellow early Christians. As Paula Gooder underlines, Paul's frailties were not 'a source of shame but ... the means by which people could encounter, more fully, the glory of Christ'.[18]

Mental health, in one sense, is not a new phenomenon; it is only the active care and nursing of mental well-being, and the terminological diagnoses to assist with this, that have recently emerged as a matter of importance. Whether we have labelled it or not, people have always struggled with depression, anxiety and so on. As such, it is not necessarily anachronistic to apply such thinking to ancient texts if these mental diagnoses did indeed exist, but without their modern categorization. That said, it seems likely that the stress of today's rapidly advancing, technological, consumerist, hedonistic, capitalist Western world may be giving significant rise to the diagnosis of mental health conditions, particularly on the younger generations entering this exhausting world.

The various lockdowns and tiering systems in the UK prompted by the spread of Covid-19 granted not only the time to write much of the material of this book, but also the opportunity for more time involving self-care. One of the primary aspects of this was exercising more. I have always had a tumultuous relationship with fitness, just as I have with my own mental health – the two have become rather intertwined. At school I dreaded every time a PE lesson popped up on my timetable, with boys radiating ideal masculinity as they kicked around footballs and lifted weights. I, for one, was much better suited to my hands tinkling on a piano, or my head stuck in a book. In recent years, however, running has become a spiritual sanctuary for me. It has become a space in which I often pray, taking in the world around me and thanking God for it. Even more, it has often helped me process the events of the past day or week, allowing space and quietness to think things through.

For years I have struggled a lot with my own journey of mental health. Whether this was because of the particular people I had surrounded myself with at times when it had been worse, or the absence of emotional men in my childhood upbringing, or a history of mental health difficulties in my family, I cannot be sure.

I have always had depressive cycles in my life; there have been some weeks on end where I would walk through the bedroom door and fall on my knees crying daily, and others where I have felt so deprived of energy, motivation and happiness that I have struggled to even get out of bed. Situations have been crippled by anxiety, where I have felt sick to my stomach to do the smallest of tasks such as picking up the phone, answering the door or seeing a friend. Days taken off work as holiday resulted in dreadful anxiety, fearful that I would have forgotten how to do my job by the time I returned. And yet, throughout all of this, there would be times when my mental health appeared to have no issues to raise.

This rollercoaster of mental well-being was exhausting, but it has also always been the crux of my problems: those times when I have felt mentally well have acted as a self-justification not to directly tackle my mental health difficulties. Phrases like 'I'm not *that* bad' and 'There will be people who have it worse than me' would fill my head. Of course, all I was doing was perpetuating a vicious cycle of emotional highs and lows. It was endless, until I found places and people who lifted my mental well-being out of the gutter. Luckily, running then became a space for me to continue to process my emotions and improve my enduring relationship with mental health for the better.

Although this is positive, I know I am still part of the very problem linking mental health suppression with masculinity. The damning statistics of men's suicide rates that we have reiterated again and again point to something deeper going on – men are afraid to speak out about their deeper issues, whether these are mental or emotional. The most significant issue is that many men believe that revealing their mental health difficulties equates to opening themselves up to a fragility of manhood. Figures like Piers Morgan, who left *Good Morning Britain* after invalidating outright the suicidal thoughts that Meghan Markle revealed she had experienced while being a senior member of the British Royal Family, perpetuate an idea that mental and emotional openness is a damaging prospect for anyone. I never had the confidence to go to a doctor to speak about my depression and anxiety. I have still never sought professional help, although I know I have grappled with my mental health enough now for it not to be a debilitating issue. Perhaps, however, if we had more people at school specifically encouraging boys to speak out about their mental health, or figures in the media telling inspiring stories of their mental health journeys rather than repudiating those of others, many boys and men, just like me, might be more proactive and honest about their well-being.

It is not as if these conversations are not needed. Having spent a couple of years working as a bartender following my period of academic study and prior to beginning ordination training, I realized how much pubs and churches have in common. They perform the same fundamental ministry of pastoral care, confession and healing. Just as many would go to a priest to talk about their problems, even more now find themselves sitting at a bar with a pint of beer in their hands. As a bartender, you tend not to pry for conversation – it just happens.

Many men, and it usually was men, would need little invitation to ramble on about their life stories, their families, their problems and their emotions. It was once a dog collar that created the sense of security for an open conversation to happen; now it merely takes a pastorally minded person behind a bar and an alcoholic beverage. It's an interesting thought that I carry with me often, as someone who has been the inviting bartender but is now journeying towards wearing that unfamiliar dog collar!

Yet it should not take alcohol for men to feel free enough to speak. All it took Paul was his faith. But importantly, the pub is considered by many to be a comfortable place to have such conversations today. It has become a haven for many men, an escape from their troubled lives. Paul similarly tried to cultivate an environment in which weaknesses were seen as an authentic and permitted part of Christian identity in the early Church communities. Perhaps, in our mission and ministry, we might want to take notes from both Paul and our pubs.

If we create more safe spaces where conversations about mental well-being between boys and men can take place, without shame or stigma, then we might start to tackle the issue head-on. I hope that one of these environments could be churches, as well as pubs. With clergy and lay people pastorally trained and waiting to listen to the problems of men, it ought to be encouraged more widely. Once men open up more freely, they will realize that mental and emotional well-being is just as important to take care of as the physical fitness they are taught to obsess over.

The implications

It is interesting to see that arguments about gender roles were a concern around 2,000 years ago on the other side of the globe, and yet are still persisting today. Just as many members of the early Church would have protested about the place of women in ministry, so many still do today. Much of the Church in the majority world or global south, for example, still do not ordain women. It is still a rather privileged Western view to think liberty for women has been wholly attained.

It breaks the hearts of many, including myself, to see the lives of so many women restricted and constrained. It shows that questions of gender are not easily solved; Paul obviously did not provide the answers, because we can see how such 'traditional' gender stereotypes have caused more harm than good. Because women were silenced regardless, their suffering was inaudible. Until relatively recent decades, it has remained so. Such instructions have always worked in the favour of men, and so it has only been criticized by the boldness of women in the last century who have grown tired of the status quo.

In some ways, the androcentric teachings of Paul and many other parts of the Bible reflected the culture surrounding them. In other ways, the New Testament was completely radical. Jesus gave a place to women that they had rarely been afforded (e.g. Luke 10.38–42), and it is thought that the early Church contained many women in leadership despite what is inferred in the Pauline texts, although this slowly declined over the subsequent centuries. But, once again, we must be cautious of simplifying Paul into a binary answer of radicalism or conservatism for the time.

Nevertheless, one of the most important questions is whether the specifically gendered teachings of these early Christian writings were meant to influence society thousands of years later. Were – and are – they issues of salvific importance? Are they fundamental questions concerning our Christian identity that we must interrogate in the texts? I am apprehensive to say yes to these questions, because I think there are much more vital aspects to living out our Christian faith: helping the poor and the outcasts, calling home those discarded by the Church and wider society, sharing unequivocal love and truly living out the gospel of Jesus. These are the things central to our faith, unbound by cultural context and unchanging throughout human history, unlike matters of gender. Yet I am thankful that those women who do feel God's calling upon their life today are able to act upon it in many countries and denominations, flourishing in their God-given ministry to this world and to the Church.

This was only one of the many challenges Paul faced in his ministry of establishing Christian communities. Yet he was honest with himself about the distress that this calling would bring on him: the weight of such a mission and, still, the joy of Christ he could share with so many. He communicated these emotions in his letters. Some may argue he is self-deprecating; others may find his open words freeing:

> Therefore, to keep me from being too elated, a thorn was given to me in the flesh, a messenger of Satan to torment me, to keep me from being too elated. Three times I appealed to the Lord about this, that it would leave me, but he said to me, 'My grace is sufficient for you, for power is made perfect in weakness.' So, I will boast all the more gladly of my weaknesses, so that the power of Christ may dwell in me. Therefore I am content with weaknesses, insults, hardships, persecutions, and calamities for the sake of Christ; for whenever I am weak, then I am strong. (2 Cor. 12.7b–10)

Perhaps Paul's notorious 'thorn in the flesh' actually refers to his ongoing unstable mental health, as he persevered in his difficult ministry. It could indeed be something different, and other answers are always welcome, but the possibility offered by this reading will be reassuring to so many Christians. Similar to the consideration of Jesus as a victim of sexual abuse as we discussed in Chapter 7, it is not insulting or sacrilegious to see our biblical heroes as struggling sufferers. Instead, it is comforting to realize that these figures also went through the troubles that many of us face today. We can resonate with their resilience.

If Paul was talking about his mental well-being, albeit in different words to those we might use, then we must learn from his candidness. Pages of his letters talk of his troubles, as he brings them all to God in hope for forgiveness, healing and revival. No wonder the sacraments of healing and confession have become so pertinent to the many denominations of the Christian faith. Perhaps we ought to recognize that confession is itself a sacrament of healing for mental well-being. Talking about the health of our heads, as well as our bodies and souls, will help us to bring ourselves even closer to the healing restoration and reconciliation of God. Though it may be difficult, we must try to encourage men to begin to communicate more freely about their emotions and mental health, whether that be in a pub, round the dinner table, or in the pew of a church. If we can, we must make men realize that a problem shared really is a problem halved. The more common men speaking out becomes, the more honest masculinity can become. If it is more honest, it has much more of a chance of being less toxic and certainly less fatal.

Notes

1 Thank you to Grace Emmett for our conversation on this.

2 See Samuel L. Perry and Andrew L. Whitehead, 2021, 'Linking Evangelical Subculture and Phallically Insecure Masculinity Using Google Searches for Male Enhancement', *Journal for the Scientific Study of Religion*, 60(2), pp. 1–12.

3 David J. A. Clines, 2003, 'Paul, the Invisible Man', in Stephen D. Moore and Janice Capel Anderson (eds), *New Testament Masculinities*, Atlanta, GA: Society of Biblical Literature, pp. 181–92.

4 Clines, 'Paul', p. 192.

5 Stephen D. Moore, 2001, *God's Beauty Parlor and other queer spaces in and around the Bible*, Palo Alto, CA: Stanford University Press, p. 170.

6 Grace Emmett, 2021, 'The Apostle Paul's Maternal Masculinity', *Journal of Early Christian History*, forthcoming.

7 Alicia D. Myers, 2017, *Blessed Among Women? Mothers and Motherhood in the New Testament*, New York: Oxford University Press, p. 100. Thanks to Grace Emmett for this citation.

8 We began to debunk this in Chapter 2, however.

9 Beth Alison Barr, 2021, *The Making of Biblical Womanhood: How the Subjugation of Women Became Gospel Truth*, Ada, MI: Brazos Press, p. 41.

10 See, for example, Joan Taylor and Helen Bond in the documentary *Jesus' Female Disciples: The New Evidence* (2018).

11 WATCH (Women and the Church), 2020, 'A Report on the Developments in Women's Ministry in 2019', https://womenand thechurch.org/resources/a-report-on-the-developments-in-womens-ministry-in-2019/ (accessed 23.10.2020).

12 There is an abundance of material concentrating on this topic. Plenty of scholarship outlines each particular circumstance specific to the city/community to which Paul is writing and what he might be addressing. For an accessible, devotional and practical resource for Christians to begin with, see Sarah Bessey, 2013, *Jesus Feminist: God's Radical Notion that Women are People Too*, London: Darton, Longman and Todd Ltd. For the specific example of the church in Corinth, see Lucy Peppiatt, 2015, *Women and Worship at Corinth: Paul's Rhetorical Arguments in 1 Corinthians*, Eugene, OR: Wipf and Stock Publishers.

13 Moore, *God's Beauty Parlor*, p. 171. Moore talks particularly here about activity and passivity in sexual relations, with one participant assuming dominance, but I think this can be broadened to the social arrangement of marriage in the ancient world too.

14 Aimee Byrd, 2020, *Recovering from Biblical Manhood and Womanhood: How the Church Needs to Rediscover Her Purpose*, Grand Rapids, MI: Zondervan, p. 230.

15 Barr, *The Making of Biblical Womanhood*, pp. 47–9.

16 Barr, *The Making of Biblical Womanhood*, p. 49.

17 Of course, in reality, there can be no Christianity without Christ. However, concerning Christianity as a social institution and organization in the form of a religion, Paul was the integral component in its formation and flourishing.

18 Paula Gooder, 2020, 'Paul, the Mind and the Mind of Christ', in Christopher C. H. Cook and Isabelle Hamley (eds), *The Bible and Mental Health: Towards a Biblical Theology of Mental Health*, London: SCM Press, pp. 74–82 (p. 80).

IO

A Manly God: Conclusion

Masculinity, God and us

Through every twist and turn of this book, we have watched the men of the Bible act in very masculine ways as well as particularly un-masculine ways. There is no easy conclusion here. There is no singular biblical masculinity for Christian men to follow, but various masculinities. We cannot use the Bible as an instruction manual on gender because there is simply too much contrast and conflict. This inconsistency, I would suggest, shows that Scripture was not designed to be authoritative on matters of gender and therefore should not be treated as such. Gender is not a matter for Christian doctrine or dogma. Despite the cultural expectations of the ancient world, the men of the Bible acted as they wanted when interacting with each other as well as with God. For some of their actions, they were blessed. Other behaviours were so toxic that they surely cannot be used as an example for us.

Though it may seem, in the words of Stephen Moore, that the 'biblical God is the supreme embodiment of hegemonic hypermasculinity, and as such the object of universal adoration',[1] the remarkable portrayals and interpretations of Jesus alone – a part of the portrayal of the Christian biblical God – appear to suggest otherwise. Milena Kirova notices the all-encompassing, and all-conflicting, hegemonic masculinities of God in the Bible.[2] She says there is no scriptural monolithic singular hegemonic masculinity of God. Further, she states that those traits of masculinity promoted as aspirations for biblical men are of too great a number to fit modern understandings and terminology of masculinity. Following on from this, I would like to assert that there cannot be any so-called 'biblical masculinity' that we should adopt as Christians. God does not embody a definitive and definably consistent masculinity, and neither do the various biblical men. Any claim to encourage 'biblical manhood' is inherently false. The Bible is too culturally complex and multifaceted in its portrayal of models of masculinity to generate some sort of gendered ideal. As such, any promotion of a Christian manhood based on the Bible is dangerous, primarily because, as we have identified, the men of the Bible are as complex as we are, often exhibiting many toxic traits just as men do today. For far too long we have replicated 'traditional' masculinity as if it were the only way for a man to be. We know that other masculinities exist, but they have simply been suppressed and I do not think God wants them to be. Just as Barr states that the notion of biblical womanhood is Christian patriarchy,[3] so is the model of biblical manhood – and both of them stifle and crush the potential we might have for human flourishing.

Masculinity studies in the wider field of theology has been growing rapidly within the last couple of decades. I hope that this book has been an accessible contribution to this field and shown its profound impact on the lives of Christians today. It is not simply conceptual or theoretical work but involves research that has a real-life impact, influencing the way in which we live on God's planet. Unfortunately, this book stands as a unique source in that it is so far the only work concerning biblical masculinity studies and their repercussions to be written for both academic *and* non-academic readers. I hope this will not be the case in years to come. Meanwhile, for those readers of a more academic mind wanting to grapple with these areas, I include suggestions for further reading in the more generic study of masculinity, as well as some with particular application in biblical studies and theology, at the end of this chapter.

We do have one rather important masculinity of the Bible

left to consider: the masculinity of God. Up to this point, I have intentionally avoided using gendered pronouns for God. If we use masculine pronouns for God, the fear is that we perpetuate the false image of God as an old man in the sky. The more we use these definite gendered pronouns, the more likely we are to identify God in that way. To be clear, God has no gender identity. Throughout both testaments of the Christian Bible, God is depicted as feminine and masculine (although only the latter has been our concern here). God has no biological form, so is not male or female either. However, for just this final chapter, I would like to use masculine pronouns for God. This is not because I believe God to be predominantly masculine or male, but because the Bible intentionally portrays him in masculine ways. In the ancient contexts in which these texts were written in, masculinity meant authority. It meant status, honour, leadership, persuasiveness, progeny and power. It meant that God was worth listening to, obeying and worshipping.

We have already learnt so much about God's divine nature through the relationship that biblical men had with him. They were always in service to God, being obedient and loyal. Those that attempted to challenge his masculine authority, such as Adam in his actions of sin, Pharaoh in his battle for control, or the Roman Empire in its violent pursuit of Jesus, always lost in the end. In the ancient world, all people would have to submit to God eventually. Why? Because he was consistently and ultimately the most masculine in such encounters.

In this way, God takes control. To ancient eyes he becomes the ultimately masculine being to which there can be no competition. That is not to say that our faith in God becomes some sort of blind following of an authoritarian leader. If that were the case, the danger could be that God enacts some sort of toxic masculinity or, at least, a few of its traits. We know through the acts and words of Jesus that we are called into a reciprocal relationship of grace and love. The idea that the God of the Hebrew Bible is one of aggression and wrath, while the God of the New Testament in Jesus is one of love, is a delusion. The God of the Hebrew Bible has many moments of mercy and compassion, while the life of Jesus in the New Testament is unimaginably entangled in violence and horror.[4] Ultimately, in an ancient world enveloped in masculinity, the way to depict a God who is in control was to make him masculine. The person of Jesus brings to our revelation another dimension of that relationship, and God is continually revealed further today through the Holy Spirit. Our relationships with our God, with faith and, indeed, with gender may have strands of likeness but are also immeasurably different. This masculine authority and control that we have seen portrayed in the biblical God tells us more about how the ancient world understood its gender politics and gendered power dynamics, and their own understanding of relating with God, than about Godself.

So if God's full authority cannot be successfully challenged in the Bible, we should not be worrying about who is more masculine or feminine and the power that it brings within our society. If gender becomes a central way in which we understand each other, we start to associate certain characteristics of power and authority with one group of society (usually men). We have seen that this leads to violence, abuse, homophobia, suppression and repression of emotions, mental health issues and even suicide and death. Surely God does not want us to be in this life of gender hierarchy? He calls us to be ourselves, as long as we are in worship of him. That is the problem that modern society faces: many do not want to submit to anything but themselves. Individualism has captivated the minds of this Western world and masculinity has become a focus of self-image and success. Most of secular society would not dare to think that there is something out there greater than humanity itself. We proclaim the gospel in a world that treats its own greed and glory as good news.

Scripture is interwoven with ancient and inevitably gendered assumptions of status, honour and authority – assumptions that are mostly irrelevant today. In the eyes of the ancient world, we have a perplexing God: one who is both hegemonically masculine throughout the Hebrew Bible and some of the New Testament too, and yet one who relinquishes all masculinity with its honour and status in Jesus who is humiliatingly crucified upon a cross. Yet let us not forget the subsequent glory that comes. Jesus rises again. With an ancient lens, perhaps his masculinity is then restored. He leaves his physical body behind and adopts a new spiritual body. As Christians we are promised the same. The way in which we act has been labelled as feminine and masculine due to our biological bodies and social behaviours. The heavenly future before us is not concerned with bodies, nor our gendered performance. Jesus leaves his behind and so will we.

Of course, our current physical bodies will largely be biologically male, female, or perhaps intersex. Our gender identities will range from transgender and non-binary to women and men. Our races will be black, Asian, white and dozens of others. Our sexualities will be bisexual, lesbian, asexual, heterosexual, homosexual and plenty more. We will be old and young, short and tall, poor and rich, able-bodied and not, and so much more. Our amalgamations of labels and self-identifications seem almost limitless. But when it comes to it, none of these bodily characteristics matter in the eyes of God. They are still an intrinsic part of our very being, characteristics that make us unique as God's creation, but they are inconsequential in terms of how much God saves and loves us.

The topsy-turvy kingdom of God that we learn about in the Bible does not really prioritize these things. God is not some casting director, looking for the right type of man, with a checklist of masculine attributes that must be achieved or performed in order to earn his love or our own salvation. Society may still give us a script of how to act as men, but God prefers a much more ad-lib method of working out his purpose in the world, taking and using us as we are, whoever and wherever that might be. There is no biblical manhood or womanhood for us to replicate. All of us, in whatever form we come, will be equal recipients of God's love and welcome, if we choose to accept it. It is in the same spirit of the song 'Born This Way' of the queer near-theologian Lady Gaga, where our part in God's beautiful creation and his love for us is not lessened or devalued by the divisions of earthly binaries and classifications.[5] We see this message epitomized in Galatians:

> As many of you as were baptized into Christ have clothed yourselves with Christ. There is no longer Jew or Greek, there is no longer slave or free, there is no longer male and female; for all of you are one in Christ Jesus. (Gal. 3.27–28)

It is important that we not only read the Bible but also engage with it properly. Academia is finding fresh and exciting insights about Scripture and the ancient world, one of them being masculinity studies. By refocusing our attention on the men of the Bible, we have discovered that there was an unspoken hierarchy of manhood in the ancient world and the remnants of it still linger in our world. Masculinity studies have unveiled even more things that the Bible has to offer us, and those lessons are much needed in today's society. But an ongoing conclusion throughout this book has been that we should not forget the context of Scripture. To do so would be insensitive to the richness that the Bible offers. The teachings of Scripture are immersed in a culture that we will never be able to claim to fully understand.

In turn, when we look at the men of the Bible, we should remember that they are not us. They share our humanity, of course, but we do not share the culture and time that they were set in. The texts that describe these men were written thousands of years before any of us modern readers walked this planet. That is not to say that these men are irrelevant, but that they are noticeably culturally situated. We too are culturally set in history, even if we are not aware of it now. Cultural understandings about gender and masculinity continually shift and are never stable. They have changed and they will continue to do so long after we are gone.

Most importantly, however, we have seen that there are some similarities between the men of the Bible and masculinity today. The issues we have discussed have been a springboard for our conversation back and forth from the modern to the ancient world. There is still a toxicity to masculinity that wants to assume power, to exclude others (particularly women), to be violent, to fear male intimacy and to suppress emotions – all of which we have also seen in biblical men. We have been foolishly taught that the men of the Bible are spotless characters that we should not hesitate to imitate, exalt and even venerate. Yet we have seen the imperfection of these men. We have seen that they are flawed just like us. If we take off the mask of grandeur that churches and centuries of theology have placed on masculinity, we realize that there are very similar men with very similar problems staring straight back at us from the pages of our Bibles, despite our differences.

One thread of hope and consistency that has followed us throughout our discussion of ancient and modern societies is that God is in control of the happenings of our lives. The ancient world may have understood this as ultimately masculine, in association with power and authority, but we do not need to. We just need to know that we are offered a relationship of love and care, regardless of our background, race, sexuality, gender, sex or any other earthly categorization, and that God is not boxed into those categories either.

God hears the cries of those men who do not want to be violent anymore, of those who cry themselves to sleep each night but are scared to be seen doing it, of those subject to homophobic abuse for just trying to be themselves, of those who are emotionally, physically and sexually abused but are too scared to speak out, of those oppressed by more powerful men who manipulate and mistreat others, and of those who just do not want to be the men that society expects them to be. God knows our every word and action, every thought in our heads, and each feeling in our hearts. He knows our very being, more than we can ever imagine, and unequivocally loves us. We should never hide ourselves from God, for we are already unhidden in his eyes.

To bring that offer of love and relationship to others, it is firstly down to us. The standards we have set for men, and the alienation that has followed from them, need to be readdressed.

We must deconstruct society's unhealthy ideals of masculinity, which means recognizing the contribution that the Bible and the Christian Church have made in constructing these worrying gendered standards. Only then will we be able to tackle the damage that toxic masculinity has done in society. Only then will we be able to offer a way of living wider and deeper than the confines of earthly constructions such as gender. We are called to live among each other as beautifully and wonderfully made humans – known and loved by God as we are, not as society wants us to be.

It means placing the responsibility in our own hands. The French literary critic and anthropologist René Girard said that 'men create their own hell and help one another descend into it'.[6] Girard is talking about violence and its nature to linger in endless perpetuation, but we can apply it to culture more broadly. If we are not careful, continuing these societal structures that indoctrinate men to be violent, emotionally suppressed, sex-ravaging humans because of their manhood can simply be seen as aiding each other into a descent of hellish and harmful gendered turmoil. In his discussion of disability theology, David McLachlan points out that the cross is a place of 'unfettered' access and inclusivity – the alienation that many disabled people feel is caused by their experiences with other people, not with Jesus.[7] In this same way, we must recognize that much of the damage caused by men and even made towards men themselves, which often acts as an obstacle to the Christian faith, is not derived from God – it is an issue of humanity and one that we must begin to rectify ourselves. Jesus teaches us to be among each other, regardless of who we are, to learn from each other and live together. Let us extend our hands out to one another, lifting each other up, and reshaping Christian men in a much healthier way within our churches and communities.

As I have outlined throughout this book, the playing out of this goal can take many forms – it is a multifaceted issue which can only begin to be resolved with equally multifaceted solutions. We will need to re-educate young boys and teenagers in their upbringing, particularly in how to deal with their own emotions, as well as how to interact healthily in future romantic and sexual relationships, physically, spiritually and emotionally. They will need to know that there are no expectations placed on them, nor on their 'manhood', for how they should be when they grow up. However, as men, they will need to treat people equally and with respect. They cannot hurt or abuse others for their own gain or satisfaction. We might want to encourage men to talk more about their mental well-being, fostering safe spaces where men feel able to discuss openly their own experiences and feelings. Many of the available helplines that are listed in the final pages of this book could help begin that process. An understanding where intimacy between men, whether platonic or romantic, could be promoted to help break down a fear of male intimacy, as well as tackling issues of homophobia. These are only some first steps.

And as Christians, the practical methods for this must impact our theologies, which includes our interactions with the Bible. I do not necessarily ask the reader to reject what they have been taught and know about the beloved biblical men that we have discussed. I do, however, suggest that these figures are questioned, critiqued and reconsidered much more often. This will not change our understanding of God, but it might alter the way in which we perceive biblical manhood. We have concluded that men in the Bible may not be so perfect, and yet God still favoured them by giving them a chance. All I ask is this: next time you read the Bible, whether by yourself, in a study or prayer group, or when preparing to preach a sermon, do not forget to draw out those passages where the man commits a wrongdoing, highlighting their capacity for change, and not forgetting to communicate the biblical lesson that men are flawed characters who are still loved, despite their frequent toxicity. This might speak to the men who are present much more profoundly than you might assume.

We have explored only a sample of examples together. Adam, the man who is privileged enough to be the First Son of God, gets arrogant in his claims to power. Are we sometimes inclined to do the same? Moses was lucky enough to be close with God but was feared by the Israelites for such masculine intimacy. Are we guilty of incriminating male intimacy today because it is not manly enough? David, the mighty king, turned out to be an unlikely choice by God, yet evolved into a murderous voyeur seeking only sexual pleasure and social status. Have we taught men to be violent and sexually consumed, without concern for others in the process? Job was stuck in a vortex of male-exclusivism, with no regard for the voice of his wife and little respect for the omnipotence and omniscience of God. Are we prone to ignore the wisdom of both women and God, to our own detriment? Jeremiah was tasked with a mission of prophetic evangelism, yet he struggled so much with the peril he faced that he wept for his people. Are we so scared to show our emotions that we do not follow the calling God has for us? The Son of God himself was not always the mighty and traditionally masculine man depicted across the centuries. Jesus' gender was bent by the Gospels and his body was broken by humanity. He was a victim of torture and even sexual abuse at the hands of the Roman Empire. Could we learn something new from the suffering man on the cross, and should we be afraid to speak out if we identify with him? Jesus was followed by twelve disciples who all had to relinquish their masculinity in order to put God first. In our lives, do we put God in the centre, or do we care more about earthly worries like reputation and pride? Paul focused so much on the ministry of spreading the gospel in communities rife with debate that his mental health declined, but he was honest enough to share these problems with his fellow early Christians. As men, should we be doing more to look after our own mental well-being, confronting the prevalent stigma and shame of doing so? And, finally, throughout all of this God remains superior. He accepts the diversity of masculinities found throughout the biblical stories and he uses them for his mission. He remains as loving and forgiving as ever, not despite the biblical men's disobedience, misconduct and transgressions, but because of them. I am sure he would want us to learn lessons from these men, from their good, their bad and all the ambiguities in-between.

So where do we begin in our journey of cultivating healthy masculinities in our churches and communities? Our first step must be to sensitively understand, genuinely appreciate and mindfully use Scripture in knowledge of its context and culture. In doing so, we will realize that the men in the Bible can speak so much more to us about our shortcomings and failures, particularly those that we have the power to change. I hope this book has helped here. Then we must give ourselves to the work of the Spirit. We must ignore the expectations that the world places on us and follow the message of Jesus. Sometimes, the toxic masculinity that has conditioned us is 'one of the biggest barriers to men accepting the gospel of Jesus Christ', because it means admitting we are weak, failed and always in need of God's transforming love.[8] It means cutting off our toxic masculinity and taking up our cross in following Jesus. But if we undertake these things and give ourselves as Christian disciples, we will see that there is no blueprint to being a man of God, only a mirror with a reflection of who we already are: the image of God. As André Louf articulates: 'God never says to us: "I love you because you are beautiful", but "I love you because you are you, however you are, and whatever your sins and wrongs".'[9]

So we must fix our eyes on what really matters, remembering that we are first and foremost the treasured flock of Christ, welcomed and embraced as we are, unfettered by the gendered expectations of this broken world. In the spirit of Psalm 139, I remind you that God searches and knows us, he is beside us when we wake and when we sleep, he formed us in our mother's womb, and we are one of his most wonderful works. In whatever way we may be wrapped up in terms of gender presentation, I encourage you to recognize that each and every one of us is a blessed gift *from* God and *of* God, for the world and for the Church, and we are continually transformed to be better servants of Christ. Once we realize this, only then can we truly live our lives by the power of God, rather than the power of men.

Notes

1 Stephen D. Moore, 1996, *God's Gym: Divine Male Bodies of the Bible*, New York: Routledge, p. 139.

2 Milena Kirova, 2020, *Performing Masculinity in the Hebrew Bible*, Sheffield: Sheffield Phoenix Press, pp. 162–3.

3 Beth Alison Barr, 2021, *The Making of Biblical Womanhood: How the Subjugation of Women Became Gospel Truth*, Ada, MI: Brazos Press, p. 216.

4 See Helen Paynter, 2019, *God of Violence Yesterday, God of Love Today? Wrestling honestly with the Old Testament*, Abingdon: BRF; and Thomas R. Yoder Neufeld, 2011, *Jesus and the Subversion of Violence: Wrestling with the New Testament evidence*, London: SPCK.

5 For more on the interface between Lady Gaga and theology, see Stephen B. Roberts, 2017, 'Beyond the Classic: Lady Gaga and Theology in the Wild Public Sphere', *International Journal of Public Theology*, 11(2), pp. 163–87.

6 René Girard, 1986, *The Scapegoat*, trans. by Yvonne Freccero, Baltimore, MD: Johns Hopkins University Press, p. 134.

7 David McLachlan, 2021, *Does This Cross Have Disabled Access? Re-thinking Theologies of Atonement and Disabilities*, Oxford: Centre for Baptist Studies, Regent's Park College, pp. 23–32.

8 Natalie Collins, 2019, *Out of Control: Couples, Conflict and the Capacity for Change*, London: SPCK, p. 246.

9 André Louf, 2002, *Grace Can Do More: Spiritual Accompaniment and Spiritual Growth*, Collegeville, MN: Cistercian Publications, p. 83.

Bibliography

Asikainen, Susanna, 2018, *Jesus and Other Men: Ideal Masculinities in the Synoptic Gospels*, Boston, MA: Brill.

Asikainen, Susanna, 2020, 'The Masculinity of Jeremiah', *Biblical Interpretation*, 28(1), pp. 34–55.

Barr, Beth Alison, 2021, *The Making of Biblical Womanhood: How the Subjugation of Women Became Gospel Truth*, Ada, MI: Brazos Press.

Bauman, Christy Angelle, 2019, *Theology of the Womb: Knowing God through the body of a woman*, Eugene, OR: Cascade Books.

Bessey, Sarah, 2013, *Jesus Feminist: God's Radical Notion that Women are People Too*, London: Darton, Longman and Todd Ltd.

Bola, JJ, 2019, *Mask Off: Masculinity Redefined*, London: Pluto Press.

Bolz-Weber, Nadia, 2019, *Shameless: A Sexual Reformation*, London: Canterbury Press.

Bonhoeffer, Dietrich, 1959, *The Cost of Discipleship*, London: SCM Press.

Brand, Russell, 2018, *Recovery: Freedom from our Addictions*, London: Bluebird.

Brenner, Athalya, 2005, *I Am... Biblical Women Tell Their Own Stories*, Minneapolis, MN: Fortress Press.

Brintnall, Kent L., 2011, *Ecce Homo: The Male-Body-in-Pain as Redemptive Figure*, London: University of Chicago Press.

Brueggemann, Walter, 2018, *The Prophetic Imagination*, 3rd edition, Minneapolis, MN: Fortress Press.

Burridge, Richard A., 2013, *Four Gospels, One Jesus? A symbolic reading*, 2nd edition, London: SPCK.

Butler, Judith, 2006, *Gender Trouble: Feminism and the Subversion of Identity*, Abingdon: Routledge.

Byrd, Aimee, 2020, *Recovering From Biblical Manhood and Womanhood: How the Church Needs to Rediscover Her Purpose*, Grand Rapids, MI: Zondervan.

Clines, David J. A., 1989, *Job 1–20*, WBC, Dallas, TX: Thomas Nelson.

Clines, David J. A., 1995, 'David the Man: The Construction of Masculinity in the Hebrew Bible', in *Interested Parties: The Ideology of Writers and Readers of the Hebrew Bible*, Sheffield: Sheffield Academic Press, pp. 212–43.

Clines, David J. A., 2003, 'Paul, the Invisible Man', in Stephen D. Moore and Janice Capel Anderson (eds), *New Testament Masculinities*, Atlanta, GA: Society of Biblical Literature, pp. 181–92.

Clines, David J. A., 2019, 'The Ubiquitous Language of Violence in the Hebrew Bible', paper presented at the Joint Meeting of Oudtestamentisch Werkgezelschap, Society for Old Testament Studies, and Old Testament Society of South Africa. Groningen, The Netherlands. Available at: www.academia.edu/37260426/The_Ubiquitous_Language_of_Violence_in_the_Hebrew_Bible.

Coleman, Peter, 2014, 'Mad With Power?', *HuffPost*, www.huffpost.com/entry/mad-with-power_b_5736728 (accessed 7.8.2020).

Collins, Natalie, 2019, *Out of Control: Couples, Conflict and the Capacity for Change*, London: SPCK.

Collins, Natalie, 2021, 'How can I teach my son to respect women?', *Woman Alive*, www.womanalive.co.uk/stories/view?articleid=3384 (accessed 6.4.2021).

Cone, James H., 2011, *The Cross and the Lynching Tree*, New York: Orbis Books.

Connell, R. W., 2005, *Masculinities*, 2nd edition, Cambridge: Polity Press.

Conway, Colleen M., 2008, *Behold the Man: Jesus and Greco-Roman Masculinity*, Oxford: Oxford University Press.

Cottrell, Stephen, 2021, *Dear England: Finding Hope, Taking Heart and Changing the World*, London: Hodder & Stoughton.

Creangă, Ovidiu, 2017, 'Introduction', in Ovidiu Creangă and Peter-Ben Smit (eds), *Biblical Masculinities Foregrounded*, Sheffield: Sheffield Phoenix Press, pp. 3–14.

Crisp, Beth R., 2021, 'Jesus: A Critical Companion in the Journey to Moving on from Sexual Abuse', in Jayme R. Reaves, David Tombs and Rocío Figueroa (eds), *When Did We See You Naked? Jesus as a Victim of Sexual Abuse*, London: SCM Press, pp. 249–59.

Crossley, James, 2018, *Cults, Martyrs and Good Samaritans: Religion in Contemporary English Political Discourse*, London: Pluto Press.

Dell, Katherine, 2017, *Job: An Introduction and Study Guide. Where Shall Wisdom Be Found?*, 2nd edition, London/New York: Bloomsbury Publishing.

Doane, Sébastien, 2019, 'Masculinities of the Husbands in the Genealogy of Jesus (Matt. 1:2–16)', *Biblical Interpretation*, 27(1), pp. 91–106.

Du Mez, Kristen Kobes, 2020, *Jesus and John Wayne: How White Evangelicals Corrupted a Faith and Fractured a Nation*, New York: Liveright Publishing Corporation.

Edwards, Katie, 2012, *Admen and Eve: The Bible in Contemporary Advertising*, Sheffield: Sheffield Phoenix Press.

Edwards, Katie (ed.), 2015, *Rethinking Biblical Literacy*, London: Bloomsbury Publishing.

Eilberg-Schwartz, Howard, 1994, *God's Phallus: and other problems for men and monotheism*, Boston, MA: Beacon Press.

Emmett, Grace, 2021, 'The Apostle Paul's Maternal Masculinity', *Journal of Early Christian History*, forthcoming.

Figueroa, Rocío and David Tombs, 2020, 'Recognising Jesus as a Victim of Sexual Abuse', *Religion and Gender*, 10(1), pp. 57–75.

Firth, Jill, 2020, 'Spirituality from the Depths: Responding to Crushing Circumstances and Psychological and Spiritual Distress in Jeremiah', in Christopher C. H. Cook and Isabelle Hamley (eds), *The Bible and Mental Health: Towards a Biblical Theology of Mental Health*, London: SCM Press, pp. 115–27.

France-Williams, A. D. A., 2020, *Ghost Ship: Institutional Racism and the Church of England*, London: SCM Press.

Gafney, Wilda C., 2008, *Daughters of Miriam: Women Prophets in Ancient Israel*, Minneapolis, MN: Fortress Press.

Gafney, Wilda C., 2017, *Womanist Midrash: A Reintroduction to the Women of the Torah and the Throne*, Louisville, KY: Westminster John Knox Press.

Gelfer, Joseph, 2011, *The Masculinity Conspiracy*, London: Createspace.

Girard, René, 1986, *The Scapegoat*, trans. by Yvonne Freccero, Baltimore, MD: Johns Hopkins University Press.

Girard, René, 2014, *The One by Whom Scandal Comes*, East Lansing, MI: Michigan State University Press.

Goldie, Terry, 2002, 'Dragging Out the Queen: Male Femaling and Male Feminism', in Nancy Tuana, William Cowling, Maurice Hamington, Greg Johnson and Terrance MacMullan (eds), *Revealing Male Bodies*, Bloomington, IN: Indiana University Press, pp. 125–45.

Gooder, Paula, 2020, 'Paul, the Mind and the Mind of Christ', in Christopher C. H. Cook and Isabelle Hamley (eds), *The Bible and Mental Health: Towards a Biblical Theology of Mental Health*, London: SCM Press, pp. 74–82.

Goss, Robert E., 2002, *Queering Christ: Beyond Jesus Acted Up*, Eugene, OR: Wipf and Stock Publishers.

Graybill, Rhiannon, 2015, 'Masculinity, Materiality, and the Body of Moses', *Biblical Interpretation* 23(4–5), pp. 518–40.

Graybill, Rhiannon, 2017, *Are We Not Men? Unstable Masculinity in the Hebrew Prophets*, New York: Oxford University Press.

Greenough, Chris, 2020, *Queer Theologies: The Basics*, Abingdon: Routledge.

Greenough, Chris, 2021, *The Bible and Sexual Violence Against Men*, Abingdon: Routledge.

Greenough, Chris, and Nina Kane, 2020, '"Blessed Is the Fruit": Drag Performance, Birthing and Religious Identity', in Mark Edward and Stephen Farrier (eds), *Contemporary Drag Practices and Performers: Drag in a Changing Scene Volume 1*, London: Bloomsbury Methuen Drama.

Guvna B, 2021, *Unspoken: Toxic masculinity and how I faced the man within the man*, London: HarperCollins Christian Publishing.

Hamley, Isabelle, 2020, 'Patient Job, Angry Job: Speaking Faith in the Midst of Trauma', in Christopher C. H. Cook and Isabelle Hamley (eds), *The Bible and Mental Health: Towards a Biblical Theology of Mental Health*, London: SCM Press, pp. 85–95.

Heacock, Anthony, 2011, *Jonathan Loved David: Manly Love in the Bible and the Hermeneutics of Sex*, Sheffield: Sheffield Phoenix Press.

Hemmings, Chris, 2017, *Be A Man: How macho culture damages us and how to escape it*, London: Biteback Publishing.

Hengel, Martin, 1977, *Crucifixion: In the Ancient World and the Folly of the Message of the Cross*, Philadelphia, PA: Fortress Press.

Hobbs, Valerie, 2021, *An Introduction to Religious Language: Exploring Theolinguistics in Contemporary Contexts*, London: Bloomsbury Publishing.

Holdsworth, John, 2010, *Lies, Sex and Politicians: Communicating the Old Testament in Contemporary Culture*, London: SCM Press.

House of Bishops, 1991, *Issues in Human Sexuality: A Statement by the House of Bishops*, London: Church House Publishing.

House of Bishops, 2019, 'Civil Partnerships – for same sex and opposite sex couples', www.churchofengland.org/sites/default/files/2020-01/Civil%20Partnerships%20-%20Pastoral%20Guidance%202019.pdf (accessed 6.5.2021).

Howes, Lewis, 2017, *The Mask of Masculinity: How men can embrace vulnerability, create strong relationships and live their fullest lives*, London: Hay House UK Ltd.

Hudson, Don Michael, 1994, 'Living in a Land of Epithets: Anonymity in Judges 19–21', *Journal for the Study of the Old Testament*, 19(62), pp. 49–66.

Hughes, Trystan Owain, 2017, *Living the Prayer: The everyday challenge of the Lord's Prayer*, Abingdon: BRF.

Julian of Norwich, 2015, *Revelations of Divine Love*, trans. by Barry Windeatt, Oxford: Oxford University Press.

Kawedo, Elvis Onyedikachi, 2021, 'Boys will not be boys: The toxic norms around masculinity we have to disband', *Indy100 Conversations*, https://conversations.indy100.com/boys-will-be-boys-toxic-masculinity (accessed 7.9.2020).

Kirova, Milena, 2020, *Performing Masculinity in the Hebrew Bible*, Sheffield: Sheffield Phoenix Press.

Koenig, Sara M., 2018, *Bathsheba Survives*, Columbia: University of South Carolina Press.

Kristof, Nicholas, 2020, 'The Children of Pornhub: Why does Canada allow this company to profit off videos of exploitation and assault?', *The New York Times*, www.nytimes.com/2020/12/04/opinion/sunday/pornhub-rape-trafficking.html (accessed 4.9.2020).

Louf, André, 2002, *Grace Can Do More: Spiritual Accompaniment and Spiritual Growth*, Collegeville, MN: Cistercian Publications.

Loughlin, Gerard, 1998, 'Refiguring Masculinity in Christ', in Michael A. Hayes, Wendy Porter and David Tombs (eds), *Religion and Sexuality*, Sheffield: Sheffield Academic Press, pp. 405–14.

McDonald, Chine, 2021, *God Is Not a White Man (And other revelations)*, London: Hodder & Stoughton.

Messerschmidt, James W., and Michael A. Messner, 2018, 'Hegemonic, Nonhegemonic, and "New" Masculinities', in James W. Messerschmidt et al. (eds), *Gender Reckonings: New Social Theory and Research*, New York: New York University Press, pp. 35–56 (pp. 48–49).

Moltmann, Jürgen, 2001, *The Crucified God*, 2nd edition, London: SCM Press.

Moore, Stephen D., 1996, *God's Gym: Divine Male Bodies of the Bible*, New York: Routledge.

Moore, Stephen D., 2001, *God's Beauty Parlor and other queer spaces in and around the Bible*, Palo Alto, CA: Stanford University Press.

Moore, Stephen D., 2003, '"O Man, Who Art Thou...?": Masculinity Studies and New Testament Studies', in Stephen D. Moore and Janice Capel Anderson (eds), *New Testament Masculinities*, Atlanta, GA: Society of Biblical Literature, 2003, pp. 1–22.

Moore, Will, 2017, 'Why the Church needs to reject the Nashville statement and embrace LGBT+ Christians', *Premier Christianity* blog, www.premierchristianity.com/home/why-the-church-needs-to-reject-the-nashville-statement-and-embrace-lgbt-christians/3794.article (accessed 2.11.2021).

Moore, Will, 2020, 'Militance, Motherhood, and Masculinisation: How is gender constructed in Judges 4 and 5?', in Helen Paynter and

Michael Spalione (eds), *The Bible on Violence: A Thick Description*, Sheffield: Sheffield Phoenix Press, pp. 90–105.

Moore, Will, 2021, 'A Godly Man and a Manly God: Resolving the Tension of Divine Masculinities in the Bible', *Journal for Interdisciplinary Biblical Studies*, 2(2), pp. 71–94.

Moore, Will, 2022a, 'Gorifying the Gospels: the treatment of crucifixion violence in film', in Michael Spalione and Helen Paynter (eds), *In the Cross-Hairs: Bible and Violence in Focus*, Sheffield: Sheffield Phoenix Press, forthcoming.

Moore, Will, 2022b, 'Being Bisexual in Church – A Balancing Act', *Via Media News*, www.viamedia.news/2022/03/01/being-bisexual-in-church-a-balancing-act/ (accessed 1.3.22).

Moskala, Jiri, 2004, 'The God of Job and Our Adversary', *Journal of the Adventist Theological Society*, 15(1), pp. 104–17 (p. 104).

Mowat, Chris, 2021, 'Don't be a drag, just be a priest: The clothing and identity of the galli of Cybele in the Roman Republic and Empire', *Gender & History*, 33(2), forthcoming.

Moxnes, Halvor, 2004, 'Jesus in Gender Trouble', *CrossCurrents*, 54(3), pp. 31–46.

Mulvey, Laura, 1975, 'Visual Pleasure and Narrative Cinema', *Screen*, 16(3), pp. 6–18.

Myers, Alicia D., 2017, *Blessed Among Women? Mothers and Motherhood in the New Testament*, New York: Oxford University Press.

Neufeld, Thomas R. Yoder, 2011, *Jesus and the Subversion of Violence: Wrestling with the New Testament evidence*, London: SPCK.

O'Donnell, Karen, 2018, *Broken Bodies: The Eucharist, Mary, and the Body in Trauma Theology*, London: SCM Press.

O'Donnell, Karen, 2021, 'Surviving Trauma at the Foot of the Cross', in Jayme R. Reaves, David Tombs and Rocío Figueroa (eds), *When Did We See You Naked? Jesus as a Victim of Sexual Abuse*, London: SCM Press

Paynter, Helen, 2019, *God of Violence Yesterday, God of Love Today? Wrestling honestly with the Old Testament*, Abingdon: BRF.

Paynter, Helen, 2020a, *Telling Terror in Judges 19: Rape and Reparation for the Levite's Wife*, Abingdon: Routledge.

Paynter, Helen, 2020b, *The Bible Doesn't Tell Me So: Why you don't have to submit to domestic abuse and coercive control*, Abingdon: BRF.

Peppiatt, Lucy, 2015, *Women and Worship at Corinth: Paul's Rhetorical Arguments in 1 Corinthians*, Eugene, OR: Wipf and Stock Publishers.

Perry, Samuel L., and Andrew L. Whitehead, 2021, 'Linking Evangelical Subculture and Phallically Insecure Masculinity Using Google

Searches for Male Enhancement', *Journal for the Scientific Study of Religion*, 0(0), pp. 1–12.

Prince, Stephen, 2006, 'Beholding Blood Sacrifice in The Passion of the Christ: How Real Is Movie Violence?', *Film Quarterly*, 59(4), pp. 11–22.

Pullman, Philip, 2017, *The Good Man Jesus and the Scoundrel Christ*, Edinburgh: Canongate Books.

Purcell, Richard, and Caralie Focht, 2019, 'Competing Masculinities: YHWH versus Pharaoh in an Integrative Ideological Reading of Exodus 1–14', in Ovidiu Creangă (ed.), *Hebrew Masculinities Anew*, Sheffield: Sheffield Phoenix Press, pp. 83–104.

Reaves, Jayme R., and David Tombs, 2020, '#MeToo Jesus: Naming Jesus as a Victim of Sexual Abuse', in Helen Paynter and Michael Spalione (eds), *The Bible on Violence: A Thick Description*, Sheffield: Sheffield Phoenix Press, pp. 282–308.

Reaves, Jayme R., David Tombs and Rocío Figueroa (eds), 2021, *When Did We See You Naked? Jesus as a Victim of Sexual Abuse*, London: SCM Press.

Roberts, Stephen B., 2017, 'Beyond the Classic: Lady Gaga and Theology in the Wild Public Sphere', *International Journal of Public Theology*, 11(2), pp. 163–87.

Robinson-Brown, Jarel, 2021, *Black, Gay, British, Christian, Queer: The Church and the Famine of Grace*, London: SCM Press.

Roose, Joshua M., 2021, *The New Demagogues: Religion, Masculinity and the Populist Epoch*, Abingdon: Routledge.

Schacht, Steven P., 2002, 'Turnabout: Gay Drag Queens and the Masculine Embodiment of the Feminine', in Nancy Tuana, William Cowling, Maurice Hamington, Greg Johnson and Terrance Mac-Mullan (eds), *Revealing Male Bodies*, Bloomington, IN: Indiana University Press, pp. 155–70.

Sexon, Sophie, 2021, 'Gender-Querying Christ's Wounds: A Non-Binary Interpretation of Christ's Body in Late Medieval Imagery', in Alicia Spencer-Hall and Blake Gutt (eds), *Trans and Genderqueer Subjects in Medieval Hagiography*, Amsterdam: Amsterdam University Press, pp. 133–53.

Slee, Nicola, 2021, 'The Crucified Christa: A Re-evaluation', in Jayme R. Reaves, David Tombs and Rocío Figueroa (eds), *When Did We See You Naked? Jesus as a Victim of Sexual Abuse*, London: SCM Press, pp. 210–29.

Smit, Peter-Ben, 2006, 'Jesus and the Ladies: Constructing and Deconstructing Johannine Macho-Christology', *The Bible and Critical Theory*, 2(3), pp. 31.1–15.

Smith, Mitzi J., 2018, *Womanist Sass and Talk Back: Social (In)Justice, Intersectionality, and Biblical Interpretation*, Eugene, OR: Wipf and Stock Publishers.

Stavrakopoulou, Francesca, 2021, *God: An Anatomy*, London: Pan Macmillan.

Stiebert, Johanna, 2020, *Rape Myths, The Bible, and #MeToo*, Abingdon: Routledge.

Tombs, David, 1999, 'Crucifixion, State Terror and Sexual Abuse', *Union Seminary Quarterly Review*, 53(1–2), pp. 89–109.

Tombs, David, 2021, 'Crucifixion and Sexual Abuse', in Jayme R. Reaves, David Tombs and Rocío Figueroa (eds), *When Did We See You Naked? Jesus as a Victim of Sexual Abuse*, London: SCM Press, pp. 15–27.

Tonstad, Linn Marie, 2018, *Queer Theology: Beyond Apologetics*, Eugene, OR: Wipf and Stock Publishers.

Trainor, Michael, 2014, *The Body of Jesus and Sexual Abuse: How the Gospel Passion Narratives inform a Pastoral Response*, Australia: Morning Star Publishing.

Trible, Phyllis, 1978, *God and the Rhetoric of Sexuality*, Philadelphia, PA: Fortress Press.

Trible, Phyllis, 1984, *Texts of Terror: Literary-feminist readings of biblical narratives*, London: SCM Press.

Trombin, Charlotte, 2021, '"Then the earth reeled and rocked; the foundations of the heavens trembled and quaked, because he was angry": Misogyny, the Bible, and Environmental Violence', paper presented at 'From the Rising to the Setting Sun: Global Perspectives on Bible and Violence' conference. Centre for the Study of Bible and Violence, Bristol. Available at: www.youtube.com/watch?v=UN-fWX2TDpE&list=PLb-pzovmK3Erf2ETe4ZvQgW6Qiyk2b8f2&index=3 (accessed 4.10.2021).

Trombin, Charlotte, 2022, 'The Lamb on Your Plate: Finding the Crucified God in the Violence of the Slaughterhouse', in Michael Spalione and Helen Paynter (eds), *In the Cross-Hairs: Bible and Violence in Focus*, Sheffield: Sheffield Phoenix Press, forthcoming.

Turner, Luke, 2019, *Out of the Woods*, London: Weidenfeld & Nicholson.

Urwin, Jack, 2016, *MAN UP: Surviving Modern Masculinity*, London: Icon Books Ltd.

Walker, Alice, 2017, *The Color Purple*, London: Weidenfeld & Nicholson.

Walters, Jonathan, 1991, '"No More Than a Boy": The shifting construction of masculinity from Ancient Greece to the Middle Ages', *Gender & History*, 5(1), pp. 20–33.

Walters, Jonathan, 1997, 'Invading the Roman Body: Manliness and Impenetrability in Roman Thought', in Judith P. Hallett and Marilyn B. Skinner (eds), *Roman Sexualities*, Princeton, NJ: Princeton University Press, pp. 29–43.

Walton, John, 2015, *The Lost World of Adam and Eve: Genesis 2–3 and the Human Origins Debate*, Westmont, IL: InterVarsity Press.

Ward, Graham, 2009, 'Bodies: The Displaced Body of Jesus Christ', in Björn Kronendorfer (ed.), *Men and Masculinities in Christianity and Judaism: A Critical Reader*, London: SCM Press, pp. 96–112.

WATCH (Women and the Church), 2020, 'A Report on the Developments in Women's Ministry in 2019', https://womenandthechurch. org/resources/a-report-on-the-developments-in-womens-ministry-in-2019/ (accessed 6.5.2021).

Weidemann, Hans-Ulrich, 2017, 'Being a Male Disciple of Jesus according to Matthew's Antitheses', in Ovidiu Creangă and Peter-Ben Smit (eds), *Biblical Masculinities Foregrounded*, Sheffield: Sheffield Phoenix Press, pp. 107–55.

Wenham, Gordon, 2015, *Rethinking Genesis 1–11*, Eugene, OR: Cascade Books.

West, Gerald O., 2021, 'Jesus, Joseph and Tamar Stripped: Transtextual and Intertextual Resources for Engaging Sexual Violence Against Men', in Jayme R. Reaves, David Tombs and Rocío Figueroa (eds), *When Did We See You Naked? Jesus as a Victim of Sexual Abuse*, London: SCM Press, pp. 110–28.

Wilcox, Melissa M., 2018, *Queer Nuns: Religion, activism, and serious parody*, New York: New York University Press.

Further Reading and Resources

Accessible further reading

JJ Bola, 2019, *Mask Off: Masculinity Redefined*, London: Pluto Press.

Tim Grayburn, 2017, *Boys Don't Cry: Why I hid my depression and why men need to talk about their mental health*, London: Hodder and Stoughton.

Guvna B, 2021, *Unspoken: Toxic masculinity and how I faced the man within the man*, London: HarperCollins Christian Publishing.

Chris Hemmings, 2017, *Be A Man: How macho culture damages us and how to escape it*, London: Biteback Publishing.

Charlie Hoare, 2020, *Man Down: A Guide for Men on Mental Health*, London: Vie Books.

bell hooks, 2004, *We Real Cool: Black Men and Masculinity*, Abingdon: Routledge.

bell hooks, 2004, *The Will to Change: Men, Masculinity, and Love*, New York: Atria Books.

Lewis Howes, 2017, *The Mask of Masculinity: How men can embrace vulnerability, create strong relationships and live their fullest lives*, London: Hay House UK Ltd.

Derek Owusu, 2020, *Safe: 20 Ways to be a Black Man in Britain Today*, London: Trapeze.

Martin Saunders, 2019, *The Man You're Made To Be*, London: SPCK.

Andrew Smiler, 2019, *Is Masculinity Toxic? A primer for the 21st century*, London: Thames & Hudson.

Luke Turner, 2019, *Out of the Woods*, London: Weidenfeld & Nicholson.

Jack Urwin, 2016, *MAN UP: Surviving Modern Masculinity*, London: Icon Books Ltd.

Academic further reading

Susanna Asikainen, 2018, *Jesus and Other Men: Ideal Masculinities in the Synoptic Gospels*, Boston, MA: Brill.

Judith Butler, 2006, *Gender Trouble: Feminism and the Subversion of Identity*, Abingdon: Routledge.

David J. A. Clines, 1995, 'David the Man: The Construction of Masculinity in the Hebrew Bible', in *Interested Parties: The Ideology of Writers and Readers of the Hebrew Bible*, Sheffield: Sheffield Academic Press, pp. 212–43.

R. W. Connell, 1987, *Gender and Power: Society, the Person and Sexual Politics*, Cambridge: Polity Press.

R. W. Connell, 2005, *Masculinities*, 2nd edition, Cambridge: Polity Press.

Colleen M. Conway, 2008, *Behold the Man: Jesus and Greco-Roman Masculinity*, Oxford: Oxford University Press.

Ovidiu Creangă (ed.), 2010, *Men and Masculinities in the Hebrew Bible and Beyond*, Sheffield: Sheffield Phoenix Press.

Ovidiu Creangă (ed.), 2019, *Hebrew Masculinities Anew*, Sheffield: Sheffield Phoenix Press

Ovidiu Creangă and Peter-Ben Smit (eds), 2017, *Biblical Masculinities Foregrounded*, Sheffield: Sheffield Phoenix Press.

Tim Edwards, 2006, *Cultures of Masculinity*, Abingdon: Routledge.

Howard Eilberg-Schwartz, 1994, *God's Phallus: and other problems for men and monotheism*, Boston, MA: Beacon Press.

Lucas Gottzén, Ulf Mellström and Tamara Shefer (eds), 2020, *Routledge International Handbook of Masculinity Studies*, Abingdon: Routledge.

Rhiannon Graybill, 2017, *Are We Not Men? Unstable Masculinity in the Hebrew Prophets*, New York: Oxford University Press.

Chris Greenough, 2021, *The Bible and Sexual Violence Against Men*, Abingdon: Routledge.

Amy Kalmanofsky, 2018, *Gender-Play in the Hebrew Bible: The ways the Bible challenges its gender norms*, Abingdon: Routledge.

Milena Kirova, 2020, *Performing Masculinity in the Hebrew Bible*, Sheffield: Sheffield Phoenix Press.

Björn Krondorfer (ed.), 2009, *Men and Masculinities in Christianity and Judaism: A Critical Reader*, London: SCM Press.

Stephen D. Moore, 1996, *God's Gym: Divine Male Bodies of the Bible*, New York: Routledge.

Stephen D. Moore, 2001, *God's Beauty Parlor and other queer spaces in and around the Bible*, Palo Alto, CA: Stanford University Press.

Stephen D. Moore and Janice Capel Anderson (eds), 2003, *New Testament Masculinities*, Atlanta, GA: Society of Biblical Literature.

Will Moore, 2021, 'A Godly Man and a Manly God: Resolving the Tension of Divine Masculinities in the Bible', *Journal for Interdisciplinary Biblical Studies*, 2(2), pp. 71–94.

Joshua M. Roose, 2021, *The New Demagogues: Religion, Masculinity and the Populist Epoch*, Abingdon: Routledge.

Francesca Stavrakopoulou, 2021, *God: An Anatomy*, London: Pan Macmillan.

Ken Stone, 1996, *Sex, Honor, and Power in the Deuteronomistic History*, Sheffield: Sheffield Academic Press.

Charities, helplines and other resources

56 Black Men, changing the stereotypes surrounding black men in the UK: www.56blackmen.com/

Barbican's 'Masculinities: Liberation through Photography' exhibition: www.barbican.org.uk/whats-on/2020/event/masculinities-liberation-through-photography

CALM (Campaign Against Living Miserably), creating awareness surrounding male suicide: www.thecalmzone.net/

Heads Up Guys, tackling men's depression: https://headsupguys.org/

MenEngage Alliance, with resources from global perspectives: http://menengage.org/

menkind podcast

Mind Out, an LGBTQ+ mental health support service: https://mindout.org.uk/resources/

Project 84, making people aware of the lives lost to male suicide: http://projecteightyfour.com/

Respect's Men's Advice Line UK, a helpline for men experiencing domestic abuse: https://mensadviceline.org.uk/

That Guy, a campaign by Scotland Police to tackle male sexual violence against women https://that-guy.co.uk/

FURTHER READING AND RESOURCES

The State of Men, *The Guardian*, a series on masculinity: www.
theguardian.com/us-news/series/the-state-of-men

Time to Change, ending mental health discrimination: www.time-to-
change.org.uk/resources

Survivors UK, offering support for male rape and sexual abuse survivors www.survivorsuk.org/about-us/

Glossary

Androcentrism The centring or prioritizing of men and their perspective. This is usually to the detriment of women.

Christology The way in which we think of, imagine or understand Christ. This usually includes the academic study of the nature and character of Christ.

Crisis tendencies A term coined by R. W. Connell: when masculinities exhibit crisis tendencies, they are shown to be always subject to change, which give a sense of danger to those who are insecure in their masculinity. These crisis tendencies give space for new or alternative ways of masculinity to emerge.

Effeminacy The presentation of a man or masculine person as womanly, feminine, effeminate or ultimately un-masculine.

Fragile masculinity A term used for those who are insecure in their manhood. As such, their masculinity is considered fragile because they dare not do anything that might threaten it, such as show emotion or be intimate with men.

Gender This is primarily a classification referring to a sociological or socially constructed label. In this way, someone usually has a gender identity (i.e. man, woman, non-binary, transgender). Someone's gender identity is commonly associated with certain roles, behaviours and appearances (such as fashion). It is in this way that someone is usually gendered as 'masculine' or 'feminine'. This is separate from one's biological sex (male/female).

Hegemonic masculinity The dominant masculinity of a culture to which men aspire. Not many men will actually embody this masculinity, but it is still the standard by which men are measured.

Hermeneutics The lenses we use and the ways in which we interpret and understand the Bible.

Heteronormativity The state in which heterosexual relationships are default and considered 'normal', thus imposing heterosexual expectations upon society. For example, our assumption of a man to be attracted to a woman, or vice versa, would be heteronormativity.

Homoeroticism The intimacy, which is usually sexual, between two people of the same sex. This is distinctly different to homosexuality which is classified as a sexual orientation. Homoeroticism, however, is a temporary description of people or an event that involves attraction between two men or two women.

Homoerotophobia The fear or abuse of those who engage in acts of male intimacy. In distinction to homophobia, this may not necessarily refer to those who identify as homosexual.

Homophobia The fear or abuse of homosexuals. This can manifest itself in many ways, such as microaggressions, assumptions and comments, as well as physical and emotional violence.

Hypermasculinity The exhibition of masculine traits to an extreme extent, usually in response to a sense of insecurity or purposelessness.

LGBTQ+ Lesbian, Gay, Bisexual, Transgender, and Queer or Questioning. The 'plus', and indeed the letter Q for queer (or those who do not conform to expectations of gender identity or sexuality), represents those people who may identify as part of this grouping or community, but who do not fit the label of these words.

Performativity This is a term coined by Judith Butler, outlining that gender is primarily enacted in actions and interactions. Through this, a sense of gender is understood after particular models of performativity are cemented. As such, there is no 'gender identity' behind a person, but gender simply lies in the way we embody ourselves.

Phallocentric The privileging and favouring of the phallus, or the male sexual organ, in societies and culture. The male body becomes superior. The term phallus can also be understood more symbolically, in which case the definition will be much like androcentrism (above).

Sex This term is used to refer to the biological identification of a person and is distinctively different from socialized gender. Sex is primarily identified by a person's genitalia and genetic makeup. Usually understood as a binary (male/female) classification, this has been disputed with work on intersex people who share biological characteristics from both male and female sexes.

Synoptic Gospels This grouping consists of the Gospels of Matthew, Mark and Luke, because they 'see all together' (from the Greek *synopsis*) and use similar sources. The Gospel of John, the Fourth Gospel, is considered separate from these, mostly due to its estimated later date and alternative sources.

Toxic masculinity A phrase commonly used for an iteration of twenty-first-century masculinity that indicates the worrying damage it inflicts on those men who embody toxic masculinity, as well as other women and men they come into contact with. Traits of toxic masculinity include violence, control, emotional repression, homophobia and others.

Patriarchy A system in which maleness is prioritized and privileged to the detriment of women, as well as to men who do not fit the ideals set in such a culture.

Queer A purposefully ambiguous word, queer can refer to several things. First, it is commonly used in academia with regard to discipline and theory, such as queer theory and queer theology. However, many people now identify as queer, meaning that they do not wish to classify themselves with a particular label but would rather remain ambiguous in gender and sexual identity. This is a reclamation of the word by the LGBTQ+ community; previously it was frequently used as a prejudiced slur.

Bible References Index

Old Testament

Genesis

I	31
1.27	32
1.28	36
2.7	37
2.21–22	37
2.25	38
3	32, 39, 43
3.5–6	44
3.6	40
3.7	44
3.8	52
3.16	41
3.23–24	45
6.11	78
17.10–14	70
19	55
32.24–30	45
32.30	53

Exodus

1.17, 20–21	64
2.2–3	64
2.3	69
4.24–26	70
7.8–13	72
8.15, 32	65
9.34	65
11.4–7	64

14	72
14.26–28	64
15.20–21	106
19.16–19	52
32.10–11, 14	51
33.11	51
33.20	52
33.21–23	53

Leviticus

15.19	87

Numbers

6.24–26	52

Deuteronomy

21.15–17	84
23.12–14	52
32.18	15

Joshua

1–2	78

Judges

4.4–10	83
4.21	78
4, 5	154
9.53–54	78
19	55, 103

Names and Subject Index

Lightning Source UK Ltd.
Milton Keynes UK
UKHW010729010822
406672UK00002B/400